T0305399

Economic Institutions and Democratic Reform

ECONOMIES AND SOCIETIES IN TRANSITION

General Editor: **Ronald J. Hill**

*Professor of Comparative Government
and Fellow of Trinity College
Dublin, Ireland*

Economies and Societies in Transition is an important series which applies academic analysis and clarity of thought to the recent traumatic events in Eastern and Central Europe. As many of the preconceptions of the past half century are cast aside, newly independent and autonomous sovereign states are being forced to address long-term organic problems which had been suppressed by, or appeased within, the Communist system of rule.

The series is edited under the sponsorship of Lorton House, an independent charitable association which exists to promote the academic study of communism and related concepts.

Economic Institutions and Democratic Reform

A Comparative Analysis of Post-Communist Countries

Ole Nørgaard

Research Professor, University of Aarhus, Denmark

ECONOMIES AND SOCIETIES IN TRANSITION

Edward Elgar

Cheltenham, UK • Northampton, MA, USA

Published by
Edward Elgar Publishing Limited
Glensanda House
Montpellier Parade
Cheltenham
Glos GL50 1UA
UK

Edward Elgar Publishing, Inc.
136 West Street
Suite 202
Northampton
Massachusetts 01060
USA

A catalogue record for this book
is available from the British Library

Library of Congress Cataloguing in Publication Data

Nørgaard, Ole.
    Economic institutions and democratic reform : a comparative analysis of
post-communist countries / Ole Nørgaard.
    (Economies and societies in transition series)
    Includes bibliographical references and index.
    1. Europe, Eastern—Economic policy—1989- 2. Comparative economics.
    3. Europe, Eastern—Politics and government—1989- 4. Democracy—Europe,
Eastern. I. Title. II. Economies and societies in transition

    HC244.N58 2000
    330.947—dc21   00–035350

ISBN 1 84064 401 X

Printed and bound in Great Britain by Biddles Ltd, *www.biddles.co.uk*

Contents

List of Figures

List of Tables

Preface and Acknowledgements

When I was enrolled in a Danish army intelligence school in 1969, I – along with 14 fellow cadets – was brought up on a digested and popular version of what I later learned was the totalitarian model of the communist systems. In 1972 I spent a few months as a student in Leningrad, with the permission of Counterintelligence, who (correctly) assumed that my language would improve, thus outweighing the security risk of a personal encounter with the enemy. My Russian language was indeed improved, but so was my understanding of the country and society I was expected to fight. First of all, I experienced a society and ordinary citizens far from the submissive and docile picture intrinsic to the totalitarian model. When I entered an academic career it was this experience that drew my attention towards the transformative potential of grass root political participation in totalitarian systems. When I later realized the constrained (although genuine) nature of this political participation, my interest was drawn towards the role of economic interest groups as agents of change in what I still considered a society mature for change. I published books on these issues respectively in 1980 and 1985.

A second outcome of my first encounter with a totalitarian system was a basic and lasting belief in the long term incompatibility of a totalitarian (or authoritarian) system of government with a modernizing society. It was an incompatibility that originated in the ridicule and contempt (rather than fear and submission), with which we (my fellow students and I) approached the KGB-types who often tailed groups of youths that included foreign students. From here stems my fundamental belief that a modernizing totalitarian (or authoritarian) system cannot survive when its educated citizens do not endow public institutions with a minimum of legitimacy and respect, and when fear is replaced with irony and sarcasm. This belief in the ultimate superiority of democracy was reinforced when I travelled widely throughout the Eastern bloc and the Soviet republics in the 1970s and early 80s, and when I spent a few months in Spain in 1975 shortly before Franco's death and the beginning of the Spanish transition. I was proven right in the late 1980s and early 1990s with the eventual (and largely peaceful) collapse of the communist systems when even the ruling elites ceased to believe in their right to rule.

It is the same experiences that provide me with a strong belief in the democratic instincts of the citizens of most post-communist countries. I believe that the communist experience effectively shielded educated citizens of post-communist countries from the appeal of any version of autocracy.

The current danger to democracy rather stems from the economic and social costs that followed the simultaneous transformation of economic institutions, costs that originate in the initial state of the systems, but – as shown in this study – to a large extent also in the economic models and strategies that have been imposed by international organizations in conjunction with local elites. This process may endanger democracy because everyday life is made so difficult for the ordinary citizen who worked for the original transformation that he withdraws from politics. Instead the political playing field is often captured by elites without any democratic credentials, but impregnated with the spirits of Byzantine politics that characterized communism, and all too willing to sacrifice (or postpone) democracy to advance any new economic blueprint. A sacrifice of democracy that has, alas, too often been encouraged by Western leaders and media, who continue to believe that democracy can only be imposed on reluctant societies by new born capitalist (or left-over communist) elites. In this context the collapse of public service and especially the educational systems may threaten the future of the new democracies when social and political decay produces a new lumpenproletariat, susceptible to populist demagogues who capitalize on social despair and search for scapegoats. Alternative modes and strategies for change of economic institutions thus become quintessential when assessing the future of regimes undergoing a simultaneous transformation to democracy and to the market.

It therefore also follows that the present study is written in the tradition of comparative politics, which Eckstein (1998, p. 513) terms a 'problem solving discipline'. I am fully aware that the generalist implication of this approach may earn me the scepticism (or even worse) of those who are searching for generalized models. The years during which I have dealt with post-soviet science have made me acutely aware of the hierarchy of science, where those cultivating first order principles are ranked (or rank themselves) above generalists who deal with complex orders: physicists versus biologists (or even worse: meteorologists!), mathematical economists versus social scientist – and (some) social scientists versus the arts. Still, as physicists have little to say about the development of species (or about the weather), and econometric theory about social development, I do not believe that generalized models or methodological one-sidedness, whether of the Marxist, the culturalist or rational choice variant, are productive when approaching the complex orders of post-communist transformation. Instead I apply a methodological plural-ism (Roth, 1987) and explore which theories and methodologies can improve our understanding of specific issues and contexts. This methodological eclecticism also applies to the level of analysis. At an early stage in the research process I realized that in order to provide adequate answers I had to move between different levels of analysis, starting with the mega-theories of global capitalism and democracy, moving through micro-level analyses of individual behaviour and meso-level theories of empirical and historical institutionalism, only to finally return to the mega-theories from whence the inquiry began. I hope that the unavoidable costs to theoretical depth are compensated for by a clearer comparative understanding of the interaction between the key variables of the study: initial conditions, strategies of institutional change, social and economic costs, political responses and institutions, and ultimately democracy. I also hope that the shifts between different levels of analysis can improve our understanding about which type of explanation is most productive at which level. Similar reservations (and ambitions) apply to the geographical scope of the study. Although the focus is on 20 post-communist countries, it was the ambition to address more general issues with implications for other regions and countries. The subset of 20 post-communist countries should therefore be perceived as a regional case study adapted to general theories and models. As argued by Peter Mair (1998, p. 331) the process of bringing together the more case- and context-sensitive advantages of the case study with general theories can perhaps also advance our comparative understanding.

As far as possible, the study is based on the analysis and interpretation of hard data – figures and estimates from international financial institutions, public opinion surveys, sociological research, electoral results and estimates of institutional performance. Some may find this addiction to numbers excessive, especially in view of existing validity and reliability problems. Still, after decades when we lacked almost any hard data for political analyses and in a field still dominated by 'soft' analyses and descriptions, I believe that hard data are necessary as a point of departure and preferable to a purely interpretative approach where conclusions are often supported more by causal (although informed) observations and selective statistics than by systematic analyses. This does not imply that the present study is the result of pure desk research. Concurrently with the research leading up to this book and on behalf of my university, I have been actively involved in a large number of the countries covered by the study as a Danish representative in EU institutions and programmes channelling assistance to former communist countries, as a manager of a Danish assistance programme and a number of bilateral university programmes. Most of the ideas that I try to substantiate in this book actually originate in first hand observations in the countries involved, and in encounters with the people who are the substance of the political and economic processes. I do not believe that there is one number, one table or one regression line that I cannot visualize or exemplify in the form of personalities, life stories, events or just casual observations made during innumerable travels and stays in the former communist countries during the last 10 years.

Hence, my first thanks go to all those people from the post-communist world who, over the last 10 years, have shared with me their thoughts, feelings and insights. The interpretations I offer in this book owe everything to those friends and colleagues who have actually lived through and, in many cases, actively participated in the events that ultimately formed the patterns described and supported by the data. I am also indebted to those who have taken the time to offer valuable comments to the draft version of the chapters in this book, among them the colleagues at the Department of Political Science who have discussed preliminary chapters, and in particular to Erik Damgaard, Peter Nannestad, Søren Risbjerg Thomsen, Martin Paldam, Karin Hilmer Pedersen, Lise Togeby, Steven Saxonberg, Lone Bøge Jensen, Märtha-Lisa Magnusson and Evald Mikkel, who commented on the final draft. Ole Hersted Hansen has provided very important research assistance. Particular thanks go to Else Løvdal for her professionalism in the preparation of the manuscript. The project was funded by a grant from the Danish Social Science Research Council, and I am also grateful for the financial support provided by The University of Aarhus Research Foundation. I also benefited tremendously from the able assistance of the library staff at the Department of Political Science.

I am grateful to all these people and institutions for their contributions. None, though, bears the slightest responsibility for the final result. This rests solely with the author.

Ole Nørgaard
November 1999

1. Emerging Democracies and the Market

'We are only beginning to understand the relationship between democratisation, inequality, environmental protection, and growth' (Stiglitz, 1998, p. 29).

The victory of the Western democracies in World War Two heralded the beginning of global democratization. It began with the democratic (and economic) institutions imposed by the victors, continued with the implantation of Western-type democratic institutions in the former colonies throughout the 1960s, proceeded to Southern Europe in the 1970s and Latin America in the 1980s. Democracy finally completed its global triumph with the as yet unsettled process set in motion by the collapse of authoritarian socialism in Central and Eastern Europe and the emerging democracies in the semi-authoritarian economic 'tigers' of South East Asia. The victory of Western democracies had always been accompanied by an attempt to universalize their economic (and social) systems, or rather, the current economic wisdom of the dominating Western powers and major international financial institutions. That was why the defeated countries of World War Two could retain their highly regulated (Keynesian) market economies, while the new third world democracies of the 1960s could proceed along semi-socialist development paths involving large state sectors and economic protectionism. The new democracies of Southern Europe were also able to gradually adapt their (authoritarian) corporatist economies to the welfare (and societal corporatist) economies of the European common market. When democratization reached Latin America and finally Eastern Europe and South East Asia, a new neo-liberal orthodoxy thrived in major Western countries and had become the dominating ideology of international financial institutions. This new orthodoxy came to guide the economic restructuring adopted by (and/or imposed upon) the 'emerging democracies' and 'emerging markets' (to use 'financial markets' jargon, which I shall continue below)[1] in Latin America, Central and Eastern Europe and South East Asia.

This new economic dogmatism was developed in confrontation with equally dogmatic socialist economies. Up to the mid-1990s it became the governing dogma about how underdeveloped (or distorted) economies were to catch up with the developed West. Until the mid-1990s the international

1

financial institutions virtually evangelized the narrow instruments of what came to be known as the 'Washington consensus'. This somehow soft packet of economics inspired by neo-liberal theory spelled out ten commandments of policy advice, the gist of which were an orthodox stabilization policy and reliance on the market and the private sector to overcome structural barriers to development (macro-economic stability, liberalization and privatization) in the pursuit of economic growth (Williamson, 1990). Social protests, political repercussions and approaching economic collapse in some countries of the former Soviet Union, however, eventually generated recognition among the 'experts' that despite their theoretical virtues, tailor-made economic blue-prints might prove counterproductive when imposed on societies that are neither prepared nor able to tolerate the austerity, the social inequalities and ultimately the societal model (type of capitalism) that were implicit conjectures of orthodox stabilization and structural adjustment programmes. The 'post-Washington consensus' that is presently evolving in response to these failures and set-backs implies that textbook laissez-faire capitalism unconstrained by the institutions of democracy is neither economically viable nor compatible with democracy in the modern world. At long last it appears that the international financial institutions are preparing themselves to share all the virtues of modern Western welfare capitalism with the 'emerging' markets and democracies – and not only the laissez-faire part of textbook abstractions. This 'emerging' approach involves employing a wider range of instruments and, first of all, a broader set of goals, including social welfare, ecological sustainability, equity and 'democratic development where citizens participate in various ways in making decisions that affect their lives' (Stiglitz, 1998, p. 34).

This book deals with two of these goals: democratization and change of economic institutions, while for the time being leaving ecological sustain-ability in more competent hands. The primary concern is to explain why some but not other countries have been able to establish economic institutions that are conducive to economic growth and welfare, while at the same time consolidating democracy. Why, to paraphrase Eric Hobsbawn, is Albania not as rich and democratic as Switzerland? (Chirot, 1989, p. 3). Which leads to a first assumption or premise underlying the following study: that in the long term (except for a very few countries with exceptional natural resource en-dowments) institutions – economic and political – determine whether coun-tries will prosper or fail in their aspirations to create better lives for their citizens. Economic institutions define the incentive structures that bring the physical, human and financial resources into productive (or unproductive) play. But politics determine whether economic institutions conducive to growth and welfare will come into existence in the first place, and whether they will distribute the collective goods in ways that are democratically sustainable. Hence, answering the question of why some are successful while others are not is very much like disentangling a Russian doll, the matrioshka: each answer to our question about what determines success or failure raises new questions. The simplest answer as to why some countries are more successful than others in generating economic development is – according to standard textbook explanations – that they have, and are better able to mobilize, the resources required for growth and development, particularly physical and human capital, and are able to spend more time learning to use new technologies (Jones, 1998, p. 138). Why, then, are some countries better able to mobilize the resources for investment and learning? Answers may be found in institutional infrastructures that favour production over diversion (corruption, rent seeking), are open to international trade and have at least some private ownership (Hall and Jones, 1996). This observation leads us to the last question: why were some countries better and faster than others when it came to disentangling economically dysfunctional institutions and replace them with the basics of a market economy that stimulates growth and welfare, all the while consolidating democracy?

A second assumption, tested in practice by the following analyses, is that a market economy, or what Pereira et al. (1993, p. 4) term 'market orientation', basically driven by individuals striving for personal economic gain, has proven superior to all other types of economic institutions so far invented. It is, however, a fiction that this assumption should give rise to specific institutional arrangements with universal applicability. In the real world the institutions of a market economy have historically been adjusted to the specific tastes, values, traditions and configurations of interests in each particular country. Hence, the evolution of particular institutions that constrain and regulate market forces and redistribute the collectively produced goods in a specific country is ultimately a political process reflecting the social values, the preferences and the power of collective interests as mediated through political institutions. The focus on change of economic institutions as the major dependent variable, however, leaves associated questions unexplained.

Figure 1.1 illustrates how change of economic institutions is in the focus of the present study but that institutional development is intrinsically interwoven with two associated issues: economic growth and welfare and democratization. Institutional change is shown to be a major factor behind economic growth and welfare in the countries in question. At the same time growth and welfare are influenced by other factors. Democracy, gaining legitimacy from growth and welfare, and consequently linked to institutional changes in the economy and to other factors, feeds back into political support for (or rejection of) continuation of economic reforms. In this vein politics becomes its own cause. While all these factors, linkages and modes of explanations should be taken into account when trying to understand the linkage between economic change and political constraints in emerging market democracies, the focus (the dependent variable) in the present study will be on the change of economic institutions. Only in the last chapter shall we return to the interaction between change of economic institutions and consolidation of democracy.

These broader goals of socio-economic development and institutional change confront political reformers and social scientists with a much more complex and challenging tasks than when the agenda was defined by the crude dichotomies between democracy/dictatorship or market/planned economies. To attain the dual goal of economic growth and welfare combined with democracy, we have to go beyond economic blueprints and normative political theory in our search for policies that meet the dual criteria of economic viability and democratic feasibility. We should not expect to find ideal solutions or blueprints but, rather, contradictions and the need to accept trade-offs between equally desirable objectives. Nor will the trade-offs be universal. What might represent democratically feasible compromises in one country may go against the values, social preferences or collective interests of another. In our search for a nexus between economic desirability and political feasibility we must consider all aspects of the democratic system: public attitudes and values, social cleavages, collective interests, institutional set up, the role of elites and individuals and the international context. These parameters ultimately decide whether specific economic policies and institutional changes are democratically feasible.

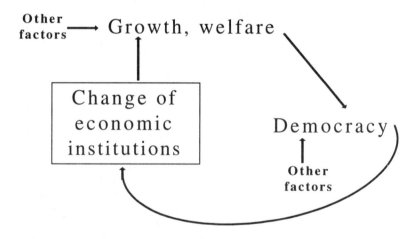

Figure 1.1. Change of economic institutions and adjacent issues.

These are of course truisms applicable to all democratic systems, East and West, North and South. But they are truisms which were neglected for a decade by those who designed economic reform strategies for many of the countries that were trying to find ways to improve their economies and the lives of their citizens. At the same time the conflict between equally desirable goals and the need for trade-offs will be much more apparent in systems undergoing rapid institutional change. This was the case in the former colonies in the 1960s when Westminster type democracies proved inadequate for countries trying to cope with ethnic tensions and the challenges of economic modernization. On this background the democratization of Southern Europe turned out to be a fortuitous episode where economic modernization seemed to walk successfully hand in hand with democratization. In Latin America food riots and other forms of overt social protests swept over the subcontinent in the 1980s, reflecting the tensions between the new-born democracies and the austerity measures induced by neo-liberal economic adjustment programmes. Furthermore, the tensions between economic reform programmes, their local applicability and the social and political repercussions fragmented the former Communist world and turned it into winners and losers of transition – countries, classes and individuals. This time, however, without provoking overt social protest, but – despite appalling human costs – the tensions were channelled into social decay or parliamentary setbacks for the champions of the free market ideology. During 1998 it gradually became clear also that the 'Tiger economies' of East Asia were plagued by institutional problems, part of which were caused by political mechanisms lagging behind economic development. While the economic turmoil seems to have initiated a new round of democratization, the political and social dynamics of the East Asian crises are, however, not yet fully understood, but also in this region the answers must be found in the intersection between (imposed) Western institutions and local cultures and patterns of behaviours in the context of a globalizing economy.

While the ambition of the present book is to add to our general understanding of the nexus between the dual goals of democratization and change of economic institutions, the empirical base of the study is more modest: 20 post-communist countries not tormented by war (which obfuscates any discussion about democracy). One reason for choosing the emerging democracies and markets of the post-communist world is that they represent the closest to a 'natural experiment' that we shall ever get in social sciences. Their economic and political institutions were largely similar under communism. Still, despite institutional path dependencies and roughly identical demands from the international community, the post-communist countries chose very different strategies when they tried to simultaneously create workable market economies and pluralist democracies. They also vary widely in their present level of success, whether measured by change of economic institutions, by the traditional standards of economic growth, by the welfare they offer their citizens or their level of democratic development.

A second reason why the post-communist system is appropriate as a starting point for more general discussions about economic change and democracy is the 'totalitarian' nature of 'Soviet type' societies. By 'totalitarian' I do not imply the kind of totally masterminded and controlled society envisaged in the classical treatise of Frederich (1954), for example. What I have in mind, rather, are the totalitarian aspirations of its leaders to transform societies. By 'totalitarian' I refer to the comprehensive transformation of society launched by the early Soviet leaders. In the process (that was more the outcome of circumstances than of any utopian socialist blueprint) they left their imprint on all spheres of society, creating a coherent and internally consistent social system for a surprisingly long period of time. It is this 'totalitarian' transformation that makes the post-communist systems suitable as a point of reference and comparison for political transformations in other emerging market democracies, because they demonstrate the same constraints and dilemmas that characterize other emerging markets and democracies. They share the legacies of protected and subsidized industries and associated collective interests with Latin America. With East Asia they share the central role of the state and exposure to fluctuation of the global capital market. They share the friction between modernization and ethnic conflict with Africa, and some of them share the prospects of European integration with Southern Europe. The trade-off between emerging markets and democracies have thus become a social sciences hot house where we can examine issues and dilemmas that, in part or on a more modest scale, torment all emerging markets and democracies. A final argument for the choice of post-communist countries as subject of a comparative analysis is that despite similar institutions, they represent very different countries on the level of society and informal institutions, called '2nd order initial conditions' below. They are also very different in other variables exogenous to but potentially important for the change of political and economic institutions, for example size, endowment with natural resources and geographical location.

In the following chapters we will leave the global view on emerging markets and democracies and focus on 20 post-communist countries in our attempt to understand why some of them, despite initial institutional similarities, have been better able than others to sustain a development that has produced institutions conducive to growth, welfare – and democracy. Our study will start in 1989 when Poland as the first communist country turned down the road of profound institutional change. It ends in early 1998 when the looming crash of the Russian financial markets endangered the fragile institutions of the whole region.

TRADE-OFFS: POST–COMMUNIST MARKETS – AND DEMOCRACIES 1989–1998

Almost since the establishment of the first Soviet type economic system its inherent deficiencies and malfunctions have been known to social scientists. From the earliest critique by ideological opponents through the dissident movement in various countries and to the mature critique developed by East European economists and the somewhat introspective analyses by former Sovietologists of reasons for the collapse (Spiegeleire, 1995: 47), the same weaknesses have been identified in explanations of the systems failure to catch up with the West. 'The treadmill of reform', as phrased by Gertrude Schroeder (1979), bears witness that the criticism also reached the ears of politicians eager to improve the efficiency of their economies for political and military reasons. As described by Schroeder and numerous other economists and political scientists, however, all attempts to change the basic structures of the planned economies failed, although especially Poland and Hungary managed to implement rudimentary reforms from the 1970s onwards. Basic reforms failed partly because they incurred unacceptable losses when old patterns of behaviour and linkages were changed, partly because they challenged powerful political and social interests integrated in a web of socio-political institutions (Kornai, 1992: Chapter 15; Nørgaard, 1985). Shielded behind the lustrous facade of communist propaganda and self-image, the managers and bureaucrats of the existing system proved stronger than reform minded political leaders when they, ex ante as well as ex post, frustrated any attempt to change economic mechanisms and priorities and adjust to the demands of an increasingly complex economy.

All this was to change when the communist systems collapsed in the late 1980s and early 1990s. From then on the full-scale replacement of the existing system with its virtual opposite, a full-fledged market economy and equally utopian democracy, gradually became the goal of most post-communist governments. Many years of totalitarian and utopian thinking synthesized with an emotional rejection of any attribute of the former system produced an intellectual and political climate that eventually excluded any attempt to formulate intermediate variants or 'third ways'. The choice of initial policies was also heavily influenced by advice and demands from Western financial institutions, at that time dominated by the neo-liberal orthodoxy of the 1980s.

This development was also reflected in the intellectual dominance of neo-classical economists. In their recommendations to East European policy-makers they drew on experience from third world stabilization and structural adjustment programmes sponsored by international financial organizations. The neo-liberal orthodoxy in a softer version epitomized by Williamson (1990) in the concept of the 'Washington consensus' expressed consensus among the financial institutions and the leading Western governments on what kind of policy was needed to overcome structural obstacles to development in third world countries. 'Although the scientific status remained somewhat unclear' (Toye, 1990), it became the ideological wisdom that came to guide the first years of post-communist economic transformation.

For the time being, the remaining 'third way' economists or area experts were left to roar in the academic jungle without visible impact on policy or politicians. At the same time, the new cohort of experts on Eastern Europe and the Soviet Union seemed to perceive the post-communist countries as virgin territory. The popular rejection of the communist system had allegedly created an institutional void where economic and political life could be created from scratch and where actors were expected to rapidly adapt to the new rules of the game in the spirit of neo-classical economics. Hence, was the logic, any expertise on communist institutions, whether hosted by academic experts or Eastern practitioners, was as obsolete as the systems themselves. What counted was a correct definition of the target situation and of the resources required to reach that target. At that time, the specific market economic model to be sought was not an issue. The Anglo-Saxon laissez-faire model was implicitly what was striven for, while the European social market economies or the Asian developmental states were considered variants of impermissible third ways.

Euphoria was not to last long. All countries soon faced dramatic and unexpected collapses of output followed by an equally critical decline in living standards and a host of other social indicators (World Bank, 1996, Chapter 4; UNICEF, 1994). In many countries the economic decline had significant political repercussions. Beginning with the autumn 1992 parliamentary elections in Lithuania and ending with the November 1995 presidential elections in Poland and the December 1995 parliamentary elections in Russia, economic hardship provoked the political return of converted communists. Though mostly paying lip service to the virtues of market economy, they were elected on platforms that promised to alleviate the burdens of the emerging economic system, whether for exposed social groups or for branches or regions threatened by foreign and domestic competition. The institutional phantoms of the past made their final clampdown with the Russian crash of August 1998, when the fallout of a global financial crisis revealed the incompatibility between rapid change of economic and political institutions in post-communist Russia.

Hence, economic and political developments after the collapse of the communist regimes soon proved the obvious: That post-communist systems were not the perceived institutional voids in which institutions as well as values, ideas and patterns of behaviour had been eradicated by the ouster of the communist regimes. To varying degrees the past, both communist and pre-communist, survived the political changes and required adjustment of institutional reform strategies. They thus repeated the lessons from third world and middle income countries: that economic reforms must not only be technically viable concerning the character of the changes initiated (policy) and the order and speed with which they are implemented; they should also be politically feasible (Williamson, 1990; Nelson, 1990b; Bates and Krueger, 1994). On the one hand, technically perfect blueprints for a new economic system that cannot be adopted by the legitimate political institutions or is stopped halfway by a recalcitrant bureaucracy can leave the system worse off than before. On the other hand, a reform design which placates all vested interests of the old system would mean no change at all. Hence, the task is to find the optimum trade-off between a reform blueprint that provides for economic efficiency and is able to obtain political support – ex ante and ex post. The economic reform strategies, however, are not applied to an abstract model of post-communist systems. They are carried out in concrete country settings with specific institutional legacies and external environments. Identical reform strategies will inevitably produce different outcomes in terms of stabilization, economic growth, institutional change, democratic consolidation and any other criterion which may be applied to measure reform progress.

The subsequent analyses on the politics of economic institutional change will proceed on two levels. The first level focuses on structural variables exogenous to the reform process, initial conditions and external environment. These variables constitute the framework conditions and are outside the control of the reformers. The exogenous variables (Naughton, 1995, p. 137) may directly influence reforms in that they make the change of institutions easier (or more difficult), regardless of the reform strategy pursued in terms of economic costs, political feasibility, and administrative capacities. Or they may provoke the adoption of a particular reform strategy which may prove suitable (or unsuitable) for local circumstances. The second analytical level focuses on the reform strategy. These strategies are ideally under the control of political decision-makers or they are the outcome of the political process, making domestic politics endogenous to any institutional strategy. The scope of options and contingent choices available to politicians are consequently defined by the structural constraints identified at the first level of analysis.

The general outline of the study is illustrated in Figure 1.2.

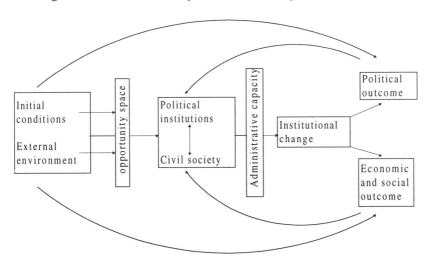

Figure 1.2. Change of economic institutions: Frameworks and determinants.

With these ambitions and preliminary definitions in mind, Chapter 2 presents the basic concepts and definitions (building blocks) and the research design (draft architecture) that will guide our subsequent search for causal models. Chapter 3 identifies the various sources of research or 'clusters of theories', leading up to the present study and the answers (hypotheses or draft architectures) provided by previous research. In Chapter 4 indicators and strategies of institutional change and their economic and social outcomes are examined. In Chapter 5 I define and assess the constraints and opportunities for action that the initial structural conditions set for the reformers. In Chapter 6 I identify the framework conditions that have made it possible for some countries to transcend the structural constraints (and associated costs), focusing on the role of political institutions, popular mobilization and elites. In Chapter 7 I discuss the role of economic ideas and their promulgators, the internal and external actors who formulate policies, focusing in particular on six countries that have performed either significantly better or worse than would be predicted based on their initial conditions. Finally, in Chapter 8 I take the experience of the 20 post-communist countries (our hot house cases) back to the global perspective on economic growth, welfare and democratization.

NOTES

1. I am using the theoretically unassuming concept 'emerging democracies' as a descriptive term to label political systems that have just 'emerged' from a non-democratic system and as a match to 'emerging markets', 'emerging' from a non-market position. Hence, the term does not carry any indication about how far they have come and how far they have to go, or whether they are in the 'transition' or 'consolidation' phase. For an account of where and how the 'emerging markets' concept originated, see Frank Partnoy, *F.I.A.S.C.O. Blood in the Water on Wall Street,* Profile Books, London 1998, pp. 68f.

APPENDIX 1. SELECTING THE CASES

The objects of this study are trade-off countries, that is, communist countries currently undergoing fundamental institutional changes. At the last count this includes a total of 30 countries:

The 15 countries of the Former Soviet Union (FSU):
Armenia, Azerbaijan, Belarus, Estonia, Georgia, Kazakhstan, Kyrgyzstan, Latvia, Lithuania, Republic of Moldova, Russian Federation, Tajikistan, Turkmenistan, Ukraine, Uzbekistan.

To these republics should further be added Mongolia, politically and military closely associated with the Soviet Union.

The 5 republics of the former Yugoslavia:
Bosnia and Herzegovina, Croatia, Slovenia, The Former Yugoslav Republic of Macedonia, The remaining Yugoslavia (Serbia).

The 8 countries of Central and Eastern Europe:
Albania, Bulgaria, Czech Republic, Hungary, Poland, Romania, Slovakia, GDR.

Asian communist systems:
China, Vietnam.

When choosing the subset for analyses to be carried out in this study, the individual countries were to meet the following criteria:

* Identifiable political and economic identities during the transition;
* In a process of double (or triple) transition: from authoritarian to democratic rule; from a planned to a market economy and (maybe) in the process towards the establishment of independent statehood:
* 'Normal' political and economic systems in the sense that the transition process should not by severely affected by non-economic and non-political factors as for example war, international blockades or natural disasters.

Taking these criteria into consideration, the GDR is disqualified because she was absorbed by the FRG; Vietnam and China are disqualified because they – so far – have only reformed their economic systems, while their political systems remain basically unchanged. Croatia, Former Yoguslav Republic of Macedonia, The remaining Yugoslavia, Armenia, Georgia, Azerbaijan and Tajikistan are disqualified because they have been affected by war, economic blockades, natural disasters – or all three. When applying these criteria we are therefore left with 20 Countries in Transition.

Countries of the Former Soviet Union and Mongolia:
Belarus, Kazakhstan, Kyrgyzstan, Republic of Moldova, Russian Federation, Turkmenistan, Ukraine, Uzbekistan, Mongolia. These countries were all integral parts of the Former Soviet Union and thus closely integrated in the economic and political structures of that country. Except for the major part of Moldova, these states were all exposed to the Soviet Communist system from the early 1920s to the break-up of the Soviet Union in September of 1991. Moldova was part of Romania in the inter-war years. Mongolia became socialist in the mid-1920s and was a close ally of the Soviet Union politically and economically until 1990.

The Baltic states:
Estonia, Latvia and Lithuania. Although they were integral parts of the Soviet Union from 1945 and thoroughly Sovietized from the late 1940s, all three countries experienced independent statehood in the inter-war years.

Central and Eastern Europe:
Albania, Bulgaria, Czech Republic, Hungary, Poland, Romania, Slovakia, and Slovenia. Except for the former Yugoslav republics and Albania which withdrew in 1968, they were all members of the Warsaw Pact. They were also, again with the exception of Albania that ceased to participate in 1961, members of CMEA, the organization for economic cooperation between socialist countries, where an agreement was made in 1964 that enabled the limited participation of Yugoslavia in the fields of finance, currency and industrial development. They had all, with the exception of Slovenia, maintained separate statehood throughout the Soviet era, and all had, again with the exception of Slovenia, vivid memories of independent statehood before independence was lost in the aftermath of the World War Two.

2. Finding the Building Blocks and Draft Designs

'Historically grounded huge comparisons of big structures and large processes help establish what must be explained, attach the possible explanations to their context in time and space, and sometimes actually improve our understanding of those structures and processes' (Tilly, 1984, p. 145).

This book is about institutional change in post-communist economies. Institutions are 'the rules of the game in society' or those constraints that 'structure incentives in human exchange, whether political, social or economic' (North, 1990, p. 3). These rules, constraints or institutions may be formally inscribed into a hierarchy of legal regulations, from constitutions down to legal codes. Institutions may also be the informal and not codified values and norms embedded in the minds of humans, or the codes of behaviour in organizations. Formal institutions may be the constructs of political actors (as in the case of written constitutions), or they are the formalized outcome of an evolutionary process (as in the case of Common Law). Informal institutions are by definition unintentional constructs in which remnants of the past survive as values, norms and codes of conduct that may – or may not – be compatible with existing formal institutions (Knight, 1992). This interface between formal and informal institutions is the topic of this study. The core issue is why some countries have been able to dissolve the (inefficient) formal economic institutions of the old system and replace them with (formal) economic institutions that provide the incentives for growth and welfare while building democracy, and others have not. A second (and much broader) question is why similar institutions have generated dissimilar outcomes in different countries. In order to answer these questions one must look into how the informal institutions of the past interact with the new institutions: the extent to which the implementation of new institutions is obstructed (or delayed) because they threaten the well-being of the population, the power and privileges of organizations, or of an elite shaped by the incentives of the incumbent system and the extent to which the new formal economic institutions generate the anticipated change in behaviour.

13

In this chapter I present an introduction to the concepts, possible causes and alternative strategies of institutional change in 20 post-communist countries; in short, the building blocks and draft design of the causal models to be elaborated in subsequent chapters: the initial conditions, external environment and affiliated political interests and actors; the opportunity space following the demise of the old regime; political institutions and state capacities and the reform outcomes, which in turn feed back into the democratic process. I also address the issue of comparability and discuss the process of generating hypotheses – draft architectures – that will help us assemble the blocks into a hopefully coherent and stable building.

INITIAL CONDITIONS

The initial conditions of a reforming economy comprise the set of economic and socio-political resources and constraints that exist when reforms are launched. They are remnants of the past crystallized into the specific structures of formal and informal institutions under which the reformers have to perform – historical opportunities realized at the expense of other options. Initial conditions are by definition beyond the control of the individual government and hence exogenous to reform policies. They are the result of certain institutional paths that reach back before the communist epoch (2nd order initial conditions) and of the socio-economic legacies of communism (1st order initial conditions). Initial conditions are also the outcome of the way in which the previous (communist) system was extricated, as the 'mode of extrication' determines which elites and political forces survive and continue to influence policy-making. The legacies of these historical phases are important to the present economic adjustment process because they impinge on economic performance and, indirectly, on the choice of specific reform policies.

Long-term institutional trajectories: 2nd order initial conditions

In most countries pre-communist history provides the symbols and alternative visions (or focal points) that, in addition to images of the Western world, represent the issues and symbols around which reformers and the population at large are mobilized (Przeworski, 1991, p. 85). In other countries we will find that informal social institutions (for example clan and family structures) have survived the formal institutions of communism (Makarenko, 1999). The historical uniqueness of each post-communist country is represented at this level of generalization. The duration of the communist regime is important to the type of ideals and symbols that are carried over from the past and the likelihood that informal civil-society institutions survive. Countries with a recent prehistory of independent statehood ex ante hold a political capital that is not available to countries experiencing independence for the first time in modern history. Similarly, will countries that can refer to a liberal democratic and economic pre-communist history have a more solid democratic legitimacy in the eyes of the population than countries in which communism replaced another variation of authoritarianism. Weber (1992) and Mytol (1997), for example, observe that a coincidence does exist between reform success and lines of civilization (Protestants and Catholics versus Orthodox versus Muslims; Western Europeans versus Eastern Europeans versus Asians). Mytol disagrees, however, that civilizational lines alone explain the variation in capacity for change. It is, rather, the degree of totalitarianism and/or imperial rule, i.e. legacies from communism, that explains the extent to which individual countries have been able to meet the challenges of transition.

The legacies of communism: 1ˢᵗ order initial conditions

All post-communist systems share the legacy of the communist mode of government, economic planning and management – from basic institutional features to more elusive characteristics – mentalities, ways of thinking and patterns of behaviour. The homogenization of the communist regimes was, however, far from complete. The variations produced by the socialist division of labour merged with the pre-communist identities to produce different starting positions that can be divided into four categories (Balcerowicz, 1995, p. 167; World Bank, 1996, Chapter 1; Dabrowski, 1996, pp. 31–32):

- Initial macroeconomic imbalances which impinge on the austerity of the stabilization policy needed.
- The formal economic system, i.e. formal decision-making institutions and implementing agencies affecting the adoption and implementation of economic policies. Some systems had – although modestly – moved away from the archetype Soviet system of planning and management.
- Economic structure, i.e. the relative size of branch and territorial output with implications for adjustment costs and for the political capability to adopt and implement institutional change. The economic structure partly reflects the degree of modernization (as measured on traditional modernization indicators), partly the degree of economic distortion (as reflected in properties which are incompatible with the new economic order, for example over-industrialization).
- Wealth measured in terms of the real value of physical capital, human capital, location[1] and natural resource endowments.

The formal economic system and the economic structure form particularly important parts in the perspective of this study, because they determine the scope of institutional change, the adjustment costs and the political impediments to change. The importance of these two dimensions can be demonstrated by the distinction between 'conservative' and 'progressive' post-communist systems, each with distinctive economic and political features. As will be shown in subsequent analyses there is a tendency that factors conducive and/or hostile to institutional change cluster around conservative and progressive poles.[2] The economic and political logic of ideal-type conservative and progressive post-communist systems is illustrated in Figures 2.1. and 2.2.[3]

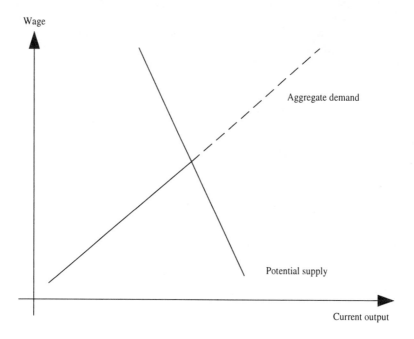

Figure 2.1. Macroeconomic adjustment in a conservative system.

The graphs describe two ideal-type post-communist economic systems characterized by the commonplace weaknesses of socialist economic systems on the verge of change: low productivity, monetary overhang, hidden inflation and isolation from Western markets. In both systems the potential supply curve illustrates the maximum amount of goods that firms are willing to produce at a given real wage level, whereas the aggregate demand curve illustrates the impact of real wages on aggregate demand. The demand curve is the dotted line to the right of the supply curve, indicating the virtual nature of a demand not underpinned by production.

The 'conservative' and rather ill-starred country (Figure 2.1) is distinguished by rigid and centralized decision-making institutions and implementing agencies. It mostly (but not always) scores high on most modernization indicators, but at the same time it has an obsolete industrial structure with extreme capital endowments. It is highly monopolized and its output is unmarketable on Western markets regardless of price. Policy

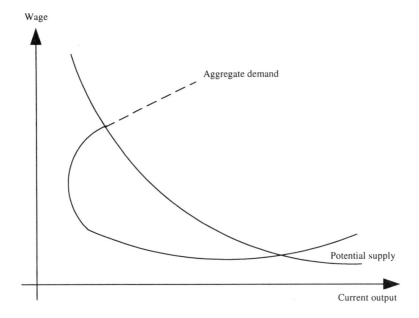

Figure 2.2. Macroeconomic adjustment in a progressive system.

choices induced by vested interests have produced major macroeconomic imbalances and human as well as physical capital is obsolete. Finally, the country is without natural resource endowments and sufficiently large and isolated to leave foreign aid and advice without a major impact on domestic political life. The low elasticity of the supply curve indicates the limited short-term effect of a fall in real wages on the output. Here entrenched monopoly positions and a lack of entrepreneurial spirit prevent a response to lower wage costs. At the same time, wages represent only a limited fraction of total costs in a system dominated by high capital endowments which makes the wage factor less important for aggregate demand. In a long-term dynamic perspective, the same entrenched positions embedded in social and political structures and the political system prevent structural adjustments which would be illustrated by an outward shift of the supply curve.

The low elasticity of the aggregate demand curve illustrates that the distorted price structure and the monetary overhang require substantial reductions in real wages in order to have an impact on domestic demand. It also illustrates, however, an unfavourable external environment where the demand for goods produced in a capital-intensive and conservative post-communist system is low, either due to the type and quality of the goods produced or because of poor market access. Hence, opening the economy to foreign markets does not help because the goods produced are unmarketable on Western markets at any price. A national government, however, has very little control over such parameters.

The 'progressive' system illustrated in Figure 2.2 represents a fortunate post-communist economy. Although plagued by the same initial ailments as other post-communist economies, it has had or been granted a place in the socialist division of labour that makes change easier. Its enterprises are relatively small and the output represents a fairly high value added. Or it may be at a lower level of modernization where industry counts but for a smaller fraction of output, and the potential for growth through development rather than institutional change thus is correspondingly greater. Under communism it experimented with various reforms which, although they did not produce capitalism, created a stock of managers who showed entrepreneurship and were capable of dealing on market terms. It also decentralized the economic decision-making process, leaving more room for individual enterprises and limiting the power of central bureaucracies. The experiments also prepared the broad population mentally for the social consequences of a market economy. This situation is illustrated in the initial high elasticity of the potential supply curve that will increase output in response to lower wages. In the long-term perspective, these initial conditions make structural adjustments less costly in terms of political and social restraints and make an outward movement of the supply curve possible. On the demand side our fortunate country is blessed with a neighbour in relation to whom cultural and perhaps linguistic kinship lowers transaction costs and simplify penetration of the market, and thus access to foreign capital. Hence, also the demand curve becomes highly elastic when the country in question is able to generate foreign demand by selling goods at low prices on foreign markets (point E) that will compensate for the drop in domestic demand. In the long term the demand curve will also move outward due to the domestic income generated by successful reforms and because the benevolent neighbour helps alleviate whatever formal barriers to foreign markets that remain.[4] Further, the financial position of the state enables it to develop – and finance – a social safety net independently of the enterprises. The state can thus, with reduced political costs, withdraw subsidies to remaining state enterprises whose workers are induced to move to the higher wages in the private sector.

Mode of Extrication as Initial Condition

The mode of transition or extrication (Karl and Schmitter, 1991; Stark, 1992) defines the institutional and political constraints under which the reformers operate. This political dimension identifies the way the old system collapsed or was replaced, and hence the extent to which the political structures of the previous system have survived to constrain the reformers. Dealing with the transition from authoritarian to democratic regimes, Karl and Schmitter (1991, p. 275), for example, define four modes: pact, imposition, reform and revolution. The typology reflects the property of the space created in a cross-field of strategy (compromise vs. force) and actors (elites vs. masses).

Table 2.1. Modes of extrication.

		Strategy	
		Compromise	Force
Actors	Elites	Pact	Imposition
	Masses	Reform	Revolution

Source: Karl and Schmitter (1991, p. 275).

The mode of extrication will ultimately determine which political forces are to have access to influence and power during and after the transition. In terms of Figures 2.1 and 2.2, the mode of extrication affects the ability of the supply curves to move outwards as indicators of structural adjustment capacities. Based on evidence from Southern Europe and Latin America, the conclusion demonstrates that the most enduring democracies were made via pacts, a top-down process in which incoming and outgoing elites compromise on terms that respect the critical interests of both parts. It is obvious, however, that respect for old elites and the structures they represent constrains the freedom of reformers to mould new institutions to their liking. Especially the incoming elite during the establishment of new economic institutions and structures that affect the distribution of power and welfare. This problem does not exist where the old elite was extricated by revolution from below or by the imposition of an alternative elite (or foreign occupational powers).

THE EXTERNAL ENVIRONMENT

The second factor that impinges on the economic transformation but is beyond the control of the individual government is the external environment. As demonstrated by the political and economic transformation after World War Two (Herz, 1982), external actors have historically had a decisive impact on systems going through rapid institutional changes. For post-communist systems the external context '... defines the room for manoeuvre, and thus both the limitations and options of the transformation process' (Hettne, 1994, p. 56). In terms of Figures 2.1 and 2.2, a benevolent environment is what makes the outward movement of the supply curve possible in the medium-term.

Economically, access to hard currency generating markets is essential in a situation when domestic demand collapses, as illustrated in Figures 2.1 and 2.2 (World Bank, 1996, Chapter 9). The existence of a market for the goods that the post-communist countries are able to provide on a competitive basis is a prerequisite for generating an export-led growth, creating the financial basis for economic restructuring. Another source of foreign finance is direct foreign investments or foreign economic aid in the form of donations, guarantees or loans.

Politically, conditionality tied to foreign aid becomes a factor in internal disputes over transition strategies. The strict economic conditions set by international financial institutions are examples of foreign actors directly interfering in domestic decision-making. The prospect of joining attractive international organizations may be an important legitimizing factor when reformers have to sell austerity to an economically vulnerable population. The most obvious example is the set of preconditions for accession of a number of Central and East European countries listed by the European Council in their June 1993 meeting in Copenhagen. Meanwhile, the transition itself also produces political groups demanding protection (Bofinger, 1995; Mau, 1996), and public opinion can swing against integration in the form of reborn nationalism. In a broader perspective it can further be argued that in the global competition between the American, the European and the Japanese mode of capitalism, post-communist economies must adapt to the type of capitalism dominating the region where they are situated (Hutton, 1995, p. 284).

Less tangible but of crucial importance is the intellectual influence from the external environment in terms of which economic reform models are brought onto the political agenda. Intellectual influence may be directly observable when policies are designed by foreign educated advisers, as was the case with the 'Chicago boys' in Chile, the 'Berkeley Mafia' in Indonesia, the MIT economists in Mexico or the Harvard economists in Poland (Williamson and Haggard, 1994, p. 565). Influence may also be exerted via training programmes provided by international institutions like the International Monetary Fund, the World Bank or the European Union. The graduates of these training seminars are those who return to their home countries ingrained with a certain economic philosophy to form technopols – technocrats that have accepted political responsibility (Williamson, 1994, p. 12). The few individuals who learn economic theories are, of course, not guaranteed ultimate influence on economic policies. International pressure in the form of conditionality is one factor behind the 'power of economic ideas', as it was phrased in a major book on this topic (Hall, 1989). The same book argues, however, that domestic variables best explain the acceptance or rejection of a certain policy – in the study referred to, Keynesian politics. Hall focuses on three domestic categories in relation to the acceptance or rejection of a certain set of economic ideas, namely their economic, administrative, and political viability (ibid., p. 13).[5] Kahler (1990, p. 58) demonstrates that Hall's approach is useful when explaining the penetration of orthodox and heterodox economic doctrines in developing countries.

THE OPPORTUNITY SPACE

A number of authors have analysed the 'structural space' (Karl and Schmitter, 1991, p. 271), the 'period of extraordinary politics' (Balcerowicz, 1994, pp. 84–87), 'honeymoon' (Williamson and Haggard, 1994, p. 571) or 'critical junctures' (Collier and Collier, 1991) that occur when the institutional constraints of the previous system have collapsed. Focusing on foreign trade and drawing on Olson's theory of collective action (1990a), Bofinger makes an identical observation when he states that 'The complete upheaval of all existing structures has above all reduced or even destroyed the power of those groups that had been dominating under the previous regime' (Bofinger, 1995, p. 21). In his study of institutional change North (1990, p. 138) addresses in particular the situation in Eastern Europe and finds that the political actor 'has been far less constrained by constituent interests', implying that the political actor 'is in the position to initiate more radical change'. Also Remmer's concept of political capital, where she sees elections as creating 'conditions that permit leaders to set aside immediate political concerns in favour of the pursuit of prevailing economic wisdom' (Remmer, 1993, p. 405) is an equivalent concept, but applied to electoral politics rather than regime change.[6] In this context I prefer the term 'opportunity space' to indicate that this period offers the political leadership relatively unconstrained opportunities to formulate and implement policies, while the character of the policies is decided by other factors.

As described in Figure 2.3, 'opportunity space' represents the phase during which the new elites possess relative freedom to establish new formal institutions. The opportunity 'space' is a reflection of the function $o = o(t)$ which expresses the readiness of the population to accept the costs of institutional changes and the inability of old coalitions and elites to block these changes. The opportunity space has three properties: length, depth and a constant. The constant ($o0$) represents the 'normal' political space where elites can act in a given society. The other two properties can be combined into four modes representing the length and depth of the period when structural constraints are reduced, as illustrated by the four curves (1–4), limited by depth ($o0$–$o2$) and duration ($t0$–$t2$). The duration and scope of the opportunity space following regime change will be contingent upon structural factors (i.e. political culture or religion, geographical location or the possibilities for national mobilization) and political factors (degree of elite continuity and mass involvement in the extrication of the old system).

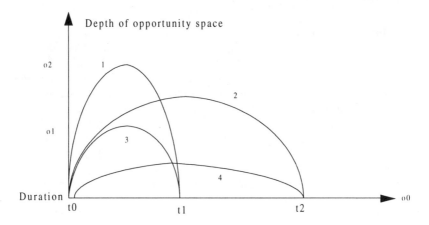

Source: Inspired by Balcerowicz, 1997.

Figure 2.3. The opportunity space.

It is while this opportunity space exists, when political constraints are relaxed and popular support peaks, that 'accidents of history' (Hansson, 1994, p. 63), 'chance' (Balcerowicz, 1994, p. 86) or the action of individuals can make a significant difference. The difference consists of the choices of certain individuals, groups or organizations who make bold decisions and thus transcend the structural constraints of the outgoing system. Or they are taken by demagogues who are able to capitalize on popular confusion and discontent while advancing their own political ambitions, irrespective of the economic impact. The 'over- and underachievers' of institutional transformation often originate in this opportunity space because the action of individuals, external actors or pure 'chance' result in institutional choices that transcend the structural constraints of the outgoing system. These choices in turn create path-dependencies (North, 1990, p. 99; Stark, 1992, p. 21) when new interests organize to match the new institutions and ultimately acquire vested interests in these institutions.

POLITICAL INSTITUTIONS AND ECONOMIC CHANGE

The change of economic institutions entails a movement from an ideal, thoroughly planned and centrally managed economic system (in effect an administrative system) to an economic system based on market actors and market signals. This transformation involves two separate stages. During the first stage the institutions of the incumbent system are dismantled by internal and external liberalization, deregulation, demonopolization and privatization.

These elements are shared by all post-communist economies. The second stage is one of institution building, during which the legal basis, regulatory bodies and institutions regulating (and modifying) the market are established. The components involved will differ from country to country, reflecting national priorities, mentalities, values and – ultimately – the type of democratic capitalism opted for. On the more concrete level, the components included in institution building will also reflect the interests and powers of social and political interests and their losses and/or gains in relation to specific components of the emerging system.

Policy outcomes are not only determined by vectors of social and collective interests and their preferences. Such interests are also processed by political institutions, in new democracies themselves subjects to intense constitutional battles (Johannsen, 1999). In these conflicts the 'political self-interest, that of both politicians and their parties, is the dominant motivation behind the choice of institutional designs' (Lijphart and Waisman, 1996, p. 244). At the same time political actors are constrained by myths about the virtues of historic or foreign institutions or by their sheer lack of analytical capabilities. In this process formal political institutions, once installed, will determine the exposure of decision-makers to popular and political pressures and structure the access of collective and social interests to the loci of power and influence. This will also be the place to resolve dilemmas of collective action by informing actors about the likely behaviour of others and by providing them the opportunity to make 'credible' commitments (Hall and Taylor, 1996). Political institutions vary in their ability to contain conflicts without political polarization or fragmentation when they are confronted with different societies and structures of interests. If the institutions are able to contain conflicts and come up with solutions that are acceptable to the interests involved, they will sustain democratic development. If the institutional design excludes or restrains major interests from the decision making process, however, democracy will be endangered because the groups might turn to alternative modes of political action which in turn might either jeopardize democracy or halt economic reforms (Weaver and Rockman, 1993). The specific configuration of political institutions also structures solutions to collective action and distributive dilemmas (Bräutigam, 1997). Particular institutional configurations will reinforce structural constraints, while others may override constraints by altering the incentives of social actors or by limiting their access to power (Bartlet and Hunter, 1997, p. 88).

Formal political institutions may be anchored in the state as the legal and administrative basis of individual rights and liberties ('level of democracy'), or they may entail the configuration of institutions, for example executive–legislative relationships and electoral provisions. Informal political institutions are based in civil society, reflecting social interests and cleavages, political cultures, values and traditions of participation. Society based intermediary institutions may also have a formal basis, however, when parties and organizations oscillate in the interface between formal state institutions and informal societal institutions.

STRATEGIES FOR INSTITUTIONAL CHANGE

The initial conditions and external environment define the context within which all reforms must be implemented, and the opportunity space creates the openings for making decisions that define the institutional and political paths of future development. The pattern of institutional change, however, is not merely a passive reflection of initial conditions as mediated by political institutions. The reform strategy, as defined by the reforming government, is instrumental. The discourse on economic reform strategies has mainly focused on two variants: the radical (or big bang) approach to economic reforms versus the gradual (or evolutionary) approach. This dichotomy has obscured what are actually four separate issues and strategies for institutional change: sequencing, scope, phasing and pace.[7] *Sequencing* has to do with the democracy or market first discussion. *Scope* is defined as the comprehensiveness of institutional change. *Phasing* is understood as a certain pattern or sequence in which the instruments are applied and *pace* is the speed at which initiatives are launched.

The issue of *sequencing* reflects the traditional concern that democracy will prevent institutional change because the social costs will impel the losers to take advantage of the democratic institutions to obstruct or hinder change. Hence the argument that the non-democratic regime should be maintained while pursuing economic reforms.

Scope encompasses two alternative strategies reflecting traditional schools of economic thought applied to post-communist economic transformation (described in further detail in Chapter 3): The neo-liberal approach favours a strong role for the market and minimal state interference in the economy, and structural changes in the economy are expected to be spontaneously generated once economic agents have adapted to the new economic institutions. The neo-structuralist approach argues for active government policies, for example in the form of industrial and social policies. The two approaches reflect not only alternative visions of how to reach a market economy. As observed by Brada (1995, p. 185) and the World Bank (1996, pp. 111, 113), they also represent alternative normative judgements as to what kind of market economy is the end goal.

Phasing describes the relative timing of the major reform components: stabilization, liberalization and institutional restructuring. The discourses have concentrated on whether stabilization and liberalization should precede institutional restructuring – or vice versa. The priority on stabilization and liberalization reflects the neo-classical concern that the major issue is to 'get the price right' and create an economic environment that will force enterprises to restructure and adapt to the new conditions and optimize the efficiency of resource allocation. The priority on institutional restructuring reflects an evolutionary or institutional perspective where the major concern is to maintain institutional knowledge and human capital in existing enterprises and institutions.

Pace reflects the well-known distinction between a big bang and a gradual approach. The former argues for rapidly launching of a critical mass of re-form initiatives, whereas the latter prefers a gradual introduction of the measures necessary for a transformation towards a market economy. Eco-nomically, the big bang approach is based on the neo-classical assumption that economic agents will relatively quickly adapt to new formal institutions once they are installed. Gradualism focuses on the slowly moving informal institutional and informational aspects of change and draws its arguments partly from evolutionary economy, partly from historical neo-institutional-ism. Politically, pace and phasing reflect alternative expectations about the way in which the general population will react to the social and economic costs of transition. The priority on stabilization, liberalization and pace assumes that it is impossible to achieve democratic support for the reforms. Hence the call for swift and comprehensive reforms which may be interpreted as a 'sneak attack' (Armijo, Bresstecker and Lowenthal, 1994, p. 168), or as 'voodoo politics' (Williamson and Haggard, 1994, p. 584). Changes are introduced before the population realizes what is going on, what may be termed 'bridge burning', in that irreversible changes are implemented before the inevitable political backlash sets in (Przeworski, 1991, p. 179). In a democratic context the feasibility of the first strategy thus hinges on the viability of this policy. It must necessarily demonstrate positive results before the next elections. The gradual approach takes the alternative perspective and fears that any economic reform which does not receive broad political support will eventually provoke a reaction that may endanger the entire reform process.

STATE CAPACITY AND STRATEGIES OF INSTITUTIONAL CHANGE

As emphasized by Eatwell et al. (1995, p. 19), the state bureaucracies of the communist systems did to a large extent acquire legislative functions due to the insignificance of the legislative organs and the absence of efficient ex-ternal control. In the economic sphere, this situation resulted in the autarchy of economic ministries which pursued narrow sectoral interests, with neither social nor political control (Nørgaard, 1985). The post-communist economies set completely new standards for the tasks to be performed by the public sector (Hesse, 1993; König, 1992; Public Administration and Development, 1993). Administrative command, control and regulation will, of course, re-main important instruments in executive policies. But they will increasingly become supplemented and/or replaced by closer collaboration between the public and private sectors, by incentives, services and provision of information, financial transfers and advice. To a varying extent, depending on the type of capitalism opted for in each specific country, we will also experience a decreasing amount of state interference, where services previously provided by the state are taken over by the private sector or third sector institutions and organizations.

In this new social and economic context, the competence of the existing bureaucracy is inadequate, both in terms of the general administrative organization and operational procedures and in terms of the skills of the individual civil servants who were nurtured in the old system. To these systemic weaknesses are further added the problems and demands engendered by the political and economic transition itself: the greater demands made on the state apparatus than in 'normal' market economies during the transition period; the fiscal crises of the state which limits the quantity as well as the quality of administration because of competition with the higher salaries paid in an emerging private sector; the political dismissal of servants of the old regime irrespective of individual skills and their replacement by often very young and inexperienced individuals.

Although the above observations are valid for all post-communist economies, 'the basic principles of socialist administrations were applied with different emphasis and in different forms in the countries of Central and Eastern Europe', as observed by Hesse (1993, p. 220). The differentiation between countries in terms of administrative legacies and capacities has implications for the launching and implementation of economic reforms (Huang, 1994, p. 445; Pachomov, 1998), and what becomes an asset in the emerging economic system may be a liability in the transition process.

This primarily applies to state capacity. A limited and poorly equipped central planning bureaucracy will introduce reforms incrementally because the leadership does not have sufficient information about the state of the economy to launch large-scale, comprehensive reforms. In contrast, a large, well-equipped and relatively competent bureaucracy provides the leadership with the bureaucratic capacities needed to launch comprehensive reforms. Once the need for reforms is accepted politically, relatively dependable information about the state of the economy gives the political decision-makers the confidence they need to launch an immediate, large-scale programme.

During the succeeding reform processes, however, the relationship between the speed of the reforms and administrative capabilities is reversed. The administrative strengths and capabilities of the well equipped system become liabilities when entrenched bureaucracies with vested interests in the old system crowd out the emerging private sector. In the administratively less developed country, in contrast, these weaknesses give the private sector room to evolve. Hence, the administrative capability, which was an asset during the initial stages of reforms, turns into a liability in subsequent stages. In the less developed countries, the situation evolved in the reverse order. The weakness of the economic administration is a liability during the initial stages of the reform process and hinders the development of any grand scheme or blueprint. In the later stages of the reform process, a weak economic administration may turn into an asset because of the fewer and weaker institutional interest groups embedded in the old system.

Table 2.2. Economic reforms (phasing, pace) in post-communist economies as a function of administrative capacity.

		Phase of reforms	
		Launching	Implementation
Administrative capacity	High	Comprehensive Big bang (sufficient information for a grand scheme)	Incremental Slow development of market relations (political opposition, crowding out)
	Low	Incremental Slow development of market relations (insufficient information for a grand scheme)	Relatively fast development of market relations (political room for development)

The tentative linkages described in Table 2.2 illustrate which linkages we may ideally expect between the administrative capacities of post-communist economies and alternative strategies of institutional change. Ideally, the two extremes represent the experiences of China and less developed parts of the former Soviet Union versus Eastern Europe and Russia. As observed by Pachomov (1998), the same contradictory logic also applies to the role of political culture. A more outspoken individualism (as for example in Ukraine) makes the transition more difficult than in Russia, where traditional collectivism makes it easier for people to adhere to common goals (or government programmes). The very same collectivism, however, makes it more difficult to make capitalism work, and individualism therefore becomes an asset in this context.

THE EFFECTS OF POLICY OUTCOMES: WHEN POLITICS BECOMES ITS OWN CAUSE

There are two possible outcomes when changing economic institutions in post-communist systems. In the short term we have seen an across-the-board contraction of GDP and a surge in inflation[8] when the economic systems adapt to new mechanisms of allocation and a new set of relative prices. In the longer term the institutional changes imply a redistribution in power and welfare. Both processes have their winners and losers and, after the revolutionary excitement has abated, we would expect them to react to the changes in relation to their balance sheet of gains and losses. A general (and static) picture of the expected winners and losers is outlined in Table 2.3. This is the general pattern which in concrete cases will be reflected in the interface between institutional strategy and the social and political interests embedded in the system at the onset of the changes. In individual countries it may be hypothesized that social and political reactions to institutional strategies produce the recursive model outlined in Figure 1.1. Political reactions to the outcomes of institutional strategies feed back into the political landscape and are processed through (or outside) the political institutions as support for or rejection of the reform strategy, and (perhaps) the democratic institutions that produced the outcomes. In political terms there will be two kinds of reaction to an institutional strategy: 1) social reactions to economic hardship and social decay; 2) institutional opposition from collective interests that stand to lose power, influence and wealth because of the changes.

Table 2.3. Winners and losers of change in economic institutions in a proto-post-communist system.

	Inflation	Institutional changes	Change of value system
Winners	Groups positioned to benefit from instability and rapid change in relative prices, traders, new financial elite, criminal structures.	Owners of privatised items (new or insiders taking control over companies). New entrepreneurs. Persons (mostly young) with marketable resources.	Meritocratic oriented groups and individuals.
Losers	Everybody on fixed incomes; Savers.	Old nomenclatura and the manager class; Traditional working class.	Egalitarian oriented groups and individuals.

Institutional change and social responses

The political changes in post-communist countries were caused by broad discontent with economic development. Dissatisfaction cut across social, ethnic and functional divides and included the broad public as well as strategic elites in industrial management, the armed forces and the political and administrative leadership. This loss of economic and welfare legitimacy paved the way for political upheavals. Among the broad population there was an imminent expectation that reforms would provide the wealth and welfare that had been squandered by the old system and regime. Disappointment with the social outcome of the reforms in turn rebounds into the political process.

In terms of equity and poverty, are the side effects of structural transformation and growth compatible with political support for a continuation of the reform process? Or will they produce a social and political reaction that revokes the institutional reforms because of 'the associated increases in income inequality and individual uncertainty'? (Roland, 1997, p. 181).

The first years of transition inevitably lead to a temporary decrease in efficiency and growth as existing patterns of allocation and distribution are being transformed. An increase in inequality is the logical corollary while the new system is generating winners and losers. In this context we must distinguish between political consequences of an increase in inequality and poverty: as resources for political action and participation and as sources of regime legitimacy (or lack thereof). One the one hand, inequality and poverty are proxies for the resources available for individual political participation. The fewer physical or intellectual resources possessed by the individual, the more time he spends on purely physical (and social) survival, and he is therefore less likely to engage in political activities. On the other hand, this very degradation of social and human values de-legitimizes the political regime and impels people to political action. Hence, when assessing the political consequences of increased inequality and poverty, we are faced with two countervailing processes: people are losing individual resources for political action while that very degradation of their lives force them to act.[9]

When choosing the statistical proxy for increased inequality and poverty, as used in this study, it is important to distinguish between the impact on human resources for political action and impact on human capabilities. Economic restructuring, inflation, the real decline in GDP, unemployment and the ensuing across-the-board decline in real incomes are the major explanations why income inequality increases and many people are pushed into poverty. Furthermore, the syndromes of transition, i.e. economic costs, environmental degradation (another legacy of the old system), individual costs of adaptation to a new political and social system and ensuing stress related factors that engender deterioration in health, aggravated by the disintegration of state and civil society, produces the deterioration of capabilities. In the perspective of this study the two-fold consequence of income inequality and poverty is that an increasing number of people lose their

Table 2.4. Social costs: Causes, results and effects.

Causes: syndrome of transition	Resources	Capabilities
Inflation; GDP-decline; institutional changes; environmental degradation; psychological stress; collapse of state and civil-society institutions.	Decrease in income; inequality; increase in income poverty.	Loss of capabilities: nourishment, shelter, literacy, premature death, social anomalies.

capabilities for full political membership of the community where they live, either because they are illiterate, in poor health, victims of social anomalies, fight for social and physical survival – or, ultimately, are unable to stay alive!

The existence of inequality and poverty may induce people to political action, which again may ultimately stop the economic reform process. It is necessary, however, to distinguish between two types of political reaction to inequity and poverty: as a response to perceived injustices and as self-defence against a social decline, putting their own life style in jeopardy. Firstly, people react to inequity (or inequality) because they perceive it as being in conflict with the basic values of society, and not necessarily because they see themselves as disadvantaged (although this, of course, will often be a corollary of the argument). They feel, for example, that the existence of beggars, homeless people and child prostitutes in the streets is incompatible with the ethical foundation of their society – or they feel threatened that they may be the next victims of the misery they see – and are thus prompted to political action. In this context, it is the feeling of inequity or poverty, 'the distance from a community shared idea about the minimum subsistence income' (Vecernik, 1995, p. 16) or the subjective poverty line (Deleeck and Van den Bosch, 1992, p. 109; Popova, 1996; Szule, 1996) that is important because feelings and perceptions rather than objective criteria provoke people to political action. 'Equity' and what constitutes acceptable levels of misery vary in different times and places, as will the statistical proxies. Also citizens' perception of what constitutes a fair distribution of economic outcomes differs over time and place, as does the relative share of those that prefer an egalitarian distribution of welfare (egalitarians) and those who are achievement oriented (meritocrats). The abstract quest for equality cannot, as stated by Barry 'be derived from anything else'.[10] It is, rather, a reflection of what historical experiences and present circumstances have defined as being legitimate levels of inequality.[11] In this context what ultimately matters if distribution and poverty induce people to political action is not the absolute level of inequality as measured by statistics and surveys, but rather whether the experienced inequality and poverty is perceived as legitimate by the citizens of a given country. Further, experiences from developing countries indicate that political reactions to unequal distribution of economic outcomes are not primarily related to differences between rich and poor (income distribution) but to the poverty profile of the individual country, that is, differences 'between the national and foreigners and among the various ethnic, tribal, and regional groups within the domestic population, which cut across statistical indices of income equality' (Lal and Myint, 1996, p. 29).

Secondly, people may react to poverty as a gesture of self-defence against human degradation. However, what makes people feel poor will differ across time and place, depending on social, economic and political development and, particularly in the post-communist countries, their frame of reference. The political response to poverty is conditioned by one's own position and felt deprivation compared to others in the same society. Also Przeworski's argument (1991, p. 91), that if consumption falls below a certain minimal level people will feel compelled to act against continued reforms to secure their own physical survival, must be understood in a relative context.[12] Hence, in that respect the relative rather than the absolute level of poverty is important. Consequently, it is not possible to define a fixed line of absolute poverty, which, across time and space, will provoke political reaction, as seems to be the implication of Przeworski's argument. What does provoke a political reaction by the poor should therefore not only be seen as a consequence of a specific income level necessary for physical survival, but rather as the income necessary for social survival. As soon as people sense that their existence as human beings within a given social context is at risk, they may be expected to react against a continuation of reforms. Although the existence of poverty may thus be an important indication of inequity, it is important to keep the two concepts and their potential political repercussion separate, because their political impacts are of different natures: inequality (and inequity) works primarily through its effect on regime legitimacy and individual uncertainty, poverty through the social self-defence initiated by those whom the economic changes have pushed below the level of what is considered a decent human existence.

All post-communist countries do share a legacy of socialist equality. They were 'indoctrinated and drilled in the ideology of equality, so that higher incomes and wealth were always considered to be unfairly won' (Vecernik, 1995, p. 13). Critical perceptions of the inequalities that followed the economic transition have therefore existed since it began. The attitude to poverty was shaped by a different legacy. Poverty was, as summarized by Milanovic, perceived as a malfunction that threatened the basic tenets, and hence the very legitimacy, of the socialist system. It was therefore – as far as possible kept hidden from the public eye – and the poor that did exist were dealt with 'not unlike in Calvinist ethics' (Milanovic, 1995, p. 5) as parasites that did not want to work.[13]

Institutional change and collective interests.

Highly concentrated actors are better able to solve the coordination problems and 'thus to pursue collectively rational rent-seeking behaviour' wield more power and influence than more diffuse and less organized and concentrated interests (Leidy and Ibrahim, 1996). As documented in previous research, the same mechanism prevented the reform of the institutions of the planned economies, despite recurrent attempts by reform minded leaders,[14] because '... over time the small groups of administrators and planners in each industry and sector were able, by inconspicuous and subtle means, to overcome the difficulties of collective action enough to collude in their own interest, even though this reduced economic performance and thereby damaged the interests of the seemingly all-powerful Politbureaus above them. A new class of subordinate officials came to enjoy spoils and powers that, in an early Stalinist phase, were possessed almost exclusively by the top leadership' (Olson, 1996, p. 20). What we saw here was the general 'logic' of collective action where one of the classical definitions by Mancur Olson remains an apt description of the conservatism of the Soviet type systems and the political problems associated with institutional change in post-communist economies (Olson, 1982, p. 166):

> '... small groups are more likely to be organised than large ones, but that (since small groups organise less slowly) the disproportionate organizational and collusive power of small groups will be greatest in lately unstable societies. The theory here predicts that the unstable society will have fewer and weaker mass organisations than stable societies, but that small groups that can collude more readily will often be able to further their common interests.'

As was made clear already in the outline in Table 2.4, reformers face dilemmas which are well known from third world countries (Haggard et al., 1995): that anti-reform forces (industrial and bureaucratic interests often associated with social losers) are well-organized, have large bureaucratic resources and are frequently close to the centres of decision-making, while the potential winners (new entrepreneurs, successful workers or specialists etc.), are relative diffuse, poorly organized and without direct access to decision-makers (Crawford, 1995; Surdej 1993; Spiegeleire, 1995; Stoner-Weiss, 1997; Leidy and Ibrahim, 1996). But the post-communist countries are different in this aspect too. Some have highly concentrated industries that can easily collude to prevent institutional changes that may contravene their interests. Other countries have smaller economic units which are easier to adjust and are likely to have more difficulties in organizing a unified front against change.

MAKING A DRAFT DESIGN

In previous sections we have constructed the conceptual building blocks needed to provide an explanation of why some countries were more successful than others in changing their economic institutions. But we still need a preliminary design of how to put the blocks together if we are to come up with answers to why some countries were more successful in changing their institutions than others. Our data and knowledge of the world of post-communism are still rudimentary, and we should have to wait for decades if we were to construct insights built on induction alone. However, in designing the building blocks, all of which are partial theories derived from the storehouse of social science theory and concepts, we have already indicated that there are preliminary maps that we can try to follow. These maps are based on the experiences of other countries in other times, and they can therefore only serve as general guidelines which must be modified, rejected – or confirmed – along the way. As will be demonstrated in the following chapter this is the course followed by the large majority of social scientists engaged in the study of post-communist economies and polities.

This study also uses previous insights, or partial theories, to guide the search for answers. More precisely, the point of departure for this study is the classical discussion of comparative political analysis in, for example, Sartori (1991) and Lijphart (1971, 1999), and further in Przeworski and Teune (1970), Szule (1996), Wellhofer (1989), Collier (1991) and Tranøy (1993); and comparative economics in, for example, Keynes (1890) and North (1990). Lijphardt, in a classical formulation, viewed the comparative method as: '... one of the basic [scientific] methods – the others being the experimental, statistical and case study methods – of establishing general empirical propositions' Lijphart (1971, p. 182). He saw the comparative method as an emergency solution due to the 'many variables, small N dilemma'. In this study we face a similar situation, where the number of variables in individual cases explaining differences in outcomes in the real world by far exceed the number of post-communist countries (Katz, 1991). Drawing on Keynes (1890, p. 334), Lal and Myint (1996, p. 5) correspondingly describe the comparative economic method as 'wider than the purely statistical inquiry (econometrics)'. They emphasize that such a view is too narrow as 'the economic methods used in practice by economists embody not only this form of quantitative induction, but also qualitative induction and, of course, deduction'.

This study applies the comparative method at two levels and from two perspectives. At the first level the comparative method is applied with a 'most different system design' on the assumption that we can find propositions that are valid across very different regions or systems. This approach implicitly guided the considerations in the introduction and previous sections of this chapter. At this level of analysis we introduce concepts and partial theories from other 'most-different' systems, and apply them as hypotheses on the subset of post-communist countries that are the subject of the present study. At the second level we proceed with 'a most similar system design'. We compare systems that were and remain similar except for those variables whose causal effects we want to explore. On this level of analysis we test partial hypotheses against available data and evidence in the form of conventional statistical cross-country regressions and focused case studies. The first level takes its point of departure in a 'most different system design' (Przeworski and Teune, 1970, pp. 34–35; Lijphart and Waisman, 1996, pp. 3–6). Hence, it is assumed that the intra-system relationship between variables is identical across the 'most different' systems involved and that the generated partial theories hold universal value across time and space. In other words, the guiding hypothesis is that specific patterns of development can be inferred from other cases across time and space. This approach is similar to what Skocpol and Somers (1980) term 'parallel demonstration of theory'.[15]

In their broad attempt to identify the use of comparison in comparative history, Skocpol and Somers distinguish between three types of comparative analysis. The first and already mentioned comparison, i.e. the 'parallel demonstration of theory', has the ambition 'to persuade the reader that a given, explicitly delineated hypothesis or theory can repeatedly demonstrate its fruitfulness – its ability convincingly to order the evidence – when applied to a series of relevant historical trajectories' (ibid., p. 176). Hence, the focus of this approach is on nomothetic variables which work across different systems and are assumed to be valid universally across time and space. The second type of comparative analysis is seen as 'the contrast of contexts'. The focus of this approach is 'the historical integrity of each case as a whole [–] that particular nations, empires, civilizations, or religions constitute relatively irreducible wholes, each a complex and unique socio-historical configuration in its own right' (ibid., p. 178). Hence, within this perspective idiographic factors overshadow nomothetic causal factors. The third type of comparative history is 'macro-causal analysis' which uses 'comparative history primarily for the purpose of making causal inferences about macro-level structures and processes' (ibid., p. 181). Within this perspective, preference is given to neither nomothetic nor idiographic variables, which are all treated similarly in the search for causal explanations of individual cases.

Skocpol and Somers see these alternative ways of using comparative analysis as supplementary and as forming a kind of research cycle (ibid., p. 180):

> 'Thus parallel comparative history tends to call forth contrast-oriented arguments when the need develops to set limits to the scope or claims of an overly generalised social-scientific theory. Contrast-oriented comparative history may give rise to macro-analytic arguments when juxtapositions of historical trajectories begin to suggest testable causal hypotheses. Finally, too, macro-analytic comparative history can create a demand for the kind of general theorising that precedes the construction of a parallel comparative analysis.'

This study applies the same logic of macro-social and macroeconomic analysis, but in a somewhat different sequence (see Figure 2.4).

At the first stage hypotheses are generated by parallel demonstrations of theory. It is hypothesized that the partial theories generated across time and space are of universal value and therefore also hold for the post-communist countries. This is the logic applied in Chapter 3. At the second level of analysis we make 'causal inferences about macro-level structures and hypotheses' that were inferred from 'the parallel demonstration of theory'. We here apply a 'most similar system design', we are dealing with 20 post-communist countries who share the path dependencies of very similar political and economic institutions and similar demands from the international environment – while they were different with regard to a number of underlying structural (1st and 2nd order initial conditions) or causal variables that ultimately explain the variation in outcomes. In this context we will concentrate 'on meaningful systemic differences' (Lijphart, 1975, p. 165) in a design that is based on a belief that, in the formulation of Przeworski and Teune (1970, p. 39), 'a number of significant differences will be found among similar systems and that these differences can be used in explanation'. This is the approach applied in the cross-country statistiscal analyses in Chapters 5 and 6.

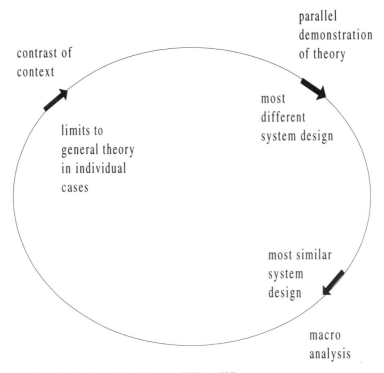

Source: *Adapted after Skocpol and Somers, 1980, p. 197.*

Figure 2.4. Research strategy and design.

As illustrated in Figure 2.4, the third stage of research is what Skocpol and Somers termed the 'contrast of context'. This phase of research involves looking for features that give each case its distinctive character. In the present study this stage will involve an attempt to identify the idiographic variables that contribute to illuminating the variation in outcome. We will concentrate on the outliers, i.e. countries that in terms of institutional changes performed significantly better or worse than predicted by initial conditions. This is the logic I follow in Chapter 7.[16] Finally, the identification of idiographic factors during the comparison of 'most similar cases' leads us back to a discussion of the universal theories generated from a sample of the most different systems originally introduced in the 'parallel demonstration of theory' stage of research. This perspective will only be taken up in the concluding chapter, where I return to the global perspective outlined in the introduction.[17]

Following Hayek (1994, pp. 142–143) and Lal and Myint (1996, p. 5), it should finally be emphasized that we are dealing with complex orders 'where the elements that have to be taken into account are neither few enough that you can know them all nor a sufficiently large number that you can substitute probabilities for the new information'. Consequently, the study of complex orders, like biology, meteorology or the social sciences, can only predict specific outcomes with great uncertainties. The best that can be achieved is 'pattern prediction, or predictions of the principle' – 'the recurrent associations of a range of effects with limited causes'. Hence, the following chapters will not be able to predict which post-communist countries will ultimately prove successful. We can only infer which countries followed institutional reforms strategies that, under their specific conditions, have proven successful.

RESTATING THE QUESTIONS

Having designed the building blocks and derived the principles needed for the construction of the final building, I can restate the main questions that will guide this study about change of economic institutions in emerging post-communist democracies.

The fundamental ambition of the following analysis is to explain why some post-communist countries – better than others – have been able to adopt and implement the change of economic institutions they all set out for when the old system collapsed. In order to answer this question we must determine the relative importance of structures and actors or, in the parlance of this book, the relative importance of 1st and 2nd order initial conditions and institutional strategies (sequencing, scope, phasing and pace of reform initiatives) in the explanation of successful institutional changes. Secondly, we should explain why some countries have been better able than others to transcend the constraints, economic and political, that were embedded in their initial conditions and (related) social and political costs and embark on efficient institutional strategies. When answering this second question we shall examine the importance of the opportunity space following the demise of the old system, the dynamics of popular support, the impact of collective interests and the role of political institutions as solutions to dilemmas of distribution and collective action. Finally, we should examine the role of internal and external actors and ideas in the choice and implementation of institutional strategies. This will take us to the impact of institutional change on economic growth and welfare and, ultimately, on democracy.

NOTES

1. Moreno and Trehan (1997) show that location is an asset in its own right, because it provides a country with access to markets and capital.

2. In this distinction, and in particular with regard to the political aspects of economic structures I have been inspired by Lal and Myint (1996). They analyse 26 developing countries, where the crucial political differences are proven to be between labour and land-abundant countries.

3. This illustration has been developed on the basis of the discussion by Amsden, Kachanovics and Taylor (1994, Chapter 2).

4. It can be argued that this scenario replicates the much criticized structuralist macroeconomic policy prescription, emphasizing growth at the expense of inflation, deficit finance and external balance. The intersection between the potential supply curve and aggregate demand thus represents an unstable equilibrium. However, my task here is only to illustrate the possible effects of initial constraints – not to discuss alternative policy measures, which are the subject of subsequent chapters. For an empirical critique of the structuralist approach, see Dornbush and Edwards (1991).

5. Kahler (1990, p. 158) summarizes the three domestic variables influencing the relative acceptance of Keynesian policies in the following way: economic viability (the theoretical appeal and problem-solving ability of a set of ideas for economic professionals); administrative viability (the degree to which a set of ideas accorded with existing administrative institutions and was feasible to implement); and political viability (the degree to which a doctrine served as an instrument for politicians in coalition-building and retaining political support).

6. Also Lenin's classical concept of a 'revolutionary situation' reflects the same idea.

7. The literature from which these concepts were derived will be presented in Chapter 3. Asilis and Milesi-Ferretti (1994, pp. 7f) address the same aspects of institutional change when applying the concepts of 'speed, depth and sequencing of reform'.

8. The reasons for the contraction and the surge in inflation have been the subject of much discussion which will be briefly introduced in Chapter 4.

9. Asilis and Milesi-Ferretti (1994, p. 8) address the same issue when they advocate 'measures that cushion the impact on the weakest segments of the population in the form of social safety nets that may enhance the political sustainability of reforms beyond moral considerations'. They forget, however that 'moral considerations' often influence regime legitimacy, and hence the political capital of government.

10. B. Barry, 'Claims of Common Citizenship', Times Literary Supplement (1989, pp. 20–26), here quoted after Lal and Myint (1996, p. 45).

11. For an introduction to this discussion, see Lal and Myint (1996, pp. 25–39) and Lal (1976).

12. See further chapter 4 for a discussion of initial income distribution.

13. In January 1918 Lenin wrote 'he who does not work neither shall he eat'. Carr (1950) quotes this as the practical credo of socialism. After Milanovic (1995, p. 5).

14. I made a modest contribution to that research in my book Politik og reformer i Sovjetunionen, Sydjysk Universitetsforlag, 1985.

15. It is also the method applied (although not explicit) by Lijphart and Waisman (1996) in their comparison of political institutions in Eastern Europe and Latin America.

16. Without here entering further into the methodological debate on comparative analyses, I make a practical case in the present study for combining the statistical approach with structured case studies, focusing in particular on the analysis and explanation of deviant cases. Building in particular on the arguments of Nissen (1998) and Coppedge (1999), I believe that Small-N comparisons and quantitative larger-N

analyses are complementary. The larger N-analysis needs the greater variety of explanatory factors that can be included in the 'thick theory' of a case study. Small-N case studies need to test and generalize their findings into 'thin theories' of statistical testing. Ideally such a combined strategy should allow the researcher to consider 'both structural factors and factors reflecting historical processes and human agency' (Ragin, 1987, p. 70). The same perspective was already in 1997 applied by Mogens Petersen in a Danish article. He wrote that 'deviant or critical case studies have the purpose of testing, refining or modifying theories, about which we know, that they cannot be applied universally ...' (Petersen, 1977, p. 244) (author's translation).

17. I do not want to engage in the discussion on 'Conceptual travels of Transiologists' or 'Conceptual Stretching' in the study of post-communist economies and democracies in this context. My position, outlined in this section and further elaborated in Chapter 3, is rather similar to that of Schmitter and Karl (1994). This article and the follow-up article by Valerie Bunce (1995a) summarizes the major issues in the discussion.

3. The Research Agenda: Old Ideas in New Bottles

'Eastern Europe's market for policy ideas, suddenly opened in 1989, was swiftly captured by an Anglo-American product with a liberal brand name. (...) it has made up for any deficiency by superb advertising and aggressive salesmanship' Gowan (1995, p. 3).

To say that research in general and social science research in particular mirrors the societal environment in which it is conducted is to state the obvious. The debacle which has tormented 'Soviet studies' for the last decade is nevertheless unique in the history of the social sciences and the humanities. Its effect on the scientific community can be compared only to major paradigmatic changes within the natural sciences. But even here the effects have always been more gradual and have diffused into the scientific community through several decades. In 'Soviet studies' the size of the cataclysm was indicated when even the name of the profession became obsolete with the disintegration of the Soviet Union.

More to the point, the collapse of the socialist systems challenged old scientific paradigms of understanding those systems and what came after without offering obvious alternatives. Although the starting point for the changes was an outspoken ideological aspiration to emulate 'the West', it soon became clear that the road from here to there (and what was 'there') was far from apparent. Consequently, research on the previous socialist systems was channelled into designs of strategies for change. While only a minority challenged the goal (however vaguely described) the strategies for reaching that goal became the major subject of research and scientific controversy. 'Transitology' became the somewhat derogatory term carrying the same flavour as its predecessor 'Sovietology'.

This chapter takes a broader view of research on institutional change in socialist and post-socialist systems. The ambition is to identify the theoretical position of alternative approaches and to explore how previous research can help us navigate in the subsequent analyses. The first section traces the development of research on socialist systems before the present process of change, as a prelude to the emergence of 'transitology'. The following sections

39

examine the contending paradigms in economic and political sciences, and the last section takes us back to where we concluded in Chapter 2: which theories or models should be the subjects of our 'parallel demonstration of theory'?

SOVIETOLOGY AND TRANSITOLOGY: GENESIS AND DISCOURSES

Like development studies Sovietology was a product of political needs. Although a few writings on the Soviet system had been published, mostly by devout (or renegade) communists, the scientific study of communist systems was a child of the Cold War. The need felt by political decision-makers in the most important Western powers generated the institutions and studies that were to produce a clearer image of what was at that time considered the 'mystery wrapped in a riddle veiled in an enigma', to quote Winston Churchill's famous phrase. During the following decades, this political birth became the main structural constraint hindering a normal cumulative insight into the workings of the socialist, communist (or whatever label one preferred) systems which had been constructed in three waves[1] of communist governments. The political constraints were revealed in two distinct development phases.

During the first phase, from the late 1940s until the early 1960s, one major factor was the origin of the first generation of Sovietologists. In the main research centres, a disproportionate share of the first generation of researchers was drawn from the pool of recent emigrants with obvious hostile feelings towards the systems they had been forced to flee. Another group of the first generation of Soviet experts was drawn from the pool of traditional historians specializing in Russian and Byzantine history. A second factor influencing the first phase of Sovietology was the type of government and private funding that was available. Although the picture was ambiguous, the American and the few European funding institutions primarily tended to fund projects focusing on the output functions of the perceived enemy (Hough, 1977). Last but not least, and connected to the funding issue, came the role played by the socialist systems as focal points. To the political right, the Soviet-type systems became an important point of negative identification and mobilization, whereas the communist left used the Soviet system as a positive point of identification. The socialist and liberal traditions vacillated between these extremes in their attitudes towards the system and the ensuing policy implications.[2]

The outcome of the political mechanisms that transformed the general political climate of the Cold War into research policy became an excessive focus on the output functions of the Soviet-type systems. The totalitarian model which in Friederich and Brzezinski's versions epitomized this approach (Friederich and Brzezinski, 1956), undoubtedly captured important parameters in countries that were being transformed by a unified party ma-nipulating a utopian ideology. However, the model was never able to integrate the social, economic and political dynamism instigated by the party itself.

The second phase of Sovietology coincided with and was partly produced by the East–West détente from the mid-late 1960s onwards. The political interest in 'humanizing' the former enemy became an important factor. The various 'theories of convergence' became the most articulate examples of this new trend. More generally this trend coincided with an increased interest in the input structures in Soviet-type systems, e.g. in discussions about the nature and impact of interest groups in the political process (Skilling and Griffiths, 1971), a trend that, with a certain time lag, reflected the break-through of the 'inputism' of behaviourism in the social sciences – at the expense of the 'outputism' of the traditional institutional approach. Another discussion in the same field was about the nature and impact of individual political activities registered in the Soviet Union in the late 1960s and early 1970s (Nørgaard, 1979). Concretely, the general climate was also in this connection transformed into projects of the kind that were likely to receive funding and thus stimulate young scientific careers. Later on, this discussion became more sophisticated in a search for (Western inspired) models of interest intermediation that could be applied to Soviet type systems (Bunce and Echols, 1980).

This development of Soviet studies was influenced by sociological and institutional factors as well. One was the generational change among sovietologists (Millar, 1995). Whereas the first generation had been either natives of the socialist systems and/or classical historians, the next generation of scholars to enter the field consisted of social scientists with solid methodological, technical and conceptual training within one of the social sciences. Hence, to a much larger extent than their (still active) predecessors in the field, they were oriented towards comparative studies and were against the implicit demonizing of the socialist systems compared to the idealized Western system which had been inherent in much previous theory. This second generation had much better opportunities for travelling to and carrying out research in the socialist system, and they had access to the social and economic data produced after the rebirth of the social sciences in the Soviet Union in the late 1960s. These trends also coincided with critical developments in the systems themselves. Especially the loosening of central control that accompanied the dismantling of the Stalinist system triggered an increased impact of latent sectoral and regional interests and the emergence of an embryonic sphere for public debate and participation (Nørgaard, 1988).

As a consequence of this development, from the early 1970s onwards Soviet studies were tormented by what was partly a generational conflict, partly a conflict between two contending paradigms. On the one hand, an in-creasing number of scholars focused on nomothetic factors, implicitly or explicitly basing their research on comparisons with other countries and systems. Behind this research was, as observed by Spiegeleire (1995, p. 50), a specific configuration of the Soviet system – actors were assumed to behave rationally within the existing institutional framework. From this perspective, issues and behaviour became comparable across systems. What differed was not the actors' motivation, but only the institutional framework.

On the other hand, a large number of Sovietologists within the traditional field of area studies continued to emphasize non-rational determinants of behaviour in Soviet-type systems. Whether driven by motivational explorations of epistemological relativism or not, they stressed the 'sui generis' nature of Soviet-type systems. At the level of politics, this approach continued to emphasize the totalitarian or top-down nature of the political system. It was this uniqueness and focus on ideographic factors that, allegedly, rendered normal cumulative comparative or theoretical analyses useless.[3]

In the late 1980s, however, Soviet studies also witnessed a new theoretical development which combined the two previous approaches, emphasizing the systemic coherence and at the same time demonstrating the relative independence of scientific thought and research from political currents. In Western Soviet studies it was the insight borrowed from new institutional theory[4] that, when applied to the Soviet-type systems, emphasized the integrative potentials of the institutions of Soviet-type systems (Stark and Nee, 1989; Nørgaard, 1992). In Eastern Europe social scientists and economists in the most liberalizing countries (especially Poland and Hungary) reached similar conclusions on the basis of empirical research on the functioning of social and economic systems (Kornai, 1992, chapter 15; Winiecki, 1990). When the systems collapsed, the latter theoretical perspective outlasted the changes. The totalitarian and affiliated institutional perspectives had focused predominately on the means of repression and control as sources of stability. When these institutions vanished during the process of change, the totalitarian model of power structures became obsolete because it soon became obvious that the core political problem was too little rather than too much control. The pluralistic approach was built on the rivalry between sectoral and regional interests that had become increasingly apparent during the last years of the Soviet-type regimes. While the existence of those interests was to become explicit during and after the perestroika period, the institutional nature of the interests proved to be different from those of Western interest groups and modes of interest mediation which had been copied by previous pluralist models of the Soviet political system (Lepekhin, 1995). At the same time, the changes occurred simultaneously with radical changes in the institutional rules of the game, which themselves became a major issue of conflict. Consequently, the insight generated from the pluralist perspective on the Soviet-type systems also lost most of its value as a source of insight into the impact of the past on post-communist developments. In this context the new and, in Soviet studies, still embryonic institutional perspective, whether in its explicit Western or implicit Eastern variant, best encapsulated the constraints and influences that they would have on future developments.[5] Its focus on formal and non-formal institutions and the functional interdependence of organizations, elite interests and mass values and expectations was to prove fruitful in the 'transitology' that replaced 'Sovietology'.

Before the collapse of the communist regimes, 'Sovietology' or 'Soviet and East European studies' had been the somewhat derogatory terms applied to research devoted to these societies. The term applied to classical Slavists and area students as well as to specialized social scientists. Yet, until the disappearance of the systems as such, the study of communist systems had remained a scientific reserve. Although social scientists with dual competence in area studies and a social science disciplines had attempted to transcend the limits of area studies since the early 1970s, the large majority of scientific articles on communist systems were published in specialized area journals, and conferences on communist systems attracted a relatively closed and narrow group of scholars. Analyses of communist systems remained infrequent in mainstream scientific journals.

During the last years of 'perestroika' and 'glasnost', the communist systems started to change radically and this process accelerated during the first years of transition when the former communist countries became a fashionable subject of study among mainstream social scientists. An increasing number of articles on post-communist transitional systems appeared in mainstream journals and gave rise to a whole new science of 'transitology' with its own journals and scientific conferences.[6] The former 'Sovietologists', of whatever brand, who had suffered the denigrating accusation of being unable to anticipate the collapse of communism which had been hanging over their heads, entered a phase of profound soul searching. As soldiers preparing to win the last war, many Sovietologists still seem to continue to fight their own Cold War battles.[7] This introspection became one among several reasons why many former experts on the communist systems played only marginal roles in the scientific debates and practical aid programmes during the first years of transition.

At the same time, the political constraints and incentives which had previously constrained and influenced the scientific inquiry into the working of the Soviet-type systems more or less vanished with the transformation of the bipolar international system. Seen in the perspective of previous paradigms, Soviet (now post-Soviet) studies entered a short phase of 'extraordinary science', to paraphrase Balcerowicz's concept (Balcerowicz, 1994, pp. 84–87), or 'opportunity space' in the terminology of this study. In this phase scientists (and political actors) were unfettered by the structural constraints of the old international systems, while the new system and structures had not yet been established. Hence, it is during such a phase of 'extraordinary science', when old paradigms are discredited, that new paradigms are born (Kuhn, 1973).

It was under these conditions that the study of post-communist regimes was captured by other researchers from different scientific fields. They took their own discourses and applied them to a new field about which we knew (and still know) very little. In most cases the results were deductive rather than inductive models and theories, speculative rather than empirical analyses and normative rather than positive theories. But it also became one of the most massive examples of 'parallel demonstration of theory' (Skocpol and Somers, 1980) in the history of the social sciences.[8] First of all, the scene was captured by development economists who transferred their experience (and debates) from developing systems to post-communist systems. Secondly, the transition systems became the object of a debate on economic fundamentals between neo-liberal (and neo-classical) economists and alternative schools of economic thinking, in particular neo-structural, neo-institutional and evolutionary economists. Thirdly, political scientists entered the field to apply political philosophy, empirical models and normative political theories to the chaotic world of post-communist politics. Fourth, the 'Sovietological' scientific community fought a rearguard battle, and were mostly preoccupied with the past while only a few clung to the traditional non-rational or sui generis approach to these societies. The present state of research is illustrated in Figure 3.1, where the dotted image of post-Sovietology indicates the gradual loss of professional identity. Together, these four obviously overlapping schools (or rather 'clusters') of thought merged into 'transitology'.

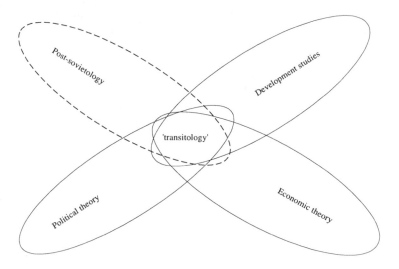

Figure 3.1. The roots of 'transitology'.

The following sections provide a broad overview of previous research on institutional change in post-communist societies. While it is obviously impossible to appreciate but a fraction of the extremely voluminous literature, the modest ambition here is to identify the major divides in the research leading up to the present study and which approaches have been or can be applied in our 'parallel testing of theories'.

THE NON-RATIONAL ACTOR APPROACH

This study is written within the context of social science, implying the recognition of generalizations applicable to societal system across regions and countries. Hence, in this context scant attention has been paid ex ante to approaches which continue to emphasize the separateness and sui generis nature of a certain range of countries.

The 'historical uniqueness' argument reiterates the traditional divide between 'area study specialists' and social scientists in a new historical context. The most recent (and strongly worded) statement of the 'uniqueness' argument is found in the Swedish book 'Hjärnridån'.[9] The core argument of this book is that the basic economic and political divide between Eastern and Western Europe has been created by their separate histories (Gerner, Hedlund and Sundström, 1995). In a fierce argument against the role of Western economic advisers in post-communist systems and their application of generalized economic models to post-communist systems, they refer to the split of Europe in 395 AD into an Eastern and a Western Roman hemisphere as the origin of present differences. This split, which has been reinforced over the centuries and most recently by the Cold War, created a path that produced fundamentally different societies based on separate values and functioning according to different logics. The Western Europeans gradually developed their present democracies and market economies, while the Eastern (but not Central) part of Europe maintained its bias towards autocracy and state controlled economies. Hence, the argument goes, no learning is possible because of the predominance of ideographic variables in the development of most post-communist systems. Only Central Europe which shares Western European cultural experience can adopt Western institutions and practices with any perspective. The very idea that development economy can be applied to countries further to the East is, allegedly, a grand illusion proved by the fallacies of Western-inspired reform policies up until now. Hence, this perspective reiterates the traditional 'historical uniqueness' argument that understanding can be achieved only through empathy and/or focus on ideographic factors.[10]

DEVELOPMENT STUDIES AND THE STUDY OF POST-COMMUNIST ECONOMIC TRANSFORMATION

When development researchers entered the field of post-communism, the most spectacular consequence was their role as advisers to post-communist reforming governments and to international financial agencies implementing Western assistance. The academic discourse on the relevance of Third World experience to the world of post-communism had surfaced in the mid-1980s (O'Neil, 1994), but gathered speed as a reaction to (and justification of) the policies pursued by transitionary governments and encouraged by the agencies of Western assistance. Hence, in most respects the political discourse on economic reform strategies in post-communist systems became a reiteration of the classic divide between orthodox and structuralist policies as pathways to development. However, the debate took off at a time when the gap between neo-classical and neo-structuralist economists had narrowed somewhat in their joint call for effective stabilization policies (Kahler, 1990). The core conflict between advocates of a state-led and a market-led structuralist adjustment strategy remained, however, under the headlines of 'Washington consensus' versus a pragmatic Social Democratic approach (Williamson, 1990; Pereira, Maravall and Przeworski, 1993), big bang versus a gradualist approach (United Nations, 1991, pp. 6ff.) or development 'with a human face' (Giovanni, Jolly and Stewart, 1987). These different approaches to the institutional barriers to development also entailed alternative values and visions of the political and economic goals of development.

References to economic transformation at other times and in other places abound in the literature on post-communist economic transformation. Likewise, post-communist cases have steadily made their way into comparative development studies (Williamson, 1993). The basic issue of comparability has, however, seldom been discussed in development literature. When for example Lipton and Sachs defended shock therapy in one of the first and most influential papers written on this issue, their version of the 'bridge burning argument' was justified with reference to 'the Argentine trap of political and social paralysis, in which coalitions of workers, managers, and bureaucrats in the declining sectors succeeded in frustrating the needed adjustments' (Lipton and Sachs, 1990, p. 100). In a similar vein, but with different conclusions and on the basis of a comparison of experiences from Southern Europe in the 1970s, Latin America in the 1980s and Eastern Europe in the 1990s, Pereira, Maravall and Przeworski (1993) argue for the application of a common 'pragmatic' economic policy as the best way to implement the necessary economic adjustment process. In a major volume on the political economy of policy reform (Williamson, 1993), an attempt was made to assess the relevance of the experiences of developing and middle-income countries for post-communist economies. This perspective was completely absent in other recent publications dealing with similar issues (Haggard and Kaufman, 1992; Bates and Krueger, 1994; Nelson, 1993) and only tentatively included in Haggard and Webb's major work on democracy and economic adjustment (1994).[11] Finally, Segbers and Spiegeleire have made cross-historical systemic comparisons in an attempt to solve the problems related to comparative or statistical inquiry into the development of post-communist systems (Spiegeleire, 1995, p. 53) without questioning the comparison as such.

Hettne (1994, p. 48) makes a clear distinction between mono-disciplinary and interdisciplinary approaches and claims the importance of conceptualizing the transformation process in a holistic way. In the context of post-communist transformation mono-disciplinary approaches, 'from authoritarianism to democracy' and 'from state to market', should be replaced by alternative interdisciplinary perspectives and Hettne identifies four: the modernization approach which regards the transition towards market economy and democratic pluralism as a 'natural evolution' signifying the celebrated 'end of history'; the Marxist approach which perceives the victory of capitalism in post-communist systems as a somehow backhanded way in which the Marxist perspective on history reasserts itself, providing the ultimate proof that the Eastern systems had nothing to do with socialism or communism in the Marxist understanding of the term; world system theory, according to which post-communism is the extension of the global market into previously protected peripheries underpinned by the values of the Western metropolises. The final approach, and the one which Hettne endorses, is that of international political economics in the tradition of Karl Polanyi, 'in which societal trans-formation is seen as movements of market expansion and counter movements of political intervention in defence of society' (Hettne, 1994, p. 48). In this manner post-communist transitions and their interaction with the surrounding world become single instances among many examples of a global trend.

Systemic similarities have been approached from a historical as well as a contemporary perspective. The historical approach was introduced in an influential Oxford Analytica paper from 1991 (Feinstein et al., 1991). This study regards post-communist transition as unique and emphasizes the possibility of partial learning from historical cases, '... to see whether any useful generalization on specific issues can be drawn from a brief survey of the historical record' (ibid., p. 3). This learning should, however, be confined to cases 'where the changes were effectively initiated from above by the state' (ibid., p. 3), thus making them comparable to what is happening in contemporary post-communist systems. From that perspective, the paper examines the transition from a feudal to a market economy in 19th century Russia and Japan, the return to market economy from fascism in post-war Europe and the transition from authoritarian autarchy in Spain after 1976. The paper argues that useful insights can be drawn from these historical precedents. This insight relates to the strategies by means of which ingrained economic patterns of behaviour and short-term expectations are changed and the ways that vested interests are controlled during the process of change. Oxford Analytica finds that the historical analogy is generated partly by the comparable structural features of the changing societies, partly by a process of learning whereby elites emulate foreign models and thus engender values and expectations favourable to economic change (ibid., 1991, p. 31).

Contemporary comparative approaches to post-communist transition have been introduced by Joan Nelson in a number of publications (Nelson, 1993; 1994a; 1994b). She explicitly discusses the issue of comparability of post-communist transition with the experiences of developing countries. Distinguishing between 'vigorous' and 'simultaneous' reformers, she does not find that post-communist systems can emulate the 'vigorous reformers' often characteristic of non-democratic regimes during a process of reform. 'The political clock cannot really be turned back' (Nelson, 1993, p. 445), and the reformers have to deal with the dilemmas that arise from simultaneous political and economic transition. In their attempts to reconcile these dilemmas, reformers in Third World countries and in post-communist systems alike have to strike a balance between two major internal and external influences: the pressure from international financial institutions and the political concerns and opposition of vested interests to deregulation and privatization. A major difference between Third World and post-communist countries is the stronger social response in the latter to social inequalities produced by social and ideological legacies of the socialist era. Another difference is the weakly developed civil society in post-communist systems. With these reservations in mind, Nelson regards the experience of Third World simultaneous reformers as highly relevant to the post-communist systems.

The issue of comparability with the Chinese economic transformation has also attracted some interest among researchers. However, Johnson (1994) expresses the broad consensus when she claims that only partial comparisons between China and Eastern Europe are possible because of the different political circumstances. The same line of argument is followed by Naughton in a number of publications (Naughton, 1995; Naughton and McMillan, 1993). In particular, attention is drawn to the larger and less developed agricultural sector in China compared to Eastern Europe, with two implications for the economic transformation. First, the less industrialized agricultural sector in China has preserved a large pool of entrepreneurship which can form the basis of a new entrepreneurial class. Second, this class will be able to develop not only agriculture but also infant industries which will ultimately be rivals to and eventually crowd out urban-based state-owned industries. In East European communism, the early enforced collectivization and industrialization of agriculture has annihilated the peasantry both as a social force and as a source of independent entrepreneurship.

Sachs and Woo (1994), Woo (1994) and Sachs (1996a and b) address three postulates in the current debate on the implications of the East Asian experience for economic reform policies in Central and Eastern Europe. The first assumption is that gradual reform strategies in East Asia outperformed shock therapy in Central and Eastern Europe. This view is refuted, and the superior results of East Asia are explained by differences in economic structure where the transfer of low efficiency rural workers to the highly efficient private sector explains the large gains in productivity and growth. In Central and Eastern Europe where state-owned industrial enterprises make up the largest part of the economy, there is no such shortcut to development. In particular, it is demonstrated that the political implications of a gradual strategy in agricultural East Asia and industrialized Central and Eastern Europe are quite dissimilar. In China the social embeddedness of the socialist welfare state is limited to the relatively insignificant state sector, because few benefits have been available to the rural population. In Central and Eastern Europe the dominance of state-owned enterprises channelled the major share of welfare benefits to the workers. Hence, the rise of the private sector is much more difficult because the workers oppose any change that might endanger the social privileges related to the previous system.

The second claim, that Asian reformers put economic reforms ahead of political reforms with superior results, is refuted by Sachs and Woo because this strategy was already attempted by Michail Gorbachev, but with disastrous results. Finally, Sachs and Woo deny that Central and Eastern Europe should have pursued industrial policies based on strong state intervention, which was crucial to Japan's post-war recovery. Central and Eastern Europe, it is claimed, 'lack the technical knowledge, experience, training, and political insulation that was vital for effective planning in Japan and South Korea' (Sachs, 1996b, p. 40).

In a later paper written with Warner (1996), Sachs pursues the same argument when they analyse the causes of the success of eight very fast growing economies and ask whether these factors can be emulated by the post-communist countries. The sources of growth that they identify are: allocative efficiency, promotion of high rates of savings and investments, technological upgrading and favourable structural endowments. The basic thrust of the article is the salience of a neo-liberal policy and the importance of favourable structural conditions. All very fast growing economies are coastal and labour-abundant. In particular, 'the abundance of labour meant low initial wages and the ability to compete internationally on the basis of labour intensive manufactures' (ibid., p. 27). In conclusion Sachs and Warner see the common ideological commitment to a universal social welfare state as the major problem which can be further amplified by accession to the EU and the adoption of the acquis communitaire of the EU. Instead the post-communist countries should aim to achieve very high growth targets by 'emulating the fiscal policies of the very-fast-growing middle-income countries. These fiscal policies include low rates of marginal taxation, low levels of current government expenditure as a per cent of GDP, relatively high levels of government investment expenditure, and pension policies based on individual saving accounts ...' (ibid., p. 51).

Balcerowicz (1995) identifies the specific properties of post-communist transition compared with 'four other major shifts' from one type of society to another: 1) Classical transition, i.e. democratization in advanced capitalist countries between 1860 and 1920; 2) neo-classical transition, i.e. processes of democratization after World War Two (the axis powers, Southern Europe and Latin America); 3) market oriented reform in non-communist countries (war economies after World War Two and a number of newly industrialized and middle income countries from the 1960s to the 1990s); 4) Asian post-communist transition (China and Vietnam). According to Balcerowicz post-communist transition is distinguished by three features: Scope, sequence and non-violence. Scope refers to the total transformation of all aspects of society compared with previous transitions, where either the political or economic systems remained relatively stable during the transition. Sequence refers to simultaneous democratization and marketization. Previous market oriented reforms had occurred under various types of authoritarian regimes, shielding decision-makers from the political repercussions of economic reforms. Under the present post-communist transition, political strategy becomes an integral part of the transition process. The non-violent character of the transition implied that most of the communist elites remained as economic and political players under the new system. Politically they stood to profit from social dissatisfaction, and economically many of them would join the emerging capitalist class.

East European economists and social scientists have also looked to Third World experiences to get inspiration to face their domestic challenges. A round table organized by the influential Russian journal *Mirovaja ekonomika i mezhdunarodnye otnoshenija* (Stol, 1994; Denisova, 1994; Karpunin, 1994; Mikhalev, 1994; Onikienko, 1994) was dedicated to the lessons learned from Third World stabilization and adjustment programmes. In the opening remarks of the issue dedicated to this topic (Stol, 1994, pp. 112–114), it is acknowledged that the developing post-communist countries have the same core problems as Third World countries with underdeveloped market structures and a hypertrophied state. At the same time, they also have the vested interests associated with the old structures. In addition the post-communist countries have to deal with a number of specific legacies of the communist era which distinguish them from developing countries. The most important differences are the vastly overgrown and outdated industrial sector and the total absence of a private sector and associated social groups and entrepreneurial mentalities.

The discussion about post-communist economic transformation strategies took off at a time when neo-liberalism dominated the political and economic agenda of most industrialized countries and international financial institutions. Hence during the first years of post-communist economic transition, most issues of discussion became a reiteration of positions and arguments that had already been on the agenda of development economics for decades.

As a descendant of the orthodox tradition and based on neo-classical positions, the neo-liberal position (the Washington consensus) on the one hand claimed that the same economic laws applied to economies everywhere – 'spread the truth – the laws of economics are like the laws of engineering. One set of laws works everywhere' as it was formulated in 1991 by Lawrence Summers, chief economist at the World Bank (Gerner et al., 1995, p. 5). At the level of policy this view argued for liberalization, marketization, privatization and a strongly reduced role of the state. Although accepting that policy choices in individual countries will be limited by the initial conditions and that the state has a certain role in the establishment of institutions and social policies, the 1996 World Development Report (World Bank, 1996) reiterated the same belief in free markets: The clear lesson of transition in both Europe and Asia is that countries that liberalize markets and preserve economic stability 'are rewarded with resumed or accelerated growth in output and productivity' (ibid., p. 43). With respect to phasing and pace, advocates of the neo-liberal position also united in unanimous support for a rapid (shock) stabilization and liberalization.

Alternatives to the neo-liberal approach also stemmed from alternative positions in development economics. The neo-structuralist tradition in development economics soon found its way into the opposition to the neo-liberal economic strategy applied to post-communist systems (Amsden, Kochanovicz and Taylor, 1994). This position, arguing that developing (and post-communist) economies are structurally different from the developed countries and from each other, asserts 'that each developing economy deserves independent analyses of its economic and institutional parameters' (Kahler, 1990, p. 48). The neo-structural position further criticizes the contradictory consequences of orthodox stabilization strategies, argues in favour of non-market/state interventions and takes distributional considerations into its policy recommendations. Hence, critique of orthodox positions generated in the discussion about the developing countries was applied to post-communist systems.

Distributional considerations have played an even more crucial role in studies sponsored by a number of UN organizations historically linked to structuralist positions (Giovanni, Jolly and Stewart, 1987). These alternative values have also been transferred to discussions about post-communist systems, where a number of studies have focused on the human costs of the transition process and implicitly on the danger of political backlash (United Nations, 1991; UNICEF, 1993, 1994, 1997). The same focus on distributional consequences, although with a more explicit political goal, is found in the 'pragmatic' or 'Social Democratic' approach introduced in a comparative study of Latin America and Southern and Eastern Europe (Pereira, Maravall and Przeworski, 1993); and with a European perspective in Eatwell et al., (1995).

Another alternative to neo-liberal positions comes from empirical studies of comparable historical or contemporary cases. Feinstein et al. (1991) and Amsden, Kochanovicz and Taylor (1994, Chapters 7–9) are representatives of those trying to learn from the development of capitalism in Western Europe, from post-war reconstruction and from the economic success stories of post-war East Asia. Drawing on a wide range of economic history and working in the neo-structuralist tradition, they all reach similar conclusions: that the state has always played an important role during periods of fundamental economic change. This conclusion applies to economic stabilization through monetary and budgetary policies, to direct intervention by means of loans, subsidies, tariffs and sector policies, and to the construction of the institutions of capitalism: banks, capital markets, legal systems, etc. The lesson is that capitalism has never developed spontaneously. It has always been nurtured by an active state, partly constructing the institutional framework of the new order, partly defending the market place against political and social forces embedded in the previous system. It takes, so to speak, a strong state to implement a reduction in the state's control of the economy. This is the 'orthodox paradox' identified by Kahler (1990, p. 55).

A few writers have taken the learning process a bit further and focused on the specific features that have made the East Asian developmental state an efficient instrument for economic growth and structural change. A cardinal concept, also introduced as a possible way of organizing the state in post-communist systems, was 'embedded autonomy', as formulated by Peter Evans in a number of writings (1992, 1995). According to Evans the East Asian states have been successful in generating structural change and economic growth by the help of an active and interventionist state because they have, on the one hand, managed to maintain a close relationship with the economic and political leaders in society, even within an authoritarian context. On the other hand, the state and its employees held an authority and prestige that made it possible to prevail over vested interests and adopt a long-term perspective on economic and societal development while escaping radical increases in inequality and poverty. Amsden, Kochanovicz and Taylor (1994, p. 210) regard this model of state intervention as a pattern that could be emulated by post-communist regimes. This line of argument has also been echoed recently in the Russian debate on the role of the state in economic development (Nikitchenko, 1999). It is strongly questioned by Balcerowicz (1995, p. 175), however, who ascribes the East Asian strategy to 'a combination of improved dispersed mechanisms' and 'special culture of government–business relationship' which cannot be emulated in other places.

This rather disparate discourse originating in development studies (itself difficult to define) on the comparability of institutional change in post-communist systems leads to two conclusion. First, while 'traditional' developing countries and even more the defeated countries after World War Two had rudimentary institutions of a market economy and civil society institutions, such preconditions were absent in most post-communist systems. Second, while the economic changes in Central and Eastern Europe are comparable to those of East Asia, these countries have only recently initiated democratization and have yet to experience the dilemmas associated with a simultaneous transformation of economic and political institutions. Third, the basic divide, originating in development studies but pertaining even more radically to post-communist economies, remains the position of the state. The question remains how big the state ought to be and what kind of role it should play in the construction of the new economic system and in the distribution of the social and economic goods and costs.

ECONOMIC THEORY AND POST-COMMUNIST INSTITUTIONAL CHANGE

Evolutionary economics has represented a second category of criticism of the neo-liberal paradigm in post-communist economic transition. Although this tradition does to some extent overlap parts of development economics, it has, in the debates on post-communist economic transition, taken its point of departure in economic theory rather than in historical or contemporary experiences. In some writings, it has merged with institutional economics (Grosfeld, 1995, p. 215; Poznanski, 1995, p. 9).

Eeg and Garretsen (1994) address the core issue when they criticize the use of neo-classical economic theory to underpin a big bang transition strategy. In doing so, is the argument, neo-liberal proponents turn to political arguments which are exogenous to neo-classical theory and can be easily reversed. Hence, 'Since general equilibrium theory has nothing to say on the best way to arrive at a full-fledged market economy, there are no sound theoretical objections against policy advisers that proclaim the introduction of a market economy (and the institutions that go along with it) overnight' (ibid., p. 4). The consequence is that political arguments are introduced and this puts the debate inside the arena of political economy. Similar arguments have recently entered the Russian discussion on the theoretical basis of the current economic transition (Shistikto, 1995; Bondarenko, 1995).

However, the most extensive writings within this tradition that deal with post-communist economic transition are from the tradition of evolutionary economics, going back to Schumpeter (1994), Nelson and Winter (1982) and Hayek (1945). Following Schumpeter, as opposed to neo-classical economics, evolutionary economics is not preoccupied with the improvement of static efficiency in equilibrium frameworks, but focuses 'on the dynamic process of creative discovery and permanent restructuring in response to changes in relative scarcities' instead (Grosfeld, 1995, p. 213).

The core issue of evolutionary economics is the behaviour of economic agents, individuals or organizations. In particular, evolutionary economics focuses on the ability of agents to adapt to changed institutional settings. Evolutionary economics does not accept the assumption of the economic actor as fully rational and fully informed. Instead it sees information as a scarce commodity and economic actors as responding on the basis of incomplete or distorted information. In that context, the organization becomes a valuable entity that through experience accumulates knowledge and information that makes it possible to screen and handle available information. Hence, whereas the neo-classical tradition claims that prices hold the most important information, the evolutionary school points to the 'tacit' knowledge of organizations. In contradiction to 'technical knowledge' which is reflected in written procedures, rules and manuals, tacit knowledge is the insight and understanding embedded in the informal structures of a company. It is, however, as pointed out by Poznanski (1995, p. 8): 'The routines, or subconscious patterns of behaviour [that] are the most essential organizational assets, for they allow organization members to "automatically" respond to variable price signals without overloading their limited computing capabilities.' From these micro-level assumptions follow two macro-level conclusions with implications for post-communist economic transition strategy, as summarized by Murrell (1992a and b).

The first and most obvious consequence of the evolutionary starting point is that gradual replacement of old structures and organizations is preferred to rapid destruction. In this respect, gradualism (institutional restructuring before radical liberalization) preserves the organizational resources of institutions and enterprises, while allowing them to adapt to a new institutional framework. Fast destruction, for example by rapid liberalization, extensive restructuring or privatization schemes will destroy the old organizations and the tacit knowledge they carry and thus ultimately reduce their ability to survive in the new environment, before new organizations and enterprises have had a chance to evolve.

A second consequence of the evolutionary approach is the emphasis on trial and error in the reform process instead of focusing on a given design or blueprint. While evolutionary economics supports the establishment of a market economy, the emphasis on the insecurity of information means that it rejects the idea of designing a desired end state (a blueprint) at the beginning of the process. It prefers to focus on the immediate and worst problems and leave further strategy to experience. From this also follows that the reform process is seen as reversible, contrary to the neo-liberal stress on commitment to the end goal. A further consequence is that small-scale experiments are preferred to large-scale changes because the costs will be less severe if things go wrong.

Critique of the evolutionary approach has been abundant. Brada (1993 and 1995) criticizes the absence of any positive stabilization programme on the part of the evolutionary economists. He also points to the historical account where capitalism has been inaugurated by the state in a top-down process and not spontaneously by self-made entrepreneurs, as claimed by the evolutionists. Furthermore, the role of the state in the establishment of capitalism has been especially important among the late modernizers, to which the majority of post-communist reforming economies belong. Grosfeld (1995) focuses on five issues which she perceives as weaknesses in the evolutionary approach as applied to post-communist economies. First, she challenges the political viability of keeping an inefficient public sector and a dynamic private sector at the same time. She believes, and finds that experience has proven, that governments will be exposed to intolerable pressures by the failing state enterprises and the new emerging private sector. Fast privatization will to some extent prevent the government from being paralysed by crossing pressures from strong interest groups in the public and private sectors. Second, she does not believe that the present state bureaucracies possess the resources and expertise necessary to carry out the restructuring, which is better left to private entrepreneurs. Third, she believes that small emerging enterprises will be financially crowded out by state enterprises with privileged access to the banking system and to state-guaranteed loans. Fourth, the economic reform process can only maintain its momentum if the emerging class of entrepreneurs holds sufficient political power. In the evolutionary scheme, however, the entrepreneurs will remain an insignificant minority vis-à-vis the managers of the state enterprises in the foreseeable future. Finally, she criticizes the evolutionists for not considering the economic and hence social costs of keeping outdated and inefficient state enterprises alive. Åslund (1994) reaches similar conclusions in his summary of the lessons of the first four years of stabilization and liberalization programmes. He concludes that it is essential that reforms are swift and comprehensive. Referring to political arguments, he states that

> 'It tends to be easier to get one big package through the political process; it is important to win the credibility for the changes that is created by a clear break; resistance need to be broken; the reform must be comprehensible so that people can understand it, learn it and support it; the paradigm of the intellectual debate needs to be transformed; the more comprehensive the package is, the more constant will the new economic system become, and the less opportunities for corruption and rent seeking will exist; a macro-economic stabilisation is best undertaken as a sudden change, breaking inflationary expectations; given the poor state of statistics and the limited predictability of the systemic changes, no precision or fine-tuning is possible in any case; and a critical mass of market-economy elements needs to be generated in order to create a functioning market.'

As can be seen from this long quotation, the core arguments against a gradual and 'institutional reform first' strategy are political, except the last two points.

Finally, a few articles have either applied the various types of new institutional perspective to post-communist systems (McFaul, 1994; Stark, 1992) or discussed the potentials of the new institutional theory as an approach to the study of post-communist systems. Bruckner (1995), for example, argues that insights from the rational choice variant of new institutional theory demonstrate the cooperation of elites 'under conditions of extreme uncertainty or information poverty will produce rigid behaviour' for three reasons, all related to institutional factors: First, institutions limit the set of choices available to those operating within them and the less information available, the more hesitant decision makers will be to take any decision. Second, because institutions are costly to establish and because they generate their own network of vested interests, they are also difficult to dismantle. Third, institutions are often created or captured by those with power and wealth and used for the promotion of particular interests, rather than some abstract national interests. From this perspective, Bruckner argues for the potentials of new institutional theory when it is used to understand the institutional (or rather constitutional) framework within which 'respect for constitutional provisions by public officials and private citizens emerges as equilibrium outcome'.

(ibid., pp. 211–212). Until now, however, most institutions in post-communist systems have allegedly been created to serve the power and interests of rent-seeking bureaucrats rather than out of concern for economic efficiency and development (ibid., p. 216).

In a recent comparative account of the role of institutional factors in China and the former Soviet Union, Solnik (1996) also applies a neo-institutional perspective to the economic reform process. Using insights from the literature on institutional economics, he discusses how reforms emphasizing the decentralization of decision-making upset the bureaucracies of centrally planned systems. Applying principal–agent theory and game theory, he concludes that 'administrative capacities matter' and that 'institutions thought to be guiding a reform can be profoundly weakened by the very reform they unleash'. Hence he sees institutional capacity as endogenous to models of reform (ibid., p. 236).[12] He further argues that the rent-seeking of local bureaucrats in the Chinese reforms was a calculated element which shielded the central bureaucracy from the centrifugal forces unleashed by the reforms. This experience where institutionalized rent-seeking gives local bureaucrats a vested interest in the existing institutions carries important lessons for the economic and administrative reforms in Central and Eastern Europe, according to Solnik. Nee and Peng (1994) reach a similar conclusion in their comparative analysis of reform in the Soviet Union and China.

The new institutional approach also calls for a gradual approach to economic reforms. The focus on formal and informal institutional barriers to change indicates the futility of any radical scheme, because change of formal institutions and rules will inevitably clash with the informal aspects of institutions (North, 1997). The outcome of this clash will be unpredictable, but in most cases produce results that are perverse in relation to the desired outcome. Hence, it is logical that advocates of institutional perspectives look to China as an example of successful gradual institutional change.

The gradualism following from both evolutionary and neo-institutional economics is complementary to the structuralist tradition in development economics as replicated in the discussions about post-communist economic transition. It should, however, be emphasized that the two approaches focus on different levels: the structuralist (and neo-structuralist) tradition focuses on the macro-level and the practical implications are related to the type of macro-economic policies to be pursued with ensuing normative implications. The focus of evolutionary economics and neo-institutional economics is on the micro-level, while the implications have to do with the pace and phasing of different adjustment ingredients rather the type of policy. Nor do the evolutionary or neo-institutional perspectives carry explicit normative connotations, as they deal with the process of change as such rather than with desired end states or blueprints.

EMPIRICAL POLITICAL THEORY AND POST-COMMUNIST INSTITUTIONAL CHANGE

While writings on macro-economic policies are abundant, research on the role of the political and political–institutional aspects of the economic transformation is still in its infancy. One reason for this is the strong focus on the immediate economic problems, while the institutional questions of democracy were considered by many to be solved once the previous dictatorship had been replaced by a democratic regime. Another reason is that on the turbulent and shifting political scene, where the links of political parties to society are often dubious, institutions change frequently and the basic rules of the game are themselves subjects of conflict, any systematic political inquiry is made almost impossible. Consequently, research addressing the political questions of economic transformation is often philosophical and/or speculative.

The first category of political theory of relevance to post-communist economic reform has its roots in the classical discussion about the relationship between economic growth/welfare on the one hand and political regimes and political institutions on the other. One of the first attempts to design a political strategy for the adoption and implementation of economic reforms under democratic conditions was made by Przeworski (1991). Drawing on the experience of Latin America and Southern Europe he prefers radical shock therapy to gradualism. Because the transitional costs will inevitably provoke a social and political reaction, shock therapy will leave the reform process further advanced than a gradual strategy, once political backlash sets in. Bruszt (1992, p. 71) later reformulated Przeworski when emphasizing that 'the dilemma is not that of the compatibility of democracy and marketization in general but that of different types of marketization, that is different paths, not to a general market economy, but to new types of democracy with different mixes of market and market economy'. Consequently, he insists that instead of studying the relationship between the democracy and the market in general, we ought to focus on the different mixtures of democratic institutions and organizational arrangements and their ability to mediate the interests of post-communist economies.

Williamson and Haggard (1994) write in the tradition of Bates and Krueger (1994) and Nelson (1992, 1993), when they attempt to identify the political preconditions for successful economic reforms on the basis of an examination of the experiences of a broad group of countries. They are the first to include policy reforms in the post-communist systems with a full chapter on Poland and a brief discussion of the experiences of Russia and Bulgaria. The book addresses the adoption and implementation of economic reform programmes, not the character of the programmes, because 'The Washington consensus is seen as policies that are good for the "first world", but that [...] are also needed to make the transition from the "second world", and that they are equally desirable for 'the third world' as well'. (ibid., p. 530). It is emphasized that 'this is not to proclaim the end of the history of economic 'thought' because of outstanding controversial issues, but that it is the political feasibility of the Washington consensus that is examined throughout the 13 cases. The attempt to generate hypotheses comprising all three worlds seems, however, to produce trivial positive results: the need for a solid political base and the existence of a visionary leader and a coherent economic team (ibid., p. 563).

The demand for 'the coherent team' is in this respect similar to the role of 'change teams' as earlier identified by Waterbury (1992). From this perspective, the falsified hypotheses seem less trivial: that authoritarian regimes are not the best at implementing economic reforms, that voodoo politics (i.e. lying to the electorate about the policy to be pursued after the elections) is not politically feasible, and that rightist governments are not superior to centre or leftist governments in implementing painful adjustment policies. Especially regarding the rejection of the 'Myth of the authoritarian advantage' (Maravall, 1994), i.e. that authoritarian regimes are better at implementing painful economic adjustments than democracies, Williamson and Haggard echo what today is a near consensus among political scientists and economists (Przeworski and Limongo, 1993). Authoritarian regimes may have an advantage during the initial phases of stabilization and liberalization policies (Nelson, 1993) and in particular under circumstances of hyperinflation (Haggard and Kaufman, 1992, p. 299) due to their greater insulation from societal pressure. According to this view, in the perspective of long-term structural adjustments democratic regimes, have proven superior, however, because of their greater political legitimacy, their better access to information and consequently because of the superior technical quality of their policies. It has also been shown empirically how presidential systems of government in post-communist systems to a larger extent than parliaments are exposed to pressure from conservative corporate groups embedded in the old economic system (Nørgaard, 1995; McFaul, 1994; Bruszt, 1992; Hellman, 1996). Identical results indicating that liberal values have a positive effect on economic growth have also been demonstrated in one of Scully's major works (1992) involving a global comparison of growth and political liberty.

These conclusions are replicated by research focusing on the role of political institutions for economic adjustment policies. On the one hand, drawing on Third World experience, it has been concluded that a strong executive (presidential system) has its advantages during the initial phases of reform when fast decisions are essential if the phase of 'extraordinary politics' is to be exploited in the institution building process and if inertial inflationary pressure must be resisted (Haggard and Kaufman, 1994; Lijphart, 1992). In the later phase of long-term structural adjustment, the efficiency of a presidential system is contingent upon close collaboration with representative institutions in constructing a political basis of reforms and creating efficient feed-back structures to the decision-making structures. Parliamentary systems, on the other hand, have the potential of forming coherent policies with a strong societal and political base and of generating the political stability that is essential to maintain positive attitudes to reforms. At the same time the incremental policy-making process characteristic of parliamentary systems makes it more difficult to act fast during the period of 'extraordinary politics' and to face the danger of political fragmentation and instability. Regarding post-communist systems, however, the impact of political institutions on economic adjustment remains almost virgin territory.

The emphasis on the overcoming of the institutional legacies of the previous system is common to these mezzo theories on political institutions in post-communist economic transition. The means is a top-down confrontational policy aiming, in essence, at an extension of the period of extraordinary politics to be used to install new political and economic institutions. This introduction of democracy by non-democratic means is what Staniszkis (1994) calls 'the dilemma of democracy in Eastern Europe'. These institutions shall, in turn, be the basis of a new path-dependency, where the new institutions generate their own and competing constituencies. Consequently, the top-down approach contains the germ of a version of democracy where competition and liberal values are emphasized at the cost of participation and collectivism.

A second approach to the political-institutional view of post-communist economic transition takes its point of departure in alternative sets of theories and values. Basically it argues that the success of transition will depend on the strength of civil society and on the level of inclusion of the forces of civil society in the politics of transition (Arato, 1990). The divide here is between the classical alternative emphasis on liberal values and elite competition versus the participatory aspects of democracy, respectively (Nørgaard, 1979). In this category we also find the scepticism which conservative political philosophers express towards the revolutionary changes inherent in the radical approach of economic change. Murrell sums up the issue when he states that '... conservatism is about how societies should change, not about where they should finish up' (Murrell, 1992b, p. 11). In this respect, the conclusions of conservative political philosophers are parallel to those of evolutionary economists, as expressed by Murrell when he refers to the writings of Oakshot, Burke and Hayek as a political argument for the evolutionary approach to economic reform.

Przeworski adopts the same perspective in a book co-authored with Peirera and Maravall (1993). Whereas his first book on Eastern Europe represented a basically theoretical approach (Przeworski, 1991), the 1993 volume also included the first empirical evidence from post-communist transition. It further differs from the first book in two important respects. First, it explicitly argues in favour of a European variant of a social market economy, here called 'a Social Democratic approach', whereas the first book did not distinguish between different forms of capitalism. Second, it explicitly adds a political dimension to the policy aspect. Also here the authors take West European experiences, and in particular post-Franco Spain and the North European welfare systems, as models. The book further supports a gradual economic transition with a broad involvement of societal and political forces, all underpinned by a social safety net. Only this type of consensual or corporatist system is allegedly able to contrive economic reforms with a technical quality and political basis that makes them viable in the long run. Hence, whereas Przeworski supported shock therapy in response to what was considered an inevitable political backlash in his first book, he supported a gradual strategy three years later based on a policy designed to avoid political repercussions.

Corporatism as a solution to the dilemma of interest mediation in post-communist economies is the subject of two major books. In the introduction to a major volume on the role of organized interests in a number of Central European countries, Wiesenthal emphasizes the missing preconditions for societal corporatism (1996, p. 5): The lack of experience, the absence of resourceful social interests as a legacy of egalitarian socialism, difficulties in the identification of interests during an uncertain period of change and the decay of oppositional movements active before 1989. Hence, in a political context where individualism, autonomy and pluralism appear to be the guiding principles, the future of corporatism in East-Central Europe hangs on the initiative and learning capabilities of the state itself (ibid., p. 55).

In their more speculative contributions Nielsen, Jessop and Hausner (1995), Nielsen (1992), Surdej (1992), and Pedersen (1992) strike a more optimistic tune when they argue for a 'negotiated economy' as the best way in which to come to terms with the institutional legacies of the past. Seeing the previous system as 'state corporatist' (Nielsen, Jessop and Hausner, 1995, p. 27), they emphasize that 'path-dependency suggests that the institutional legacies of the past limit the range of current possibilities and/or options in institutional innovation'. A 'negotiated economy' (corporatism) is seen as the system best able to accommodate the institutional legacies of state socialism. The 'rules of the political game, i.e. constitutional matrix of the political system [and] the actual political decision-making processes' are seen as subjects of political choice. Hence, also here the initiative of the political level or state representatives and not societal interests are expected to be the founders of the system.

ISSUES AND OPTIONS IN POST-COMMUNIST INSTITUTIONAL CHANGE

In the previous sections I outlined the major issues and divisions in research on institutional change in post-communist systems. While referring to only a fraction of the publications in the field, the survey attempted to identify alternative approaches to institutional change and the resulting strategic options facing reformers. The options and strategies are outlined in Table 3.1.

Table 3.1 summarizes the major differences between a neo-liberal approach (here summarized as the Washington consensus) and its alternatives. In the changing of economic institutions the divide reflects a difference between the (neo-liberal) expectation that if formal institutions (especially prices) are brought in order, economic behaviour will rapidly adapt to the new rules of the game. For political reasons changes should be fast to prevent political opposition from regrouping to block the process and stabilization/liberalization should consequently precede institutional changes. The alternative views are more concerned about the survival of institutional resources or the collision between formal and informal institutions. In particular they want to preserve organizational capital by a slower process, by emphasizing institutional evolution rather than changes imposed by premature liberalization. The differences are eventually reflected in the implicit type of capitalism opted for: the Washington consensus is tuned to the Anglo-Saxon laissez-faire type. The more open-ended alternatives, with an emphasis on active state involvement lean towards the West-European[13] type of

Table 3.1. Issues and options in post-communist institutional change.

	Washington Consensus	Alternatives	
TYPE OF CAPITALISM	ANGLO-SAXON	WEST-EUROPEAN	EAST ASIAN
ECONOMIC CHANGE			
Phasing	stabilization/ liberalization first	institutional change first	institutional change first
Pace	fast	slow	slow
Scope	minimal state, maximum market	active state	active state
Social solidarity	low	high	high
POLITICAL CHANGE			
Political liberties	extensive	extensive	restricted
Institutional arrangement	executive dominance	legislative dominance	executive dominance
Popular participation	low	high	low
Type of decision-making	elite pluralism	corporatist/consocial	corporatist
Sequencing	democracy first	democracy first	economic change first

welfare-capitalism or the Asian developmental state, both of which limit inequality and poverty.[14] The approach to political changes reflect the same basic assumptions and strategic pathways. The unspoken assumption of the Washington consensus is that people have to be demobilized in order to pave the way for economic change. Politics should be left to the emerging elite or new capitalists embedded in a strong executive. The alternatives argue for a participatory and consensual type of democracy channelled through strong legislative or consocial institutions. Further, the East Asian approach historically implies an economic-reform-first approach, initially limiting democratic rights and popular participation. These options and strategic pathways to change will guide the following analyses and the concluding discussion of which mode of capitalism is applicable to the real world of post-communist societies.

NOTES

1. The three waves of Soviet-type systems were: the re-establishment of the Russian empire in the Soviet Union in the early 1920s; the systems established in Central and Eastern Europe in the aftermath of World War Two and finally a number of Third World countries that tried to emulate the Soviet model after decolonization in the 1960s. In the following I use the terms (post-) 'socialist' and 'communist' as synonyms to describe the group of countries I deal with, although I do of course recognize the conflict with Marxist theory.

2. For further discussion of the intricate links between the perception of the Soviet-type systems and domestic politics in Western Europe, see Ole Nørgaard, Per Carlsen and Nikolaj Petersen, 'Danish Ostpolitik 1967–1993: Breakdown of Stability – Unknown Challenges', in Carsten Due-Nielsen and Nikolaj Petersen (eds.), *Adaptation and Activism. The Foreign Policy of Denmark, 1967–1993*, Dansk Udenrigspolitisk Institut, DJØF Publishing, Copenhagen, 1995, pp. 133–162. Further references to literature on the policy aspect of the images of the Soviet system are quoted in this article.

3. Spiegeleire also claims that 'area specialists have a definite "corporate" interest in claiming special status for their region: if the study of that region requires not only certain linguistic or other area specific qualities, but also psychological gifts of empathy, it obviously becomes much easier to shield the profession from "outsiders"' (Spiegeleire, 1995, p. 52).

4. The 'New Institutionalism' is as yet a relatively imprecise approach, where both prior assumptions as well as the concept of 'Institution' differ. Peters (1999), for example, distinguishes between normative, rational choice, historical, empirical and sociological institutionalism. 'Institutionalism' in the present context comes closest to the historical variant with its emphasis in the impact of historical institutional legacies (formal and informal) on present developments. See also Hall and Taylor (1996) and Steinmo, Thelen and Longstreth (1992).

5. In this connection, I disagree with Spiegeleire when he states that 'we are somewhat surprised by the fact that many of the scholars (undoubtedly inspired by the new institutionalism) seem to be focusing most of their attention on the institutional aspect of the transformation in these societies ...'. He claims that 'ultimately institutions are made by political actors, and therefore we feel our analytical energy is better spent by focusing it

on those actors'. I think his definition of new institutionalism is inadequate because it misses the crucial interplay between institutions, structures and actors.

6. Some journals should be mentioned: *Communist Economies and Economic Transformation, The Economics of Transition, Journal of Communist Studies and Transition Politics,* and *Transition.*

7. I owe this observation to Stephan de Spiegeleire, who offers an extensive list of references to literature on the post-Sovietological debate on the factors behind the collapse of the Soviet system (Spiegeleire, 1995, p. 47).

8. For a presentation and discussion of the concept of 'parallel demonstration of theory', see Chapter 2.

9. The title is a pun on the similarity between the Swedish words *hjärne* (brains) and *järn* (iron). Hence, the title actually means 'the brain curtain', but is pronounced like 'iron curtain'.

10. Surprisingly, a somewhat similar argument enters the recent book by Ágh (1998a) when in an otherwise empirically very stringent book he emphasizes the cultural legacies, going back to the Ottoman occupation, as a deeper parameter that divides East-Central Europe from the Balkans. A difference that allegedly in the latter results in a top-down approach and a predominance of nationalist–communist values, as compared to East Central Europe.

11. The book has one chapter on post-communist institutional change: Poland: The Political Economy of *Shock Therapy* by Simon Johnson and Marzena Kowalska. Post-communist cases do, however, play an insignificant part in the introduction by the authors.

12. Solnik here reiterates my own argument. See Chapter 2.

13. Dahrendorf calls this model 'the Rhineland model', reflecting that this is basically the societal model realized in Northern Europe. Here quoted after Nagle and Mahr (1999, p. 288).

14. For further discussions about these alternative versions of capitalism see for example Rhodes and Apeldorn (1997) and Albert (1993).

4. Institutional Strategies and their Outcomes

'... poverty is a principal and probably *the principal obstacle to democratic development*' (Huntington, 1993).

Institutional strategies are the initial and subsequent choices that set the course for the phasing, pace and scope of institutional reforms. The success of institutional strategies are measured by their capacity to generate change with a minimum of social costs or distributional consequences that (in a given country at a given time) are intolerable to the population or the strategic elites of a new democracy. But how do we measure institutional change and the economic, social and political outcomes? And how do initial and subsequent choices of phasing, pace and scope affect economic and social outcomes? These questions are addressed in this chapter. The first section sets out to find valid proxies for 'institutional change' and 'economic, social and political costs'; the second section portrays and examines the empirical relations between institutional strategies and their economic and social consequences for our 20 post-communist countries from 1989–98, while alternative (political) causal models of the observed patterns are discussed in the final section.

THE PROBLEM OF MEASUREMENT

Previous research on the changing of economic institutions in post-communist countries has basically used two approaches. The first was to define success in terms of a continued implementation of reform initiatives, whatever their character (Pereira, Maravall and Przeworski, 1993, p. 3). In this perspective successful institutions are those that are able to adopt and implement policies that were the end vision of the institutional designers. Such an approach, however, tells us more about the efficiency of the administrative system than about the rationale of the economic reforms as such. As argued by Peters (1999, p. 73), it is very nearly tautological, because 'if institutions are defined as being based on ideas they cannot also be evaluated on how well they perform the activity of using ideas'. Finally, the valuefree implication of this approach does not correspond to the premise of this study, where the survival of democracy is defined as a criterion for success.

A second approach has been to measure the general level of success as the arithmetic average (in some cases using weighted variables) comprising the main fields of institutional change as estimated by expert panels: liberalization, stabilization and structural adjustment. This approach was primarily applied by organizations with the necessary institutional resources needed for a comprehensive appraisal of institutional changes in a range of countries: The World Bank (1996), de Melo and Gelb (1996); EBRD (1994); IMF (Citrin and Lahiri, 1995), Ernst & Young (Financial Times, October 24, 1994, p. 3) and a number of policy research institutes. In particular The Heritage Foundation, The Fraser Institute and Freedom House have broad circulations.[1] But only Freedom House has so far focused specifically on post-communist countries in their recent 'Nations in Transit'.[2] In the economic section it deals with privatization and details the legislative and actual state of privatization in each country. The ratings (comparative or ordinal) are achieved through a three step assessment process involving examination of available data and subjective assessment by country experts.

Only a few individuals, for example Sundakov (1994), have attempted a similar approach. Sundakov also uses structural indicators when he focuses on the central role of prices in a market economy and suggests three types of indicators that reflect the structural transformation independently of the aggregate indicator: the role of the price system in the allocation of resources (absence of subsidies), decentralized price formation and the role of competition in imposing discipline on market participants. At the political level, Western countries and institutions initially focused on indices of stabilization and liberalization. They did not turn their attention to institutions until the late 1990s.

Although it is appealing because of its ability to measure reform progress, this second approach contains a number of illusions. First, there is the illusion of identical goals based on the assumption that all countries are moving in the same direction. Whereas market orientation (Pereira et al., 1993, p. 6) is obviously the general aim for all post-communist systems, the exact type aimed for may be different, as described in chapter 3. Second, the illusion of reliable indicators means that indicators are treated as objective and quantifiable variables. However, what might at first glance look like hard data that may be used for making firm verdicts are actually subjective judgements open to different interpretations. Third, the illusion of coverage is based on the assumption that the indicators employed cover the transition process in its totality, whereas in reality they cover it only partially. Finally, the illusion of similarity assumes that identical criteria carry the same weight in all post-communist countries. But when we look for the critical indicators that signal irreversible changes in fundamental structures in the real world, they may turn out be different from one country to another, depending on initial structural characteristics. Despite these shortcomings the following analysis will apply the second variant. I shall not attempt to present a final verdict but only a tentative conclusion which should ultimately be seen in conjunction with the democratic feasibility. In this sense I emulate and extend the approach suggested by Peirera, Maravall and Przeworski (1993, p. 3): 'to remain skeptical until an economy exhibits growth under democratic conditions'.

Among the great number of attempts to measure institutional changes in post-communist countries, the most significant and widely used indices have been those designed to support Bank policies by the EBRD and the World Bank. In their annual report for 1994 (EBRD) the EBRD developed a number of 'transition-indicators' meant to support bank policy towards individual countries. This approach has been continued with minor amendments and refinements in subsequent annual reports. The approach was adopted by the World Bank (World Bank, 1996; de Melo and Gelb, 1996), who produced a retrospective index going back to 1989. Both indices are constructed on the basis of expert judgements.

The World Bank cumulated index of economic liberalization is based on annual assessments of (additive) institutional changes in three spheres:

- internal markets (liberalization of domestic prices and abolition of state trading monopolies);
- external markets (liberalization of foreign trade and currency convertibility);
- private sector entry (small and large scale privatization and banking reform).

It is an open and relative (ordinal) scale indicating the movement away from the old system rather than the proximity to any ideal type of market economy.

The EBRD transition indicator is a cumulative index measuring the movement towards a 'modern Western market economy' of unspecified brand in four spheres:

- enterprise development (small and large scale privatization and enterprise restructuring):
- markets and trade (price liberalization, trade and foreign exchange system and competition);
- financial institution development (banking reform and interest rate liberalization, security markets and non-bank financial institutions);
- legal reforms (extensiveness and effectiveness of legal infrastructure) from 1995.

The EBRD scale is closed, with the maximum value assigned to those that have reached a level on a par with Western market economies. Despite the somewhat different logic and the larger number of especially institutional variables included in the EBRD index, both indices measure the same process, reflected in a 1994 bivariate correlation between the two indices of

0.91 (significant on the 0.01 level). With all the caveats related to the use of two separate indices based on subjective judgements, the following analysis will build on the World Bank assessments (from 1989 to 1994) and EBRD assessments (from 1995 to 1997).[3] With reference to the terminology introduced in Chapter 2, I will dub these two measurements of institutional change respectively 'scope94' and 'scope97'.

The measurement of economic, social and political costs which is expected to feed back into the political process of the new democracies represents the second aspect of 'institutional change'. First, the magnitude and character of costs may cause social and collective interests to support (or impede) ongoing institutional changes. International organizations and national authorities have produced a huge amount of statistics that decipher the social costs that succeed the institutional changes in post-communist countries.[4] The costs have been translated into a large number of statistical proxies ranging from nutrition, income levels, accidents and alcoholism to fertility, mortality and suicide rates, some of which are only of indirect relevance to the present notion of democratic feasibility.[5] As discussed in Chapter 2, people may protest against a certain policy if it decreases their personal social or economic situation (income or job security) or if they are generally dissatisfied with the social development of society. But they do not protest if they are drunk, dead – or maybe not even born. Hence, we will apply broader proxies for social costs that are closely related to – and one of the underlying causes of – the other indicators of social decay: inflation, decline in GDP, increase in poverty and inequality.[6]

A second consequence of institutional change may be the impact on the power and privileges of incumbent elites. In socialist societies collective interests were not independent associations. They were the centralized bureaucracies that managed sectors of the planned economy and competed during the planning process and when the plans were implemented. It was a recognition of the bureaucratic notion of competing interests that led to the attempts to decipher political structures in the concept of 'state corporatism' (Bunce, 1983). These bureaucratic elites, endowed with huge bureaucratic resources and closely integrated into the political system had, before the political changes, managed to sabotage all attempts by reform minded leaders to reform the political institutions (Nørgaard, 1985). These collective interests also became the major opponents to the 'market oriented' institutional changes initiated by post-communist reformers.[7] Liberalization would force the enterprises to adapt to new relative prices and to face a hitherto unknown competition from domestic and foreign enterprises, while stabilization was likely to harden budget constraints when fiscal policies were tightened. Privatization was a challenge to the previous de-facto ownership by managers, and marketization and decentralization to the power of planners and bureaucrats in the central ministries. In this process the interests of workers in enterprises that were unable to meet the demands of the changing environment concurred with that of the managers and the central bureaucracy, thus forming the basis for a powerful alliance against change, as they had done in the past. In this process the phasing, pace and scope of reforms were important parameters that would determine whether the old economic elite would be able to benefit from the disequilibrium of the economic transition and recycle themselves into positions in the new system, whether other emerging economic elites could amass fortunes at the expense of the broad population or whether the changes would proceed with some minimum of social solidarity.

Political consequences or repercussions from social and economic costs will be felt when (if) the continuance of reforms is jeopardized by the protests of socially exposed groups, by incumbent elites – or by an alliance of both. Or the consequences may be the reverse, that reform of economic institutions is continued at the expense of democracy, that democracy (civil and political rights, participation) in a given context proves incompatible with economic reforms.

INSTITUTIONAL CHANGES AND THEIR CONSEQUENCES

Table 3.1 described a typology of institutional strategies revolving around three dimensions: scope of institutional changes, the pace of changes and the phasing of reform initiatives, all of which ideally are under control of the decision-makers. As discussed in Chapter 3 there is, however, a logical affinity between most of the strategic options that reflects fundamental assumptions about how social and political change proceeds: Fast reforms are associated with a stabilization/liberalization first policy and an ultimate vision of a grand scope of reforms reflecting a quest for a laissez-faire type capitalism with minimal state intervention. Slow reforms are associated with a structural-reforms-first policy and stronger state involvement, leaning towards a welfare – or Asian type of capitalism. These are of course theoretical abstractions. In real world circumstances institutional strategies along the three dimensions reflect political bargaining rather than logical constructions, and strategies will include conflicting elements. Having (constructed) three bivariate variables this ultimately leaves us with 8 alternative institutional strategies (the possible combination of strategic choices). Below we first describe the scope, pace and phasing of institutional changes in our 20 post-communist countries and then the associated economic and social costs (see also Appendix A 4.1).

Figures 4.1 and 4.2 reveal two key developments. First, there are four echelons of reformers when measured on the basis of their aggregated institutional reforms in 1997 (scope97):

- The front runners who reached a total score above three in 1997, and on some variables are on a level with developed market economies. In this group we find the Central European countries: the Czech Republic, Hungary, Poland, Slovakia and Slovenia.

- The Baltic States Estonia, Latvia and Lithuania are almost on the same level as the Central European countries.
- East European countries lagging behind: Albania, Bulgaria and Romania. Mongolia also belongs to this category.
- Former Soviet Republics that lag behind to varying degrees: Belarus, Kazakhstan, Kyrgyzstan, Moldova, Turkmenistan, Ukraine and Uzbekistan. In this group only Russia approaches the level of the Central European countries

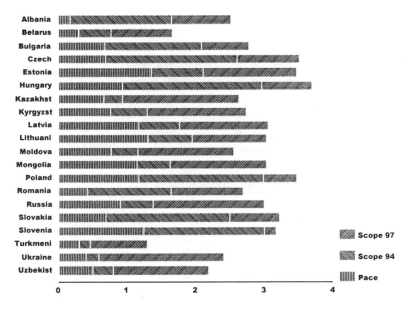

Sources: *'From Plan to Market', Policy Research Working Paper 1564, World Bank, Policy Research Dep., Jan. 1996. Transition Report 1994–97, EBRD, UK.*

Figure 4.1. Pace, scope94 and scope97.[x]

Second, while the countries of Central Europe have converged those of the Former Soviet Union reveal much greater differences. Third, we are generally witnessing a progressing development where the large majority of countries are steadily moving forward. But there are exceptions, however, reflecting economic and political obstacles to which shall we return in later chapters. Between 1996 and 1997 Albania saw a decrease in the general index caused by a drop in scores on banking and legal reform because of the collapse of the pyramid schemes. Belarus experienced a significant set-back

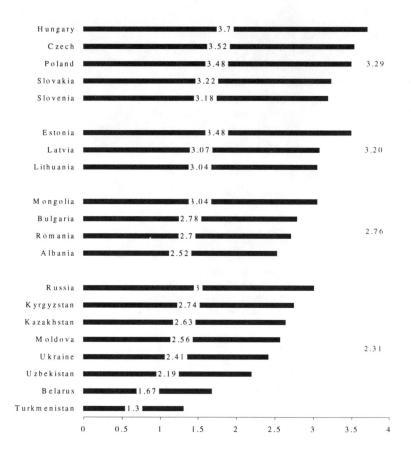

Note: The bars indicate scope97 for individual countries. The regional means and standard deviations are above each group.

Sources: *'From Plan to Market', Policy Research Working Paper 1564, World Bank, Policy Research Dep., Jan. 1996. Transition Report 1994–97, EBRD, UK.*

Figure 4.2. Regional patterns of transition.

in a wide range of structural reforms between 1995 and 1997, when the Lukashenka government re-intervened in the economy, introducing price controls, restricting currency convertibility and reintroducing subsidies to certain industries. During the same period Kyrgyzstan experienced a minor set-back due to a temporary suspension of privatizations and problems with the privatization of land. Between 1996 and 1997 Latvia fell back because of problems with company accountability towards shareholders, i.e. protection of minority shareholders. In 1997 Moldova dropped back in legal reform due to a lack of clarity in the laws concerning shareholders' rights. Slovakia fell back between 1995 and 1997 because they reintroduced import restrictions, wage regulation, state support for loss-making enterprises and restrictions on financial trading. Uzbekistan fell back on a broad range of indicators in 1997 because of setbacks in banking reforms and large scale privatization, the reintroduction of trade restrictions and a multiple exchange rate regime. In the period observed, however, these are the exceptions. On the whole all the countries have been moving in the same direction although at very different speeds, as seen in Figure 4.1.

The countries, however, proceeded in different orders, as described in Table 4.1 which shows which countries launched stabilization and liberalization before privatization – and vice versa.

Table 4.1. Phasing of reforms.

Stabilization/Liberalization first	Privatization first
Albania, Czech Rep., Estonia, Hungary, Latvia, Poland, Slovakia, Slovenia	Belarus, Bulgaria, Kazakhstan, Lithuania, Moldova, Romania, Russia, Turkmenistan, Ukraine, Uzbekistan, Kyrgyzstan

Source: *'From Plan to Market', Policy Research Working Paper 1564, World Bank, Policy Research Dep., Jan. 1996.*

Table 4.1, where I attempt to summarize a general processes that is much more complex than depicted here, shows that most of the countries in Central and Eastern Europe and the Baltic states stabilized and liberalized before they initiated comprehensive structural reforms, whereas the countries in the former Soviet Union that have reformed in most cases began with privatization, while stabilization and liberalization were delayed.

Finally, the empirical data on scope, pace and phasing of institutional changes largely meet our theoretical expectations, that liberalization/ stabilization is primarily associated with fast institutional reforms (pace) and that fast reforms in turn are linked to comprehensive institutional changes (scope) (Table 4.2).

Table 4.2. Correlation between scope, pace and phasing of institutional reforms.

	Scope(97)	Pace	Phasing	Scope(94)
Scope(97)	1.000			
Pace	0.726**	1.000		
Phasing	– 0.464*	– 0.234	1.000	
Scope(94)	0.858**	0.594**	– 0.655**	1.000

*Note: *significance at the 0.01 level; **significance at the 0.05 level*

An examination of macro-economic imbalances (inflation) and economic contraction (GDP development) from 1989 to 1997 reveals a basic divide between most republics of the Former Soviet Union and (most) countries of Central and Eastern Europe (Appendix A 4.2). As seen in the table all former Soviet Republics experienced periods of very high or extreme inflation which lasted longer than in Central and Eastern Europe. Only the Baltic Republics break the pattern as former Soviet republics who were actually able to bring down inflation to Central European levels, albeit with Lithuania as the least successful. In Eastern Europe Bulgaria and Romania were the least successful with an average inflation at the same level as most former Soviet republics. This pattern is replicated with regard to the economic contraction following institutional reforms. The GDP dropped most dramatically in the former Soviet Republics, who were also slower to resume growth. Here the Baltic states are on a level with the other parts of the former Soviet Union. The main exceptions are Uzbekistan whose GDP contraction is on the same level as Central European countries; and Romania, Bulgaria and Albania who experienced negative growth rates in last phase of the period studied.

Before considering the links between the macro-economic variables and transition indicators, it should be emphasized that we cannot say anything definite about the causal relations. We may, as is done in the following, hypothesize that control of inflation may spur growth. Still, it is also possible that it is growth, which is known to be caused by a host of factors, that generates the policies which put a stop to inflation. Hence, as observed by Coricelli (1997), the following analyses should consider that 'the correlation between transition indicators and performance should be seen as a two-way relationship within a truly dynamic framework', where the specific nature of the two-way relationship will vary over time and between countries.

With this ambiguity in mind, simple regression analysis demonstrate that average inflation is an important predictor of growth, but that inflation beyond a certain level does not significantly increase the negative effect on growth (the relationship is loglinear), as seen from Model 4.1.

However, inflation and growth are also consequences of institutional strategies, as described in the previous section. Assuming that decisions about phasing (in what order things should be done) is made prior to decisions about how fast to do it (pace) and about how far to go (scope), we can analyse the relationship between institutional strategies (phasing, pace and scope) and their economic consequences (inflation and GDP) in a path model (Figure 4. 3) (Asher, 1976).

Model 4.1.

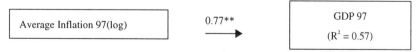

Average Inflation 97(log)   0.77**   GDP 97
                                   ———▶   ($R^2 = 0.57$)

*Note: **significance at the 0.05 level.*

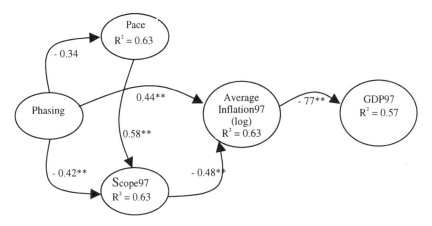

Figure 4.3. The effect of institutional strategies on economic performance (beta coefficients).

*Note: **significance at the 0.05 level.*

Figure 4.3 shows how decisions about institutional strategies may affect economic outcomes in terms of inflation and GDP-development. A basic observation is that contrary to what we would expect, decisions about phasing (liberalization or privatization) are not necessarily related to the pace of reforms, illustrating the cases where initial decisions to liberalize would not be carried into full reforms, as we saw in for example Albania, Slovakia and Romania. Looking into the effects of phasing we see the expected relation between decisions to liberalize before privatization and the eventual defeat of high inflation, albeit not as strong as should be expected.[9] Pace (the decision to initiate reforms fast) by 1997, does not have a direct impact on inflation (97log), but is a strong determinant of the eventual scope of reforms, which does have a major impact on the defeat of inflation. Inflation is in turn a crucial factor behind the resumption of growth. In short: Those who decided to liberalize before they privatized stabilized faster and those who stabilized faster also resumed growth earlier.

Turning to the social costs of institutional strategies, Figure 4.4 and Table A 4.3 describe initial level and the increase in poverty and in inequality from 1989 to 1994, the last year for which reliable data are available.

Figure 4.4 illustrates huge but also widely different increases in inequality and poverty in most of the 20 countries. Only conservative Belarus escaped a registered increase in inequality and Slovakia in poverty. In the rest of the countries the increase in inequality varies between a modest 4 point increase in Latvia to an amazing 17 (Estonia), 20 (Slovakia) and 24 (Slovenia). Also poverty has increased to varying degrees, the Czech Republic, Hungary and Slovakia being at the lower end. Most republics of the Former Soviet Union have seen between 40 and 60 per cent of their population sink into poverty.

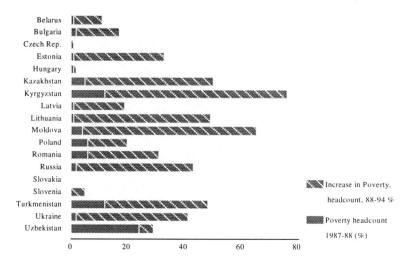

Figure 4.4. Initial level and increase in poverty.

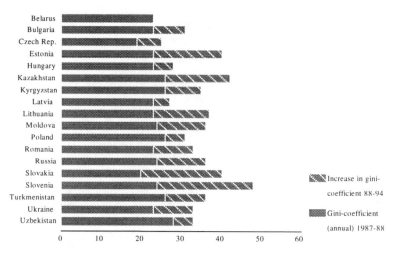

Sources: Policy Research Working Paper 1564, World Bank, Policy Research Dep., Jan 1996.

Figure 4.5. Initial level and increase in inequality.

The relationship between social costs and alternative institutional strategies is illustrated in the path model in Figure 4.6.

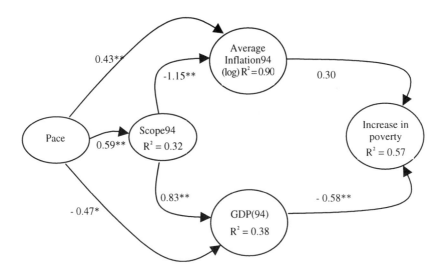

Figure 4.6. Social costs of institutional strategies (beta coefficients).

*Note: *significance at the 0.01 level; **significance at the 0.05 level.*

Figure 4.6 illustrates how institutional strategies affect social costs. The model does not include increase in inequality (GINI) as the association has been deemed too weak. The immediate causes of increased poverty are average inflation (log) and GDP-development that each account for a share of the increase. Fast reforms have an indirect positive effect on poverty through its negative effect on GDP-development. Faster reforms provoke a drop in GDP, which again increases poverty. There is, however, a compensating positive effect from pace which generates longer term growth and thus alleviates poverty: Fast reforms in general induce comprehensive reforms, which again decrease inflation, generate growth and ultimately alleviate poverty. This is the 'valley of tears'[10] defined in statistical terms, where short term costs are compensated for by long term gains. The pattern identified here is identical to the one described by Lal and Myint (1996, p. 138), who by cross-country regressions on 22 developing countries showed that growth reduced poverty in absolute terms but has no discernible effect on income distribution. Slightly different patterns can be observed between republics of the former Soviet Union and countries of Central and Eastern Europe. Whereas the GDP-decrease is the main cause of poverty increase in the former, inflation accounts for the major part in the latter. In Central and Eastern Europe there is actually a minor positive relation between growth and increase in poverty indicating that GDP-growth is insufficient to save those whom the increased inequality push below the poverty line.

Finally, it can also be hypothesized that the reason why inequality is not associated with institutional strategies and the unexplained variation in poverty should be sought in the redistribution which takes place through the surviving (from socialism) social security net. While available data show that poverty is in fact alleviated in countries that redistribute a larger share of their GDP though the social system, the same does not hold for inequality. As seen from Table 4.3, there is no discernible effect of the share of GDP allocated to social expenditures and the development in inequality. Hence, the present data confirm the observation (Milanovic, 1995) that as under communism, social transfers have remained unfocused and unable to dampen the increase in inequality.

Table 4.3. Simple correlation between social expenditures (per cent of GDP) and poverty and inequality, 1992–1996.

	Soc. Exp. 1992	Soc. Exp. 1993	Soc. Exp. 1994	Soc. Exp. 1995	Soc. Exp. 1996
Poverty	– 0.648*	– 0.396	– 0.549*	– 0.641**	– 0.648**
GINI	0.131	– 0.031	– 0.012	– 0.021	0.028

*Note: *Significance at the 0.01 level; ** significance at the 0.05 level.*

Sources: *Gini: Human Development Report 1997, UNDP; own estimates based on IMF Staff Country Reports.*

CONCLUSION: SEARCHING FOR CAUSAL MODELS

Looking into the relations depicted in Figure 4.1 a first observation is that high inflation is detrimental to growth, in this context primarily because it increases uncertainty for investors (Jones, 1998). The negative relationship between inflation and foreign direct investment in post-communist countries has been well documented in a number of studies (Stern, 1997). The initial inflationary pressures in post-communist economies stem from three general factors (Bartlet, 1996): First, cost-push pressures were generated by a contraction of supplies (in Eastern Europe in particular from Russia) and the full or partial opening of the economy to world market prices. Second, the socio-political disruptions attending the demise of communist governments generated high inflationary expectations in the populations. Third, while government expenditures in most countries changed relatively little during the first years of transition, revenues decreased rapidly when the central authorities lost control with enterprises and regional governments. In many cases, the deficit was covered through inflationary spending by the central bank. Furthermore, the initial under-valuation of a number of new currencies in newly independent states (especially the Baltic States) contributed to inflationary pressures (Saavalainen, 1995, p. 10). The combination of these factors fuelled the high inflation. In Russia and other republics of the former Soviet Union consumption was kept artificially high for political reasons, generating vast disequlibria and inflationary pressures that exploded in 1992 after the disintegration of the Soviet Union. In addition to spiralling inflation the dramatic decline in production illustrated (although probably exaggerated) by the GDP figures in Table A 4.2 was caused by the abrupt disruption of links between enterprises in the previously highly integrated socialist economies when CMEA was abolished in 1992, and even more when national borders were raised following the collapse of the Soviet Union. These new more or less protected markets came into existence simultaneously with the opening to competition from Western producers and when abrupt shifts in relative prices left whole industries without markets and/or suppliers. Internally the change from plan to market based mode of allocation and the abrupt change of relative prices were the major causes that produced the initial drop in production.[11]

Moving left in the model, a second observation is that an initial decision to liberalize before structural reforms will decrease average inflation. But more surprising is the very weak relation between initial decisions about phasing and pace. Our expectation would be that those who decide to liberalize before instituting structural reforms (phasing) would also move faster (pace). This is not generally the case. Rather, we should see the initial decisions about phasing and pace as discrete choices, each with their own subsequent consequences which reflect social and economic contexts. The initial decision about pace is very important to the eventual comprehensiveness (scope) of reforms. The decision to launch early comprehensive reforms apparently removes some of the obstacles (social, political and economic) to a continuation of structural reforms, thus substantiating a core argument of those favouring the 'shock therapy'. The model also demonstrates that scope and inflation are closely related although the direction of influence is not self-evident. Does the continuation of liberalization and the initiation of structural reforms restrain the inflationary basis of the economy? That would make the decision about pace the crucial initial decision. Or is it control of inflation that makes a continuation of structural reforms possible? That would make the initial decision about phasing most important. There is probably no definite answer to these questions, as observed in the previous section. This observation also applies to the link between the initial decision about pace, where Figure 4.6 demonstrates that fast reforms increase the initial social costs in terms of poverty and GDP-decline, in Central and Eastern Europe reflecting a decline in heavy industry as a prelude to growth in new non-state enterprises. It is this private sector growth stimulated by fast stabilization and privatization that later more than compensates for the poverty engendered by fast initial liberalization.

Hence, if we focus only on the economic dynamics of institutional strategies, fast and comprehensive reforms that initially focus on liberalization rather than structural reforms have proved superior. Although this institutional strategy incurs higher initial losses (GDP and inflation) and social costs (rise in poverty), it induces renewed private sector growth which more than compensates for the initial growth in poverty. However, the world of post-communism is far from this ideal-type economic world, depicted in the two models. Not all countries were willing or able to follow the wisdom inferred from Figure 4.3. The challenge is to understand why. Why did some countries, in particular countries of the former Soviet Union, neglect to launch the institutional strategy that apparently brings superior results in terms of growth and alleviation of social and economic costs? Why did they choose strategies that apparently brought protracted inflation, decline in GDP and a dramatic increase in poverty and related social costs?

Answering these questions takes us to the sphere of politics. If we want to understand the roots of initial and continued inflation, decline in GDP and associated social costs, we should focus not only on economic causes but, as it was argued in the structuralist debate in the 1970s, look for 'deep-seated social and political – rather than purely economic – explanations...' (Kahler, 1990, p. 40). We should recognize that '... the relative capacity of different types of regimes to stabilise is a function of the political dynamics and the underlying inflationary pressure in the first place' (Haggard and Kaufman, 1992, pp. 272). In this context we must consider how social and political conflicts and narrow elite interests may translate into inflation, cost-push, monopoly or oligopoly pricing practices. In particular, we should recognize that distributive coalitions or narrow collective or elite interests might be so powerful that the policies needed to stabilize, to renew growth or to alleviate poverty prove politically infeasible. In short, social responses and political interest must be seen as endogenous to any model on institutional strategies in reforming economies.

These insights from third world stabilization programmes are also reflected in competing perspectives on the political economy of institutional change in post-communist economies: one focuses on the political response of the early losers (large group), a second on the power and interests of the early winners (narrow group), while a third perspective emphasizes the configuration of (democratic) political institutions as mediators between competing interests.

The first approach focuses on the social and political implications of initial decisions about pace and phasing. In all post-communist countries the victims of inflation were people on fixed incomes, those with high money balances (savings) and inflexible costs. Enterprises that had inelastic demands (raw materials, energy) for their products stood much stronger than those without this advantage. In this scenario the exposed groups will use their newly won democratic powers to block or impede reforms. This is the expectation (and fear) that, in the early 1990s, dominated the supporters of a shock strategy as the only way to implement institutional changes before the victims of reforms would form the political movements that allegedly would halt (or impede) further reforms (Przeworski, 1991, pp. 136ff; Lipton and Sachs, 1990). The social and political obstacles will consequently vary between countries, reflecting the initial disequilibria, the initial competitiveness of the economy and consequently the economic and social costs that will be generated by institutional changes.

Causal model I:

Initial disequilibria
and competiveness   ➤   social costs   ➤   institutional strategy

This approach (explanation) is summarized in Causal model I linking initial conditions to social costs, which is again reflected in the eventual choice and implementation of institutional strategies. This is essentially the participant democratic model outlined in Figure 3.2 because popular sentiments about social costs are assumed to be translated into choice of institutional strategies. The initial context and the subsequent economic and social costs of institutional change consequently constrain the range of institutional strategies available to decision-makers (De Melo et al., 1997).

A second approach focuses on the role of an economic, administrative and political elite for initial and subsequent policy choices. Well-situated elites stood to be harmed by fast reforms but at the same time they were best able to benefit from initial and continued disequilibria. In this perspective continued inflation becomes a symptom either of a political stalemate, of rent-seeking or both (Åslund et al., 1996). In this scenario the incumbent nomenclatura elite (in association with new elites) reaps the benefits of delayed liberalization and stabilization, for example cheap credits, arbitrage and the control of foreign trade. That such rent seeking did in fact take place is well documented (ibid.). These economic, social and political interests were the potential losers if effective stabilization policies were implemented, either by effective and/or fast liberalization, stringent monetary and fiscal policies (phasing) or fast track privatization. Causal model II illustrates this approach:

Causal model II:

Initial disequilibria and
competiveness   ➤   collective elite interests   ➤   institutional strategy

In this model social costs are not included because it is the interests of relatively insulated (but competing) elites that guide the choice of policies. This mirrors an elitist version of democracy, as outlined in Table 3.2.

Finally, a third approach focuses on the role of political institutions. Proceeding from the traditional discussion about the connection between regime type and economic reforms and growth, this approach analyses the impact of democratic institutions on institutional strategies. Rather than the traditional democracy–dictatorship dichotomy, the question here is how the configuration of democratic institutions structures the access and influence of competing collective interests during the conflicts over institutional strategies.

Causal model III.

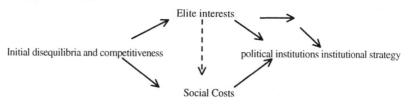

In this causal model both elite interests and social reactions are parts of the model translating social and political interests into choice of institutional strategies, where institutions provide the intervening structure that determines the power and influence of alternative groups on economic decision-making. The model does not exclude that the elite simultaneously pursues a strategy of rent-seeking, as indicated by the stippled arrow.

However, before we can examine the relative validity of the three causal models (in Chapter 6) we must consider the impact of initial conditions on institutional strategies. In particular we must know the relative weight of the constraints (economic and social costs) and opportunities (assets in the transformation of economic institutions) facing the political actors. This is the topic of the following chapter.

NOTES

1. For the most recent publications in series of research see Kim R. Holmes, Bryan T, Johnson and Melanie Kirkpatrick, 1997 Index of Economic Freedom, The Heritage Foundation/Wall Street Journal, 1997, The Heritage Foundation/Wall Street Journal–Dow Jones & Co. Washington, D.C./ New York, 1997. James D. Gwortney and Robert A. Lawson, 1997, Economic Freedom of the World, 1997 Annual Report, The Fraser Institute, 1997. Richard E. Messick and Kaku Kimura (eds), World Survey of Economic Freedom, 1995–96, Freedom House, 1996.
2. Adrian Karatnycky, Alexcander Motyl and Boris Shor (eds), Nations in Transit 1997, Civil Society, Democracy and Markets in East Central Europe and the Newly Independent States, Freedom House, 1997.
3. One further argument for using the two different indices in the same analysis is that the later we move in the process of institutional change, the more important becomes the institutional variables (in the EBRD index), while liberalization (as in the World Bank index) has greater salience in the early stages of institutional transition.
4. UNICEF and UNDP's publications, in particular, have received broad coverage. See UNICEF (1997) and UNDP (1999) for the latest survey and for references to previous publications.

5. One can of course also apply an ethical or moral perspective on these issues. That, however, is not the task of the present study. In Chapter 2, I discussed the political aspects of moral judgements which can also be applied in this context.

6. The validity of GDP-development, inflation, poverty and inequality as proxies for social costs is demonstrated by their relatively high (bivariate) correlation with the ultimate proxy: decreased life expectancy. The correlation of life expectancy (1995) with increase in poverty 1988–94 is 0.7 (significant at the 0.01 level), with average inflation 0.6 (significant at the 0.05 level) and with increase in inequality 1988–95: 0.6 (significant at the 0.05 level). Source: UNDP 1997.

7. There were obviously also other collective interests that survived the change, e.g. the military, the police and scientific institutions. They were, however, not directly hit by the institutional changes in the economy, but indirectly when the economic decline radically reduced their budgets.

8. The cumulated liberalization index (CLI) is the cumulated weighted average of 0 to 1 rankings of the following three categories: Internal markets, external markets and private sector entry. Each country's weighted average for year 0 is then added to the score in year 1, taking into account the former years of reform.

EBRD transition indicators are a calculated average of each country's score on nine different parameters. The score ranges from 1 indicating little or no progress in reform, to 4 indicating almost complete reform of the area concerned. Additionally, a category 4* is used when the specific country has attained a level of development comparable to most advanced industrial economies. In order to include this category in the figures we denoted 4* as 4.33 when calculating the average score. In the 1997 Transition Report many of the scores have been assigned either a + or a – sign which levels the possible scores while indicating that a country is on the borderline between two scores. Numerically we have added 0.33 to plus-scores and subtracted 0.33 from minus-scores. The scores on the calculated average are the same as for the single indicators ranging from 1 to 4.5. The 1994 Transition report measured only six indicators while subsequent reports operate with nine. The three additions concern developments in financial institutions and legal reform. Due to this expansion of indicators some of the countries have gone down in overall ratings from 1994 to 1995.

Pace is calculated as the Cumulated Liberalization Index at the end of year two after the initiation of reforms.

9. The model uses (log) inflation to account for the cases of extreme inflation in the Former Soviet Union.

10. The term first used by Przeworski (1991).

11. It is not the purpose of the present book to analyse the economic causes of the initial inflation or the dramatic drop in GDP. Both issues have been the subject of an extensive economic literature. For a references to relevant literature focusing on alternative causes, see Pei (1996, p. 134).

APPENDIX 4

Table A 4.1. SCOPE94, SCOPE97 and PACE.

Country	SCOPE94 World Bank Indicators	SCOPE97 EBRD Indicators	PACE
Albania	2.30	2.52	.24
Belarus	1.07	1.67	.41
Bulgaria	2.90	2.78	.94
Czech Rep.	3.61	3.52	.95
Estonia	2.93	3.48	1.90
Hungary	4.11	3.70	1.31
Kazakhstan	1.31	2.63	.92
Kyrgyzstan	1.81	2.74	1.05
Latvia	2.45	3.07	1.64
Lithuania	2.72	3.04	1.83
Moldova	1.62	2.56	1.07
Mongolia	2.27	3.04*	1.60
Poland	4.14	3.48	1.64
Romania	2.29	2.70	.58
Russia	1.92	3.00	1.26
Slovakia	3.47	3.22	.95
Slovenia	4.16	3.18	1.74
Turkmenistan	.63	1.30	.41
Ukraine	.80	2.41	.54
Uzbekistan	1.11	2.19	.68

Note: The figure for Mongolia*, which is not included in the original EBRD Transition Report, is our own estimate based on evaluations made in accordance with the individual categories in the EBRD Indicators. The estimate is based on following publications: Economic Parameters: Mongolia – Background Paper, *IMF Staff Country Report No. 95/11, IMF, Washington D.C., Jan. 1995,* Mongolia – Recent Economic Developments, *IMF Staff Country Report No. 97/92, IMF, Washington D.C., Oct. 1997,* Mongolia – Selected Issues, *IMF Staff Country Report No. 99/4, IMF, Washington D C., 1999. Legal Parameters:* Developing Mongolia's Legal Framework, *Asian Development Bank, http//:www.adb.org/Work/Law_Devt, October 1995.*

Sources: Col. 1: 'From Plan to Market', Policy Research Working Paper 1564, World Bank, Policy Research Dep., Jan. 1996, Col. 2: Transition Report 1997, Table 2.1 and Box 2.1, Col. 3: Own estimate based on Col. 1.

Table A 4.2. Economic development 1989–1997.

Country	Inflation in peak year %	Average inflation 2–1997	Inflation, latest annual (1997)	GDP. First year positive after initiation of reform	GDP – deepest slump (1990–97) 1989=100	GDP-index 1989=100		
						1995	1996	1997
Belarus	2220.00 (94)	847	64.0	5	62.62 (95)	62.62	64.37	70.81
Kazakhstan	1879.90 (94)	755	17.4	5	60.21 (95)	60.21	60.51	61.78
Kyrgyzstan	854.60 (92)	222	25.6	5	52.17 (95)	52.17	55.09	58.50
Moldova	1276.00 (92)	237	11.8	1	36.13 (96)	39.19	36.14	36.60
Russia	1353.00 (92)	290	14.7	6	58.06 (96)	59.73	58.06	58.29
Turkmenistan	3102.40 (93)	1386	84.0	No pos. growth yet	39.38 (96)	41.19	39.38	40.25
Ukraine	4735.20 (93)	1220	15.9	No pos. growth yet	36.27 (97)	41.63	37.47	36.27
Uzbekistan	1568.00 (94)	466	45.0	5	83.36 (95)	83.36	84.69	86.73
Estonia	1069.00 (92)	40	11.3	4	59.82 (94)	62.39	64.89	71.96
Latvia	951.30 (92)	39	8.4	3	49.73 (93)	50.93	52.36	55.50
Lithuania	1020.50 (92)	111	8.8	4	52.85 (94)	54.07	56.83	60.24
Mongolia	268.40 (93)	100	36.9	3	75.25 (93)	81.83	83.95	86.47
Albania	225.20 (92)	60	32.1	4	60.13 (92)	78.52	85.67	79.67
Bulgaria	1089.40 (97)	266	1089.4	5	73.29 (93)	76.18	67.87	62.85
Czech Republic	59.00 (91)	18	8.4	4	76.64 (92)	83.86	87.30	88.34
Hungary	34.80 (91)	24	18.3	5	81.89 (93)	85.53	86.64	90.10
Poland	585.80 (90)	35	15.0	3	82.21 (91)	98.56	104.57	111.78
Romania	256.10 (93)	141	154.8	4	74.99 (92)	84.54	87.83	82.04
Slovakia	59.00 (91)	18	6.2	5	73.81 (93)	82.45	88.22	93.25
Slovenia	210.00 (92)	17	9.1	2	82.85 (92)	93.36	96.26	99.82

Sources: *IMF: World Financial Outlook, 1999.*

Economic Institutions and Democratic Reform

Table A 4.3. Inequality and poverty.

Country	Gini-coefficient (annual)			Poverty headcount (in percent)		
	1987–1988	1993–1994	Increase 1988–94	1987–1988	1993–1994	Increase 1988–94
Belarus	23	22	–1	1	11	10
Kazakhstan	26	33	6	5	50	45
Kyrgyzstan	26	35	9	12	76	64
Moldova	24	36	12	4	65	61
Russia	24	36	12	2	43[1]	41
Turkmenistan	26	36	10	12	48	36
Ukraine	23	33	10	2	41	39
Uzbekistan	28	33	5	24	29	5
Estonia	23	40[2]	17	1	33[3]	32
Latvia	23	27[4]	4	1	19[5]	18
Lithuania	23	37	14	1	49	48
Albania	n.a	n.a.		n.a.	n.a.	
Bulgaria	23[6]	31[7]	8	2[8]	17[9]	15
Czech Rep.	19	27	6	0	<1	1
Hungary	23[10]	28	5	<1[11]	2	1
Poland	26	31[12]	5	6	20[13]	14
Romania	23[14]	33[15]	10	6[16]	32[17]	24
Slovakia	20	20[18]	0	0	1[19]	1
Slovenia	24	29	5	0	0	0

Notes: 1: Expenditure based measure. 2: Expenditure based, 1989. 3: Expenditure based, 1995. 4: Expenditure based. 5: Expenditure based. 6: 1989. 7: 1992. 8: 1989. 9: Expenditure based, 1992. 10: 1989. 11: 1989. 12: Expenditure based. 13: Expenditure based. 14: Expenditure based. 15: 1989. 16: Expenditure based. 17: Expenditure based. 18: 1992. 19: 1992.

Sources: Branko Milanovic, 'Poverty, Inequality and Social Policy in Transition Economies', The World Bank, Policy Research Department, Transition Economics division, November 1995, Policy Research Working Paper 1530. Transition Report Update, European Bank for Reconstruction and Development, April 1997.

5. Context or Institutional Strategies: The Role of First Order Initial Conditions

'Structures restrict as well as enable. Structures restrict and condition the choices and actions of social agents, but they also allow certain types of behaviour and shape opportunities for social action' (Sørensen, 1997, p. 37).

The previous chapter analysed the economic and social consequences of alternative institutional strategies. This chapter takes the analysis one step back and attempts to explain the framework within which these contingent choices are made. Were they the outcome of decisions by sovereign and insulated reformers? Or are they rather to be understood as reflections of initial systemic structures that leave politicians with no or very few options? This is the basic question we address in this chapter. To recapitulate, in this context first order initial conditions or structures are conceived as the structural legacies of the incumbent socialist system that at the inauguration of institutional changes distinguishes an economy and society from other systems. As initial conditions they are by definition outside the control of reformers, but represent the economic, social and political context within which they have to launch and implement institutional changes. Proceeding from these preliminary definitions, section one will conceptualize the concept of internal conditions, while section two will estimate the effect of initial conditions on respectively institutional changes and outcomes. Below I will make an attempt to substantiate causal models that reflect the political constraints and opportunities identified through the statistical analysis.

CONCEPTUALIZING INITIAL CONDITIONS

Everyone who has spent time in what used to be the world of 'real existing socialism' has probably had the same ambiguous feeling of familiarity tinged with abnormality of what we saw and experienced. On the one hand, we enjoyed the company of highly educated people, admired their educational systems, the high tech performance in space, the smoothly running public transport systems in the major cities and the scientists at the frontier of research in their respective fields. And if on the night before the October parades you happened to be in Moscow's Gorkij Street, you could almost physically feel the power of a technologically advanced war-machine when the panzer of the Kirov regiment practised for the next day's performance. They were, in other words, 'modern' in the sense we knew from our own part of the world.

On the other hand, we also sensed that something was definitely not the way it was in the West. The lenient attitude towards work duties among even the best educated people struck anybody who went there to do serious work, as did the absence of individual responsibility for collective tasks, whether social or economic. The low quality of consumer goods was a persistent source of jokes and income when we sold our worn out jeans at excessive prices. Those of us who visited industrial production facilities felt ourselves taken back to the beginning of the industrial revolution, were it not for the excessive number of workers and administrative staff often preoccupied with matters that seemed far removed from production. And then there was, of course, the synthetic consensus promulgated by the strictly controlled and excruciatingly boring mass media. Although it was at times shared by the majority of the population, this (politically opportune) consensus still concealed real conflicts of interests. The imposed consensus was also reflected in the absence of any serious political science, and in particular social science.[1] And then there was the phoney political system. You would visit the party offices of what was not really a party but a Mafia-like structure of power penetrating all formal institutions and organizations. You could observe sessions in parliaments that were actually rubber stamps for decisions taken elsewhere. One could attend rallies and demonstrations that were in fact public relations stunts for party policies, and at elections you would observe political participation that had nothing to do with conveying citizens' complaints and demands to centres of political decision making. And the 'public organizations' were not really public but top-managed state organizations that propagated official policies to various segments of the population. One also felt the perverted perceptions of the Western world which were not only political propaganda but permeated the minds of large sections of the population and hampered contact with the outside world, political, social and commercial. In short, seen from the 'modern' Western world these countries were 'distorted' in some strange and incomprehensible way.

There were obviously degrees. In the Soviet Central Asian republics you felt that the traditional questions of development were still very much present and that huge economic gains were obtainable with more industry, better infrastructure, better education or updated production technology. When visiting the Huta-Katowice metal complex in Poland you sensed that these enterprises were of such a nature that they could never compete in a liberalized and open economy, while the Czech tool-making factories or the furniture factories of Estonia reflected old traditions of craftmanship and skills that stood a chance on Western markets with updated designs and technologies, better management and marketing departments. Walking around in (or just around) Ceausescu's monstrous palace, for which one fifth of ancient Bucharest had been demolished, you definitely sensed that you were in a politically very 'distorted' country' that tolerated such excessive waste of scarce resources. In countries like Poland, Hungary and the former Yugoslavia you would despite official propaganda still experience a rudimentary civil society, in some cases centred around an independent church, in other cases surviving because of the ineptness, corruption or fragmentation of the political leadership. And if your timing was right you would experience how this dormant civil society was able to explode into real demonstrations, of creating real citizen organizations and institutions, as happened in Hungary in 1956, in Prague in 1968 and in Poland in 1980–81. This perspective of relativity also applied to the attitudes to the surrounding world. In the midst of Siberia or any other part of the Russian countryside you felt that Moscow was the only economic and political centre of importance and recognized that most people believed that they were better off than the exploited masses of crises riddled Western capitalism. Talking to a beautiful woman of Bulgaria or Bosnia you already felt yourself half way between Europe and the Orient. In Hungary and Warsaw you were mentally closer to Vienna or Frankfurt than to Moscow. You would also sense that the propaganda had the reverse effect of what was intended because people believed that Western life styles were the only solution to all their complaints about everyday life. In the Baltic states you would, despite the very real presence of Moscow and their affiliates, still sense a dormant longing for the Western world of which they had been part before they were absorbed by the Soviet Union in the wake of the World War Two.

This exposé of impressions from longer stays, jobs or short visits to all corners of the former socialist world could be continued indefinitely. The question is, however, whether the indistinct sentiments I describe of separate spheres or dimensions of the socialist world can be applied in order to define more precise and measurable aspects of the initial conditions confronting post-communist reformers, capturing what may be termed 'modernization' and 'distortion', with subsequent impact on institutional choices and social and economic outcomes?

A first argument in support of such an approach is that these are in fact the dimensions that arise from previous research into factors behind post-communist institutional change as surveyed in Chapter 3. This observation is most easily applied to traditional concepts of socio-economic modernization. Whether we focus on the political scientist's search for the connection between socio-economic development and democratization (Hadenius, 1992; Diamond, 1997) or on the economist's search for factors behind growth (Jones, 1998; Lal and Myint, 1996) it has been on the same groups of variables: education, application of modern technology, development of infrastructure, social differentiation and professional specialization. In this perspective the socialist path of development did produce a 'modern society' according to our normal understanding of that concept. It raised the level of education, produced an achievement oriented culture, and promoted technological development, infrastructure and means of communication. These features are all assets in contemporary aspirations to change economic institutions and survive in a new international context.[2] The development perspective has generated alternative causal models connecting initial development to the prospective for change and growth. Gerschenkron (1962) sees relative backwardness as an asset that can be exploited in a rapid catch-up when backward countries emulate organization as well as technologies in a learning process. The same perspective is the substance of the Sachs–Woo theorem outlined in Chapter 3, and focuses in particular on the efficiency gains obtained via migration of workers from a rural inefficient state sector to a modern private urban industry. These discussions also gave rise to the hypothesis that initial social inequalities, empirically associated with lesser development, impede institutional change and economic growth (De Melo and Gelb, 1997; Rodrik, 1996; Persson and Tabellini, 1994; Deininger and Squire, 1997; Alesina and Perotti, 1994), reflecting that greater inequalities imply increased social conflicts during the change of economic institutions. A contrasting argument is the Kuznets hypothesis that inequity is likely to increase during the early stages of development before declining when per capita income rises towards Western levels. The implications in relation to this study are that lesser development will be a liability because institutional changes in such an environment increase inequality and poverty and hence the social and political obstacles to a continuation of reforms (Lal and Myint, 1996, p. 39; Deininger and Squire, 1997; Kuznets, 1970).

Secondly, the socialist path of development also produced a number of unintended consequences, however. These have now proved incompatible with new 'modern' economic and social systems, the standards of which they must emulate when entering international markets. The post-communist economies and societies are 'distorted' in the sense that they not only have to develop their institutions (as do all developing countries), but also to dismantle the institutions of the incumbent system. The components of 'distortion' are certainly not only products of communism. In most cases communism reinforced the features of 'relative backwardness' that kept some countries at the periphery of West European development (Chirot, 1989; Gerschenkron, 1962; Berend, 1995). Like 'modernity' 'distortion' is an integrated concept and its appearances in different societal spheres is empirically connected, for example to industrial structure, technological backwardness, egalitarianism, anti-market attitudes,[3] cultural parochialism and anti-democratic political cultures. Kornai (1992: Chapter 15) describes this interconnectedness in his classical analysis of the cohesiveness of the socialist political, economic and social systems. He describes the socialist economic system (or rather the socialist system in toto) as a Weberian ideal-type integrated structure involving a hierarchy of five spheres of appearance.

At the core is the power of the communist party and the dominant position of the official ideology, penetrating (and legitimizing) all spheres of activity. On the second and third level (derived from the first level), the system is manifested by the dominant position of state and quasi-state property and by bureaucratic coordination (as opposed to market coordination) of the economy. Finally, these underlying structural properties find their concrete expression in the systemic properties of plan bargaining, soft budget constraints, the quantitative drive, weak responses to price signals and in the output characteristics: forced growth, deficit of consumer goods, labour shortage and 'unemployment on the job', economic autarchy etc. Yet it is the first sphere of the ideologically legitimized power structure that embodies the 'genetic code' of the whole system (ibid., p. 361), guiding all action in the other spheres. Kornai uses this description of the socialist system to explain the failures of previous reforms, when reformers attempted to change the economic structure without changing the power structure or the official ideology. Seen in the context of this study, the implication of Kornai's theory is that the concrete socialist (and post-socialist) country has been a more or less true reproduction of Kornai's ideal type socialist system, that the cohesiveness and embeddedness of the countries will be different, and change correspondingly more or less difficult. In short: the more closely a country resembles Kornai's ideal type socialist system, the more distorted it will be.

The concept of distortion (with various descriptions) has been applied by researchers using different variables in different contexts. McKinnon (1991) for example suggests that the number of goods allocated by central authorities is a valid indicator of the degree of centralization of an economy, and hence how far it must go in order to meet the requirements of a decentralized market economy. He also suggests that the accumulation of stocks indicates the rigidity of economic management because enterprises in planned economies continue to produce rather than curb production.[4] Pei (1996) suggests that the level of centralization in decision making and the coverage of the socialist welfare state might serve as proxies for the 'completion' of socialism. De Melo et al. (1997) pursue an identical objective when they estimate the importance of initial conditions in the determination of policy choices and the channels through which initial conditions might affect policies, inflation and growth. Using principal component analysis they identify two clusters of variables by the degree of macro economic imbalances at the beginning of transition and the degree of structural distortion. Without going into the very complex argument, their conclusion is that institutional change (policy reform) depends on initial conditions, political change and regional tensions,[5] that initial conditions are also important to performance and that adverse initial conditions are associated with slower economic liberalization. Finally, Popov (1997, 1998) also used the concept of distortion which he operationalizes by using a composite index constructed on the basis of the initial structural attributes of the socialist economy.[6] He is the only one who includes level of development as contrasted to distortion when he argues, following Sachs and Woo, that lesser developed socialist systems escaped distortion precisely because they are underdeveloped. This perspective reflects a problem which is common to these attempts to identify the impact of initial conditions, namely that they only look at distortion (under different names and with different proxies) as constraints that may hinder structural adaptation. They do not see or recognize the assets that the 'modernity' part of the socialist path of development also created.[7]

Modernization and distortion are in the present sense abstract dimensions or factors and their existence can be registered through a number of inter-dependent and interacting variables, some of which are ingrained structural parts of the factors and some of which are measurable only through their effects. Both are relative concepts because they are measured in relation to the existing mode of modernity in developed Western countries. They respectively represent opportunities and constraints for change, not agents of change (to which we shall return in Chapter 7). Modernity provides an opportunity for change because it renders societies permeable to new ideas, and mutable in the sense that incipient structures will support (and benefit from) the transformation to a modern society in the Western sense. Distortion has the opposite effect, in that the transformation becomes more costly and difficult, economically, socially and politically. The short term direct effects of distortion follow from those initial properties of the economy that directly influence the performance of the economy in its ability to meet new institutional demands under changed relative prices. This is the supply side response where the existing micro-foundations of the economy collide with new institutions. Assets in this micro-foundation (modernization) are properties that are compatible with and represent positive factors in the construction of a new economic system in the form of viable enterprises, modern infrastructure and an adequately trained and motivated work force. Liabilities (distortion) are those structural traits of the economy or society that have the opposite effect and inhibit competitiveness in the new environment where enterprises – with the change in relative prices – in extreme cases are value extracting and where the costs of adaptation in any case are greater than the potential benefits, where education and training as well as mentalities and values are inadequate or unsuitable and where infrastructures do not meet the needs of the new pattern of trade and other forms of economic interaction. Hence, distortion and modernization entail economic assets and liabilities that indicate how the present economy will fare under new conditions and what the social and political costs of adapting to the new environment will be. They will show whether the challenge is one of traditional development or whether it is a simultaneous process of destruction and construction of institutions.

Distortion and modernization may also have a short-term indirect effect in that it becomes more or less difficult to adopt and implement the necessary institutional strategies. This is their political aspect, reflecting the political and social interests and values affiliated with economic structures and initial societal conditions. Level of distortion will also determine the mode of political behaviour, because capacities and experiences from the socialist era (the embeddedness of the systems in Konai's sense) will shape the mentalities, values, attitudes and behaviour to (and within) the institutions and practices of a new democratic system. If less developed, pre-modern institutions may colonize the institutions of a new democracy. If distorted, experiences with the phoney institutions and organizations of the communist era generate distrust in organizations and institutions that appear to be replicas of communist institutions and organizations. In sum, if organizations and informal institutions of the incumbent system survive they may use their strength within the new institutional framework.

INITIAL CONDITIONS, INSTITUTIONAL CHOICES AND OUTCOMES

Following the argument that initial conditions are a blend of modernity and modernization, 9 variables were subjected to exploratory factor analysis (Kim and Mueller, 1983, 1984).[8]

Modernization is represented by four variables: 'Telephone lines' is a proxy for infrastructural development; 'Average years of schooling' indicates the educational level of the general population and is also used as a preliminary proxy for administrative capacity; 'television' is a proxy for means of communication between population and leadership, while 'per cent urban population' indicates occupational profile, in particular the fraction not working in agriculture. Together these four variables are assumed to reflect a structural factor of modernization that is a potential asset in the transformation to a market economy.

Distortion is represented by five variables: 'Monopoly' describes the share of very large centrally managed enterprises, in the Former Soviet Union defined as the percentage share of 'All-Union Enterprises' and in Central and Eastern Europe as the share of enterprises with more than 5,000 employees. 'Share of trade within the CMEA area' reflects the functional specialization of the economies within the socialist division of labour, and hence the expected scope of the initial shock when trade linkages disintegrated with the collapse of CMEA and the Soviet Union; 'Years under Central Planning' is a summary proxy covering all aspects of the 'completeness' of socialism, from organization to mentalities and the social and political embeddedness of the socialist system; 'repressed inflation' is a proxy for the relative scarcity of goods, and hence the relative distortion of the production in relation to real demand, while 'black market premium' indicates the expected and perceived real value of the currency and thus the level of distortion of the national economy in relation to the relative prices that would come into effect in a liberalized economy. The last two variables should be seen as a combined effect of structural distortions in the economy and policy mistakes during the last years of socialism. Together these five variables are assumed to reflect a structural factor of distortion that would be a liability in the transformation to a market economy.

The values 'Modernization' and 'Distortion' are described in Appendices A5.1 and A5.2. When subjected to factor analysis they identify two major factors representing 'modernization' and 'distortion' respectively.[9] Two composite indices were then constructed on the basis of these factors, respectively representing modernization and distortion for the 20 countries (see Appendices A5.3 and A5.4). The definition of the two sets of initial structures (factors) provides us with four clusters of countries, as illustrated in Figure 5.1.[10]

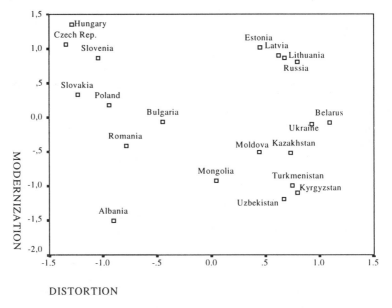

Figure 5.1. Distortion and modernization: four clusters.

- In the upper left corner a cluster of countries that are highly developed and little distorted consisting of Central and East European Countries: Hungary, Czech Republic, Slovenia, Slovakia and Poland.
- A cluster in the upper right corner consisting of developed but distorted countries of the former Soviet Union: The Baltic States, Russia and – at the lower end of modernization most distorted of all – Belarus and Ukraine.
- A cluster in the lower right corner consisting of less developed and distorted countries of the former Soviet Union, in particular the

republics of Central Asia: Kazakhstan, Turkmenistan, Kyrgyzstan and Uzbekistan. Also Moldova and Mongolia approach this cluster.

- A cluster consisting of three outliers. Albania and Romania are relatively less developed. Their inclusion in the cluster illustrated as less distorted has to do with their relatively lower initial macro-economic imbalances produced by isolationist economic policies, while they still have very large enterprises. This is particularly so in the cases of Albania and Romania. Bulgaria's position between the former Soviet Republics and Central and Eastern Europe perfectly illustrates her position as the '16th Soviet Republic', economically very closely integrated into the Soviet economic orbit. The same applies to Mongolia at a lower level of development.

Further, the 'modernization' and distortion' indices were used as independent variables in a regression analysis to predict our dependent variables: pace (the speed of reforms), scope97 (institutional reforms at the end of 1997) and scope94 (institutional reforms at the end of 1994), inflation (stabilization),[11] GDP-development and poverty. The following models illustrate the results.

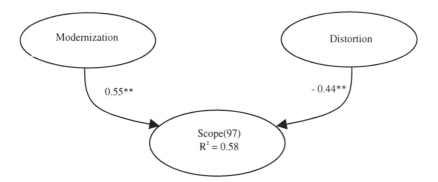

Figure 5.2. Initial conditions and institutional development.

Equation 5.1. Beta values in parentheses, Adj. R–square = 0.58.

Scope(97) = 2.81 +0.38*Modernization (0.55**) – 0.30*Distortion (–0.44**)

T-values: 31.72   3.54   –2.82

*Note: * Significance at the 0.01 level; ** significance at the 0.05 level.*

Figure 5.2 and Equation 5.1 show that the development of economic institutions has a relatively high level of dependence on initial conditions. Combined the two factors explain about 58% of the variation in institutional development. Modernization predicts higher levels of achievement and distortion predicts lower levels of achievement in institutional development.

We can further refine the argument by introducing pace as a bridge between initial conditions and institutional development, as seen in Figure 5.3 and Equation 5.2.

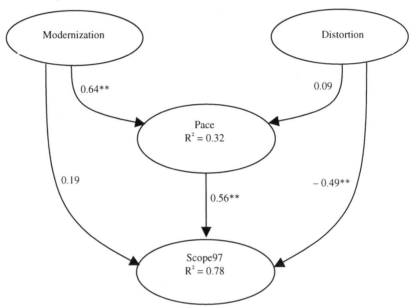

Figure 5.3. Initial conditions, pace and institutional development.

Equation 5.2. Beta values in parentheses, Adj. R– square = 0.78

Scope(97) = 2.09 + 0.13* Modernization (0.19) – 0.34* Distortion (–0.49**) + 0.66* Pace (0.56**)

T-values   11.1   1.31   –4.31   4.06

*Note: * Significance at the 0.01 level; ** significance at the 0.05 level.*

Figure 5.2 and Equation 5.3 demonstrate that modernization has a strong impact on pace, whereas the impact on institutional change (scope97) is indirect. Distortion has no impact on pace but a relatively strong negative impact on institutional change (policy). Hence, 'modern' countries are more likely to carry out fast and therefore comprehensive reforms, while 'distorted' countries are less likely to initiate institutional changes at all. Distortion, modernization and pace explain about 78 per cent of the variation in institutional change (scope).[12]

It is more complex to decipher the connection between institutional strategies and social costs. Only inflation has a relatively clear connection with distortion as shown in Equation 5.3.

Equation 5.3. Inflation 97(log). Beta values in parentheses.

Average Inflation 97(log) = 3.18 + 0.53* Distortion (0.73**) − 0.34* Scope97 (− 0.32)

T-values   11.3   17.82   − 3.41

Adj. R-square = .089

Note: * Significance at the 0.01 level; ** significance at the 0.05 level.

High average inflation is connected with initial distortion and negatively connected with the scope of reforms. The more distorted the economy, the higher the initial costs in terms of high inflation. In contrast, comprehensive institutional reforms (in particular internal and external liberalization) formed by initial conditions and the pace of reforms, will result in lower average inflation. Here, as assumed in the previous chapter, we cannot say anything definitive about the line of causation.

Regarding GDP-development and increase in poverty the bivariate regressions shown in Table 5.1 indicate that increase in poverty is related to level of distortion, whereas institutional change (scope) has no impact.

Table 5.1. Explaining social costs (beta values).

	R-square adjusted	Distortion	Scope94
Drop in GDP 1989–1994	0.40	0.69**	0.01
Headcount 1988–1994	0.35	0.73**	0.09

*Note: **Significance at the 0.01 level.*

These figures, however, cover a more complex relationship between initial conditions (distortion), pace of reforms (pace) and the scope of reforms in 1994 (scope94).[13] If we control the effect of pace for the effects of scope, the pace of reforms is also related to increase in poverty, although it has no significant effect in its bivariate relationship with increase in poverty. The implication is that the pace of reforms has diametrically opposite effects on the increase in poverty depending on the initial distortion. This implies that countries that launch fast reforms but are unable to sustain them (for reasons to be explained in subsequent chapters) face the greatest social costs, while those that are able to continue reforms soon recover with lower inflation, increased GDP and alleviation of poverty. Countries which do not reform at all face approximately the same costs as those who launched comprehensive reforms but failed.

Hence, if a new variable 'scope94-pace' describing the difference between scope and pace is regressed on distortion it produces an R-square of 0.91 (F = 189, 786, Sign. − 0.000). This indicates that the ability of fast reformers to stay on course depends on the initial level of distortion. Consequently:

- Comprehensive structural reforms increase the risk of social costs if they cannot be implemented or continued;
- Countries that cannot implement reforms are the most distorted.

These considerations can be expressed in the two equations (beta-values in parentheses):

Equation 5.4

$$NEGGDP = 45.0 - 10.9*SCOPE-PACE(-0.66**)$$

T-values   (9.82)   − 3.76)

(R^2 Adj. = 0.41)

Equation 5.5.

$$POVERTY = 45.1 - 15.1* SCOPE-PACE94 - (0.18**)$$

(R^2 Adj. = 0.42)

*Note: * Significance at the 0.01 level; ** significance at the 0.05 level.*

Equations 5.4 and 5.5 indicate that distortion is closely related to the economic and social costs of institutional change. To understand this argument it is necessary to involve Equation 5.2 which shows that distortion is unrelated to pace but negatively associated with scope97. Hence, whereas the chance that specific countries will launch fast reform (pace) seems unrelated to their level of distortion) their ability to implement reforms (scope94) has a strongly negative connection to their initial distortion.[14] The implication (depending on initial distortion) is that social and economic costs can simply be so great that they cannot be implemented in a democratic context. Fast reforms may have a positive effect on ultimate institutional changes and ultimate performance, but they carry high immediate costs in terms of decline in GDP (NEGGDP) and increase in poverty. And the higher the initial level of distortion, the higher the up front economic and social costs.[15]

Demonstrating the patterns that link initial conditions to institutional change through the relative effects of institutional strategies and social costs only takes us part of the way in our attempt to explain the change of economic institutions on post-communist systems. More specifically, it does not explain why these patterns exists. A search for the answers takes us to the political dimensions on constraints and inducements for institutional change in emerging democracies.

FIRST ORDER INITIAL CONDITIONS AND INSTITUTIONAL CHANGE

The previous analysis demonstrated the existence of two factors linking initial structures to institutional strategies and economic and social performance. Modernization has a direct positive impact on the systemic capacity to adopt and implement fast reforms (pace), with a subsequent (but hence indirect) positive impact on stabilization, institutional change (scope) and ultimately performance in terms of GDP-growth and alleviation of poverty. Distortion has a negative impact on GDP-development and poverty in countries that launched but were unable to carry through comprehensive institutional changes. So far, however, I have not discussed the routes of influence whereby 1st order initial conditions constrain or induce the adoption and implementation of institutional strategies. This chapter examines these hypothetical routes (or paths) of causation, distinguishing between the effects of modernity and distortion and electoral versus corporate (elite) channels of policy making.

THE STRUCTURAL BASIS OF POLITICAL RESPONSES

In the previous section it was argued that the inclusion of value systems and mentalities would strengthen the validity of the distortion and modernization factors, but that comprehensive data covering the countries included in this analysis are not at present available. Yet when analysing the political repercussions of the economic and social costs of institutional strategies, the response will be the combined result of the scope of costs (resulting from initial conditions and institutional strategies) and the values and attitudes of the population involved. Based on data covering only some of the countries involved,[16] this section makes an attempt to measure and hypothesize about the effect of mentalities and values that in this context will be perceived as part of the initial structural conditions of each country.

A first route of influence whereby the initial conditions can influence performance is through structural ability to adopt fast and efficient institutional strategies (pace and scope) with subsequent impacts on growth and mitigation of poverty. In concrete terms, this influence is represented by the political forces that reflect but do not reproduce the structural features of the economy and the political experiences of a particular country. Level of modernization has a positive impact on systemic capacity to adopt efficient strategies at an early stage in the process. As seen from Figure 5.3 and Equation 5.2 level of modernization influences institutional performance (scope) through pace, i.e. the capacity to adopt fast and comprehensive policies. A first observation is that this pattern is in conflict with the Sachs-Woo hypothesis (generated by a comparison of Russia with China and supported by Popov (1997)) that low level of development opens for direct mobility between inefficient agriculture and efficient private industry, which in turn generates rapid growth and development. While this mobility is a theoretical possibility, institutional rigidity, at least in the short run, has not made this a general path of development. Rather, the described pattern probably reflects that a high level of modernity facilitates the adoption and implementation of radical institutional strategies.

But how do we explain that change of economic institutions is so heavily dependent on level of modernization? We can hypothesize the following linkages: Firstly, the existence of a modern infrastructure makes it administratively easier to implement any strategy. Secondly, concentration of the population into urban centres makes it easier to communicate new policies to broader segments of the population, while we also know that conservative attitudes to institutional reform are primarily concentrated in rural area. This hypothesis is supported by Figure 5.4 showing popular attitudes to economic reforms in rural and urban regions.

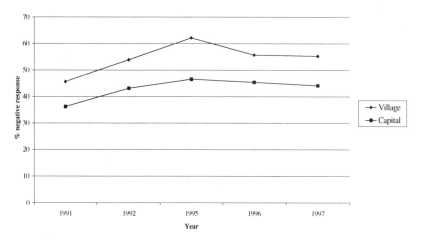

Source: EastEurobarometer, subsequent years

Figure 5.4. Negative attitude to market reforms by type of community.

Thirdly, a higher educational level as an integral part of modernity probably makes it easier for the population to comprehend and support the visions contained in a radical reform strategy. Resonating Lipset's (1959)[17] argument on why modernity promotes democracy, and on the basis of a number of empirical surveys, Frentzel-Zagorska and Zagorski (1993, p. 719), for example, conclude that '… the powerful impact of education suggests that intellectual ability to understand and define the country's general situation is an important factor in evaluating the government's policy options either positively or negatively. Better educated people tend to think in terms of the more far-reaching policies necessary for the success of reform (…). Less educated people are perhaps more inclined to react to immediate threats to their jobs and living standards, thus they are more ready to demand governmental involvement in shaping the standard of living.' This argument is supported by Figure 5.5 which shows that support for market reform depends on level of education.

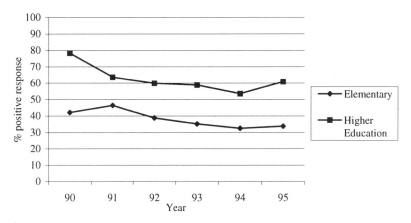

Source: EastEurobarometer, subsequent years.

Figure 5.5. Education and support for market reforms.

The positive relationship between level of modernization and ability to adopt and implement institutional changes (pace) can also be understood from the perspective of the higher levels of initial inequality and poverty that characterize less developed and more rural societies, as discussed in a previous section.[18] This observation confirms more comprehensive studies which indicate that unequal economies characterized by high levels of initial inequalities will experience lower rates of growth and in general lower rates of poverty reduction (Deininger and Squire, 1997; Persson and Tabellini, 1994; Asilis and Milesi-Ferretti, 1994). As discussed by Deininger and Squire we can hypothesize two routes whereby initial distribution influences the adoption of certain policies and economic outcomes: First, a political mechanism whereby the poor vote for redistributive politics. Such a policy entails higher taxes and lower investments and generally block or impede the desired institutional reforms. Second, a skewed income distribution is often associated with higher polarization of a society, making it harder to reach decisions on policy measures, making policies less efficient. Third, a route works though financial markets. Access to credits depends on the ownership of assets that can be used as collateral. In unequal economies fewer persons have access to such collateral and are unable to make investments, resulting in lower stocks of human and physical capital and, as a consequence, lower growth. In the present sample of countries the political channel appears to be the most likely route of influence between initial inequality and institutional strategies.[19] The initial absence (and subsequent fragility) of financial markets does not make this a likely route of linkage, although it cannot be excluded that initially more equally distributed wealth (and absence of poverty) will make it easier to implement certain types of privatization, financially and politically. A more severe problem has been unclear titles to land, real estate and production facilities which has delayed privatization in many countries.[20] Finally, we can add the observation made by Przeworski (1991, p. 177), that when a major part of the population is on the brink of absolute destitution, they will, for pure survival (physical or social), oppose any policy that they believe will further reduce their living standards. We can also add the observation made by De Melo and Gelb (1997). Comparing initial inequalities in China and Russia they emphasize the importance of income disparities in the immediate post-reform period for capital leakage, when high income groups in Russia buy foreign goods and export capital, as compared to China where domestic consumption pre-dominates because of less income dispersion.[21] Capital leakage will drain the country of capital, decrease investment and growth and hence support for reforms.

Distortion is also reflected in values and mentalities. It seems reasonable to perceive a high degree of initial egalitarianism and low average support for the introduction of a market economy[22] as structural features of a society that filter objective changes in economic welfare and distribution and produces subjective attitudes. Political effects will thus become a relative concept in the sense that it has to deal with a perceived conflict between ingrained social values and the distributional effects of economic reforms, as discussed in Chapter 2. Here we discussed egalitarianism as an integral part of the socialist value system. We can hence hypothesize a positive associa-tion between level of egalitarianism and distortion. However, our data for a comprehensive comparison of egalitarian attitudes in our 20 countries are insufficient. The World Value Studies, however, cover 11 countries, pre-sented in Figure 5.6, where the height of the bars indicates egalitarian attitudes in the countries included in the survey.

The graphic indicates that value systems in distorted economies are more egalitarian than in less distorted economies.[23] In effect, the political resent-ment to the across-the-board increase in inequality and poverty (as described in Chapter 4) will be greater in a more distorted contry than in a less distorted country. The consequence is ultimately reflected in a negative relationship between level of egalitarianism and institutional change.[24] Further research is needed to include more cases and study how deeply ingrained egalitarian attitudes are, if they are the result of long historical trajectories or communist socialization, or whether they are changeable in the short term.

We can further assume that the general level of market support (but not the dynamics of support) represent a second structural circumstance that will condition the popular response to the effects of market institutions. There is a clear negative relationship between egalitarianism, as measured in the equindex, and support for the market through the 1990s.[25] Average level of support 1991–1997 for market reforms varied widely among the post-communist countries, as shown in Figure 5.7.

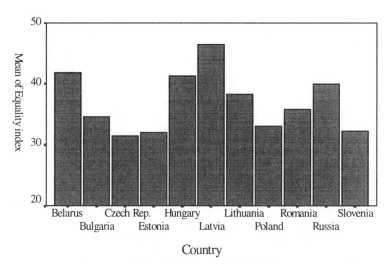

Country

Note: The bars measure 'equindex'. Equindex summarizes variables 250–256 in World Value Studies. The higher the bars, the higher the level of egalitarianism. The index measures the extent to which responses are influenced by egalitarian values, i.e. the cumulative percentage of responses located below the four extreme egalitarian values on the 1–10 scale. The equindex hence represent an estimation of the range of egalitarian values in the individual countries based on the 6 variables. See Appendix A 5.5.

Source: World Value Studies:
http://www.za.unikoeln.de/research/en/eurolabor/el_other.htm#Values.

Figure 5.6. Egalitarianism in 11 countries.

Figure 5.7 reveals a clear picture where the non-Baltic former Soviet republics show a notably lower level of average market support than the other post-communist systems, making it generally more difficult to adopt and implement market institutions in a democratic context in those countries. In Chapter 6 I return to the different levels and dynamics of market support.

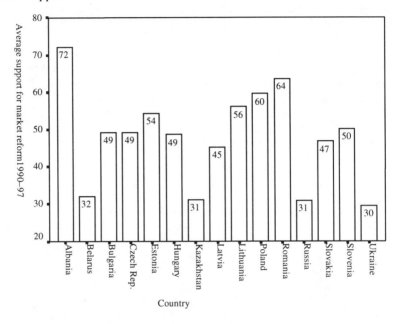

Source: EastEurobarometer, subsequent years.

Figure 5.7. Average support for the market.

The electoral effects of social and economic costs

Unlike other parts of the world that have experienced radical economic and social decline, post-communist systems have never, with a few exceptions, experienced mass or 'food' riots.[26] This apparent tranquillity may be explained in several ways. First, despite the rise in poverty and inequality described in Chapter 4, they have never reached the extreme levels found in other regions of the world. This is partly a result of the still existent rudimentary welfare system, partly the private sector being delayed in maintaining occupation and the social services associated with the enterprises. Second, the fragmentation of civil society under communism makes it difficult to organize collective action because of the lack of solidarity in and between groups. The absence of experienced organizers and collusion between managers and unions make it difficult to organize at enterprise level. Exit to the unregulated black (or grey) economy has served as a faster and more remunerative option for resourceful persons than organization of collective protests. Finally, the victims of extreme poverty are those with few individual resources: the old and marginal groups, largely hidden from the public eye in the endless suburbs or the countryside. Consequently, as summarized by Greskovits (1998, p. 87) '... voice has been biased in favour of using democratic procedures for protest rather than the rest of the repertoire of contention'. People see elections as the only feasible channel of political action. Do elections, the choice of government and ultimately policies, then reflect the impact of social and economic costs on institutional change?

To examine if this is a channel through which initial conditions (and in particular distortion) constrain institutional change, however, we face the daunting challenge of substantiating these direct or indirect linkages in a specific societal context:

objective and subjective economic social costs → attitude to reform → support for anti-market parties → government changes → policy changes

We should be able to show that people's attitudes to initiation and continuation of economic reforms (as filtered by their values and mentalities) are shaped by the objective or perceived benefits or costs, that these attitudes in turn are transformed into support for anti-market parties inclined to halt, slow or soften reforms and that support for anti-market parties, where it is converted into government participation, actually results in a reversal or moderation of reforms. While it is impossible to perform confirmative analyses of all these linkages in this context because that would require detailed country studies and time series that do not yet exist, the intention of the following analysis is to identify the broad patterns that appear from an analysis of available data.[27]

The effect of real economic and social costs on attitudes to reforms

People do not react to abstract institutional strategies. They react to the social consequences engendered by such strategies. One possibility is that they react to the general decline in macro-economic aggregates, decline in GDP, high inflation and the associated decrease in average living standards found in the path analysis in Chapter 4.

As discussed in Chapter 2, social and economic development can influence attitudes on two levels: on the aggregate level by influencing people's judgement of the overall development, and on the individual level where the subjective economic and social situation will be important. On the aggregate level, if the thesis of the political effect of economic and social costs hold, we would expect that over time there should be an increasing correspondence between development in support and general economic and social development. If we analyse the dynamic relationship between economic and social costs as expressed in development of GDP and inflation and popular attitudes in the 15 countries for which there exist survey data, we obtain the picture reflected in Table 5.2.

The negative GDP-index values for 1991–1993 show that during these years, support for the market is strongest in the countries where the GDP-decline is strongest (Central and Eastern Europe) and where support for the market is determined by non-economic factors during the phase of extra-ordinary politics. In the later stages the relationship turns positive because GDP increases in countries where the populations are positive towards the market and decreases in countries with stronger negative attitudes. An analysis of the data behind the regressions in Table 5.2 indicates, however, that whereas support for market reforms declines with a few exceptions, the ranking between countries does not change over time. This indicate that GDP and inflation rather than support changes and that other factors than relative development of GDP and inflation determine the attitudes to market reforms.

Table 5.2. Bivariate regressions of economic development on support for market reforms.

Year	Adj R-square	GDP-index	Inflation (log)
1991	0.012	− 0.333	–
1992	0.406	− 0.690**	− 0.685**
1993	0.366	− 0.497*	− 0.717**
1994	0.258	0.086	− 0.564**
1995	0.325	0.112	− 0.581**
1996	0.194	0.566*	0.020

*Note: *Significance at the 0.01 level. ** Significance at the 0.05 level.*

Source: EastEurobarometer.

This picture only shows, however, that it is not the relative magnitude of economic decline that determines people's attitudes. However, a rough negative (but of course not significant) correspondence between GDP-decline, inflation[28] and market support does exist.[29] Only in a few cases do political currents reverse or invalidate the relationship. The implication is that it was not generally the relative magnitude of economic decline that generated an increasing number of market opponents. It was general disappointment or frustrated expectations filtered through the initial value system (average market support and egalitarianism) in conjunction with political currents (to which we return below) that gave rise to the increased opposition to market reforms. Here time itself appears to be an important factor.[30]

Perception of cost, expectations and support for reforms

A second possible relationship between social cost and institutional change has to do with people's personal experiences. They may react because they see their own personal situation improved or threatened. We would therefore expect the reactions to be most negative in the more distorted countries where the populations faced the highest immediate economic and social costs of institutional change. To the extent that people tend to react to their personal experiences rather than general societal developments, we would then expect an increasing correspondence between experience of subjective economic situation and support for continuation of market reforms as the revolutionary excitement dwindles. These predictions also follow from Hirschman's 'tunnel theory' (Hirschman, 1981). His argument is that in the initial stages of regime changes people are willing to accept greater inequalities including a relative decrease in their own social and economic status because they expect that the success of others, produced by increased social differentiation, bodes well for their own future opportunities. Hence, we can hypothesize the pattern outlined in Figure 5.8.

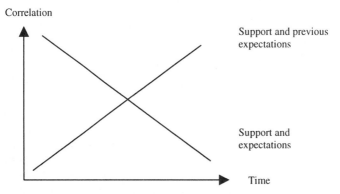

Figure 5.8. Past economic situation, future expectations and support for the market.

If the argument about the increasing salience of one's own subjective economic situation holds, we would expect the correlation between experience of own economic (financial) situation and support for the market increases ower time, and vice versa the importance of future expectations to decrease as illustrated by the two lines in Figure 5.8.[31] The data show that even though the correlation does have the right sign in most cases, the quotients are rather small and only in the most 'market naïve' countries do we find a situation which is somewhat similar to the pattern in Figure 5.8.[32] This applies to the increasing salience of past financial situation, the importance of which increases significantly over time in Belarus, Albania and Bulgaria, all highly distorted and medium developed countries. Regarding future expectations we only recognize the expected pattern in Bulgaria and Belarus where we find a clearly decreasing impact of future expectations on attitudes to reforms. Hence, to the extent that popular support for the market is influenced by real economic development, disappointment about the general socio-economic development or general disappointment rather than individual experience or expectations is what influences attitude.[33]

Market opposition and party choice

The next linkage in the attempt to link economic development to policy outcomes is the connection between attitude to market development and party choice as measured by vote intention in the 1996 EastEurobarometer Survey.[34] The question is whether the economic and social effects of the market economy will turn people against the further development of market institutions, or other issues have started to dominate the political agenda. To answer this question, Table 5.3 links attitude to market reforms to voting intention in the 15 post-communist countries in 1996.

For each country, as many parties as is necessary to count about 50 per cent of those advocating anti-market attitudes are included. The first two columns in the table give the region and the country, the third column the party name followed by party type. The next two columns describe the distribution between positive and negative market attitudes within each party and the last two columns the party's share of those responding negatively and positively to the market. If attitudes to the market remain a salient issue we would expect anti–market votes to congregate in major anti-market parties. If other issues dominate the political agenda we would expect anti-market votes to be distributed equally among more parties.

The table reveals four clusters of countries that largely resonate the four clusters of institutional progress identified in Figure 4.2. In Central Europe, in particular in Hungary, Poland, Slovakia and Slovenia, anti-market attitudes are generally equally distributed among the major parties and market attitudes no longer appeared to be a decisive element in party choice. In Hungary this represents a change from the 1994 elections, where the socialist party received 56 per cent of the anti-market vote. After that, however, the party continued a neo-liberal economic policy, and was punished by the disappointed (and frustrated) anti-market voters who moved to other parties and in particular the right-wing Independent Smallholders Party, which in 1997 captured 33 per cent of anti-market votes. Also in Poland the Post-communist Left Alliance (SLD) was brought to power in the 1993 elections but was punished by disappointed voters who in general are becoming more supportive of the market. The same picture applies to Slovenia

Table 5.3. Market attitude and party choice 1996.

Region	Country	Party	Party-type	% votes	Attitude to market in the party		Party's share of total pos./neg. market attitudes	
					Pos.	Neg.	Pos.	Neg.
Central Europe	Czech Rep.	Czech Social Dem. Party	4	31.9	30.0	70.0	22.9	38.4
		Communist Party of Bohemia and Moravia	1	9.0	4.4	95.6	1.0	14.7
		Civic Democratic Party	4	29.1	76.0	24.00	52.9	12.0
	Hungary	Independent Smallholders	3	20.4	52.4	47.6	18.9	22.4
		Hungarian Socialist Party	1	24.6	62.6	37.4	27.2	21.3
		Alliance of Young Dem.	4	17.2	58.0	42.0	17.5	16.7
	Poland	Union of Real Politics	2	28.5	77.1	22.9	28.0	30.5
		Movement for the Reconstruction of Poland	4	25.6	83.0	17.0	27.1	20.3
		SLD	1	12.5	68.1	31.9	10.9	18.6
	Slovakia	Movement for a Democractic Slovakia	2	26.0	43.6	56.4	22.1	30.1
		Party of the Dem. Left	1	10.9	48.2	51.8	10.3	11.6
		Christian Dem. Movement	4	13.1	59.7	40.3	15.2	10.8
		Slovak National Party	2	6.8	42.9	57.1	5.7	8.0
	Slovenia	Liberal Democ. of Slovenia	4	46.1	57.4	42.6	47.8	43.9
		Slovene People's Party	3	15.9	50.5	49.5	14.5	17.6
		Social Democratic Party	1	13.0	50.0	50.0	11.7	14.5
The Baltics	Estonia	Estonian Pensioners	4	11.1	54.8	45.2	9.0	15.6
		Estonian Centre Party	4	12.0	58.2	41.8	10.3	15.6
		Farmers Assembly	3	7.5	40.5	59.5	4.5	13.9
	Latvia	Democratic Party 'Saimnieks'	4	16.9	40.4	59.6	12.9	21.4
		Latvian Way	4	12.3	50.0	50.0	11.7	13.1
		For Fatherland and Freedom	2	17.2	71.7	28.3	23.3	10.3
		Farmers Union	3	7.1	50.0	50.0	6.7	7.6
	Lithuania	Homeland Union	4	34.5	69.4	30.6	38.7	27.7
		Lit. Soc. Dem. Party	4	8.8	43.2	56.8	6.1	13.1
		Lit. Center Union	4	16.4	70.7	29.3	18.7	12.6
		Lit. Dem. Labour Party	1	6.0	36.7	63.3	3.5	9.9

Table 5.3 continued

Region	Country	Party	Party-type	% votes	Attitude to market in the party		Party's share of total pos./neg. market attitudes	
					Pos.	Neg.	Pos.	Neg.
South Eastern Europe	Albania	Socialist Party	1	14.0	53.3	46.7	8.7	47.1
		The Democratic Party	4	57.9	93.8	6.2	63.0	26.0
	Bulgaria	Bulgarian Socialist Party	1	23.4	28.9	71.1	11.1	42.5
		Union of Democratic Forces	4	50.3	74.2	25.8	61.3	33.2
	Romania	PSDR	1	12.3	54.8	45.2	8.6	24.8
		Christian and Democratic National Peasants Party	3	37.8	86.9	13.1	42.3	22.2
		The Great Romanian Party	2	11.2	62.3	37.7	9.0	19.0
Former Soviet Union	Belarus	Belarussian Communist Party	1	20.2	30.9	69.1	11.0	32.5
		Belarussian Popular Front	4(2)	18.4	74.0	26.0	23.9	11.1
	Kazakh.	Communist Party	1	39.4	18.6	81.4	21.7	48.3
		Democratic Party	4	18.6	52.6	47.4	29.0	13.3
	Russia	Communist Party	1	35.2	10.7	89.3	12.6	44.8
		Honour and Motherland	4	16.0	37.3	62.7	20.0	14.3
		Russia is our Home	4	17.1	45.9	54.1	26.3	13.1
	Ukraine	Communist Party	1	29.4	16.9	83.1	15.0	36.6
		Democratic Party	4	25.3	47.0	53.0	35.9	20.1
		People's Rukh	4	8.2	39.5	60.5	9.8	7.4

Notes: Party type refers to the following classification: 1: Post-communist party; 2: Nationalist Party; 3: Agrarian; 4: Other.

Source: EastEurobarometer 1996.

where 'Liberal Democracy' (The Former Communist Youth Organization) has been in government since 1992 and where market attitudes do not seem important. In Slovakia too the anti–market vote is distributed among several parties but with Meciar's national-populist Movement for Democratic Slovakia in 1996 capturing 30 per cent of the anti-market vote. The same picture was seen in 1997, whereas Meciar's defeat at the polls in 1998 indicates that some of the market supporters may have left his party. The most deviating case in Central Europe is the Czech Republic where there is a clear division of market supporters and opponents between Václav Klaus' Civic Democratic Party and the Social Democratic and Communist Party. This reflects the increasing economic problems in the Czech Republic, which also in 1997 produced the most significant general market support among all the countries studied. It also reflects that the Communist Party is the only non-reformed post-communist party in the region, which helps explain the extremely low support for reforms among its members. With the possible exception of the Czech Republic it seems that the salience of the market issue is decreasing in central Europe. There are three possible causes: First, the market as a general economic system has been accepted and attitudes to market consequently reflects attitudes to the policies of the incumbent government, rather than market principles as such. This would also explain the Czech anomaly. Second, the frustration with post-communist parties pursuing neo-liberal policies has made the voters homeless, which also explains the decreasing turnout at subsequent elections.[35] A third possible cause is probably to be found in the approaching EU-membership which generates another picture of a 'social market economy' than the laissez-faire image that dominated the vision of the coming economic system in the early stages. The Baltic States to a large extent replicate the Central European picture, and market attitude does not seem to be a decisive issue in party choice. Over time the anti-market vote has demonstrated great volatility and wandered between all parties, irrespective of ideological and social profile. Apart from the fledgling party structure it also reflects an overlay of other issues, in particular foreign policy and (in Estonia and Latvia) attitude to large national minorities. The only prospective exception is the Estonian pensioners who seem to attract an increasing share of the losers of the economic transition, in 1997 20.5 per cent of the anti-market vote. In South Eastern Europe Albania, Bulgaria and Romania, the general very high level of support (due to political factors) is associated with a concentration of anti-market attitudes in the successor parties to the communist parties. The same picture but even more pronounced is found in the former Soviet republics of Belarus, Russia, Kazakhstan and Ukraine, where the communist parties concentrate a very large share of anti-market attitudes, indicating the strong persistent salience of the market issue in these countries.

In conclusion, it seems reasonable to hypothesize that already by the mid–late 1990s the market issue had largely disappeared from Central Europe and been replaced by the humdrum controversies of everyday politics in democratic capitalism. We see a similar situation in the Baltic states where the minority issue and relations with Russia continued to dictate the political agenda. Hence, only in South Eastern Europe and the non-Baltic former Soviet Republics did the market issue in different contexts remain in the centre of the political agenda, and support for post-communist parties continued to be an indication of popular attitudes to the installation of a market economy.

Elections, governments and policies

In the early 1990s it became a myth that the economic and social costs engendered by the economic transformation in post-communist countries would return the ex–communist parties to power, thus reversing or at least slow down the ongoing change of economic institutions. As summarized by Åslund, Boone and Johnson (1996, p. 264) this impression was nurtured by the electoral successes of the ex-communists in Lithuania in late 1992, by the defeat of pro-reform parties in Poland and Russia in late 1993, in Hungary in May 1994, in Bulgaria in December 1994, in Estonia in March 1995 and Latvia in late 1995. By 1996 seven out of fourteen pro-reform parties in Central and Eastern Europe had lost elections to more or less mutated ex-communist parties. However, as subsequent developments have shown, this was not a return to communist practices. The previous section indicated that the link between market attitudes and party choice is, at least for the Central European and Baltic countries, uncertain and we have taken this as an implication that part of the explanation is that allegedly market-sceptical parties, or parties that allegedly would soften the social consequences of market transition, nevertheless continued the institutional changes at a pace that was indistinguishable from that set by their predecessors. Table 5.4 shows the three countries where we allegedly saw a pro-Communist backlash in the mid–early 1990s.

First, the table demonstrates that in all cases electoral support was magnified by the majority electoral systems, when votes were converted into parliamentary seats. The organizational strength of post-communists compared to other parties also played an important role in mobilizing voters. Second, the table shows that at the time post-communist parties were perceived as bulwarks against unacceptable effects of the market and that they attracted a larger share of market sceptics than other parties. However, most of the parties soon lost support (as shown in Table 5.3), leading to their defeat at the subsequent election. Defeats that partly reflected their inability to pursue basically alternative policies under the constraints of international institutions, and partly that no government, irrespective of policy, has been able to stop the social differentiation and decay portrayed in Chapter 4. It is only in the former Soviet republics (outside the Baltic) that the successor-communist parties have been able to maintain the initial image, which Wesolowsky (1995) aptly describes as 'seeking to rebuild the shattered social fabric by maintaining some minimal social commitments and by offering some protection to state enterprises which face political discrimination under World Bank tutelage.' The parties had also managed to maintain a communicative interaction with large social groups which were ignored or abandoned, as Wesolowsky points out, by neo-liberal elites. In most countries outside the non-Baltic former Soviet Union, the successor parties lost this foundation and electoral policies have been dominated by a pendulum effect that has little to do with economic ideology.

Table 5.4. Market attitudes and government changes in selected countries.

Country	Elections	Parties in government after election	% of		Attitude to market among voters of the winning parties around election in %. Other parties in parentheses.	
			Votes	Seats	Pos.	Neg.
Albania	29 June and 6 July 1997	Socialist Party, Social Democratic Party and Democratic Alliance	58.1	70.3	62.0 (92.6)	38.0 (7.4)
Bulgaria	18 Dec. 1994	Socialist Party, Agrarian National Union and Ekoglasnost	50.0	59.5	31.5 (63.9)	68.5 (36.1)
Czech R.	20 June 1998	Social Democratic Party	32.2	40.6	30.0 (47.4)	70.0 (52.6)
Estonia	5 March 1995	Coalition Party and Rural Union	32.2	40.6	74.4 (69.3)*	25.6 (30.7)*
Hungary	8 May 1994	Socialist Party and Alliance of Free Democrats	52.7	72.0	57.9 (76.2)**	42.1 (23.8)**
Lithuania	25 Oct. 1992	Democratic Labour Party	44.0	51.8	80.6 (92.0)***	19.4 (8.0)***
Moldova	22 March 1998	Democratic Convention, Block for the Democratic and Prosperous Moldova and Party of Democratic Forces	46.2	58.6	Na.	Na.
Mongolia	30 June 1996	Democratic Union Coalition	45.0	65.8	Na.	Na.
Poland	19 Sept. 1993	Democratic Left Alliance, Peasant Party	35.9	65.9	54.3 (82.4)**	45.7 (17.6)**
Romania	27 Sept. 1992	Democratic National Salvation Front	27.7	34.3	34.8 (52.0)***	65.2 (48.0)***

* Autumn 1995 survey used for these figures, due to coding problems in the 1994 survey. The stronger than average support for market to the market–sceptic parties is in this context probably related to pro-government sentiments.

** Autumn 1994 survey used for these figures due to coding problems in the 1993 survey.

*** Autumn 1991 survey used.

Sources: EastEurobarometer, Subsequent years.

This is also reflected in the absence of indications that electoral outcomes and change of governments have a significant impact on the speed of institutional changes. In Lithuania the former communists, then attracting the majority of market-sceptics, won the late 1992 elections but were defeated in the subsequent elections of 1996. During the four years of ex-communist rule Lithuania made substantial progress in reform as measured by the World Bank cumulated liberalization index (CLI) (from 1.05 to 2.72) (see Appendix A 4.1). Lithuania maintained the same pace of reforms in the 1992–1995 period. So the change to an ex-communist government was not reflected in the progress of reform of economic institutions. In Poland the post-communists (SDL) returned to power in late 1993, carried into power by the market sceptic vote. At that point Poland was one of the leading reforming countries. Poland had a CLI at 3.28 in 1993. In 1994 the CLI was raised by 0.86, the largest yearly increase registered in the entire post-communist period. After 1994 Poland ranked third on the EBRD index and climbed to a second place in 1997, only surpassed by Hungary. In comparison with the Czech Republic where the ex-communists never returned to power, Poland increased its ranking from 1996 to 1997 while the Czech Republic has remained at the same level from 1994 to 1997. Hence in a comparative perspective, the four years of ex-communist government in Poland did not impede reforms. Hungary had a government of ex-communists from 1994 to 1998, also carried into power by market-sceptics. In the 1994 elections the socialist party won a third of the vote. In 1994 Hungary was at 4.11 on the CLI measure, ranking third overall. In the following years Hungary climbed the EBRD scale from 3.33 (94) to 3.78 (98), resulting in a first place of all the countries surveyed. Also here the return of socialist government did not impede the pace of reforms. In this context Bulgaria is the only country where we see a rough correspondence between reform pace and a reform-sceptic government. From 1990 to 1991 and again from 1994 to 1997 Bulgaria had a socialist (ex-communist) government with a parliamentary majority. In 1991 Bulgaria ranked fourth on the CLI measure. But in 1994 when the socialists regained power Bulgaria dropped to seventh place. From 1991 to 1994 Bulgaria increased 2 points on the CLI measure, whereas little progress was noted after 1994. In 1997, however, a dissatisfied population ousted the ex-communist government because of economic problems (hyperinflation surged in 1997).

A reform sceptic government came into power in Estonia in 1995. Until then Estonia had reformed very rapidly, on a level comparable to Central European countries. After 1995 Estonia's progress continued, however, and by 1997 she had surpassed Slovenia and reached the Polish level, as measured by EBRD. This indicates that Estonia's line of reform has progressed unaffected by the change of government in 1995. In Latvia a government dominated by ex-communists (although not a direct successor party) came into power in late 1995. Until then Latvia had progressed at a speed comparable to Estonia's, but was lagging one year behind. After 1995 also Latvia increased on the EBRD index and at the same rate as the other countries.

In a number of countries reform-sceptic parties in Central European and Baltic Counties were voted into government as a reaction to the social and economic hardships of the institutional transformation. But once in government they did not make any difference in most cases. And in many of the remaining former Soviet republics, where we have indications that anti-market sentiments were the strongest, economic reform policies were in most cases outside the reach of parliaments but in the hands of strong executive presidents.[36] In that perspective, it seems unlikely that it was through electoral policies that initial conditions set the pace and scope of institutional change. Hence, the present data and analysis lend support to the general 'ineffectiveness of popular opposition' in reforming economies, as argued by Geddes (1995, p. 66). Rather, the linkages have to be found in the interface between government institutions and corporate interests.

In that respect, the extraordinary resilience of democratic commitment by ordinary citizens and in particular by the losers of transition in post-communist countries comes as a positive surprise. As hypothesized by Weingast (1995) and also observed by Gowan (1995, p. 52), the extreme right has fared much worse than feared, and did not benefit from the social protests against reforms, as shown in Table 5.3.

Corporate power and institutional change

If the general populace affected by the change of economic institutions cannot influence the pace and scope of reform, who can? The answer is probably to be found in the positions and interests of the structures that under socialism linked major corporate interests to government institutions and produced what at that time became known as 'institutionalized pluralism' or 'directed corporatism' (Nørgaard, 1985). At the initial stage of reforms, the nature of these links, the general competence of the government bureaucracy and their compatibility with the new demands fostered by the emerging economic system is the most likely channel linking initial con-ditions to institutional change. As described in Chapter 3 government bureaucrats and enterprise managers are among the possible losers of institutional transformation: Market coordination will leave the Gosplan executives redundant and threaten managers unfamiliar with the rules of the market game. Hence, both groups have strong incentives (and resources) to block or impede reforms. This anti-reform coalition will in many cases be joined by workers and communities whose existence (in particular in dis-torted economies) depends on the survival of enterprises threatened by the market reforms. They can also expect the support of those groups and individuals who are motivated by the egalitarian value system, which – as shown – to varying degrees has become embedded in the socialist countries. Only the general educational level of the population at large and the bureauc-racy tells us whether we can expect this corporate barrier to reform to be adjusted by the ability of the citizens to understand and accept the long-term implication of the changes. In this respect we may follow Bates and Krueger (1994, p. 180) and hypothesize that general level of education (in this context average years of schooling) represents a reasonable and valid proxy for a better trained workforce and a more competent bureaucracy, politically compliant and technically capable of implementing institutional reforms.

However, the most important channels of influence are the constraints on institutional change due to the power and influence wielded by corporate interests and the asymmetry of power that favour these groups. The role of collective action dilemmas (Olson, 1965, 1996) in the adoption and imple-mentation of institutional changes has been observed by a number of authors, (Crawford, 1995; Surdej, 1993; Spiegeleire, 1995; Bofinger, 1995; Leidy and Ibrahim, 1996). Distorted post-communist economies represent extreme cases of collective action dilemmas, where the losers of transition possess many political resources and the winners – if there still are any – few. In this perspective, the chieftains of the huge corporations within various sectors (All Union Enterprises in the former Soviet Union) are the ones who will most likely solve coordination problems and pursue collective interests. They are relatively few, localized in the decision-making centres of the country, possess the bureaucratic resources necessary to work through corporate channels, are – in most cases – members of the previous nomen-clatura network with easy access to government and they enjoy the political support of the large number of workers and communities dependent on the survival of these enterprises. In such a system there are numerous admin-istrative bottlenecks, and resistance to reforms by a small number of firms and regions is sufficient to block institutional reforms. Even if institutional reforms have been decided upon, there are many veto points where actors can use their organizational resources to block further action, typically by withholding information and creating procedural delays (Pei, 1996, p. 136). The influence of these groups in particular is great in countries with con-centrated and very large industries and where industry makes up a large share of the total economy. In their discussion of trade liberalization Leidy and Ibrahim (1996), for example demonstrate how this influence is manifest in the allocation of various subsidies, maintenance of government mon-opolies and various import privileges. Some of the countries which inherited the most concentrated industrial structures were also among the slowest to liberalize especially foreign trade. Spiegeleire (1995) uses the same ap-proach to depict the political role of Gazprom in Russia. In a comparative analysis of four Russian regions: Nizhny Novgorod, Tyumen, Yaroslavl' and Saratov, Stoner-Weiss (1997) demonstrates that concentration of the economic structure is positively related to political performance, because huge enterprises are able to overcome collective action dilemmas and to cooperate with local governments.[37] It is through these corporate channels that the incumbent elite can manoeuvre to protect their enterprises and, in some cases, also reap the benefits of delayed stabilization, cheap credits, controlled foreign trade and other sources of rent seeking.[38] Against the political power of these corporate elites who collude with the workers and the company towns that host their declining industries, the potential supporters are to be found among technocrat specialist, political idealists, emerging (perhaps not yet existing) industries and general long-term social interests in a more efficient economy. In any case, in the distorted eco-nomies of our study this represents a support that is in its infancy, and thus far diffuse and without firm institutional basis.

This approach is further sustained by emerging Russian research on the role of economic interests in economic policy making. Distinguishing be-tween 'corporate interests', 'clientism' and 'parentalism' (ethnic or regional groups) Makarenko (1999) is one of the first to map the linkage of interest groups to branches of the state administration and their impact on economic policy making. His preliminary conclusions confirm the observations made in numerous Western analyses of the devastating impact of these groups on governmental ability to pursue a coherent policy (McFaul, 1994; Jensen, 1998). Similar conclusions are reached by Brada (1995) on the role of 'Eastern European Corporatism' and by Kuz'min (1998) on 'Corporate Capitalism' in Russia.

However, the scarcity of empirical research on corporate influence and rent seeking in transitional economies indicates that this is a field where further research is needed. This especially applies to the actual and prospective role of societal organizations (trade unions and professional organizations), business organizations in economic policy making and state administration.

CONCLUSIONS

This chapter has examined the effects of first order initial conditions (the communist legacy) on the choice and implementation of institutional strategies. As a first step I identified two underlying structural factors, both stemming from the socialist path of development. These two factors, distortion and modernization, respectively constrain and provide opportunities for institutional change. Modernization was shown to provide opportunities for fast reforms that again led to more comprehensive reforms. Distortion was shown to impede the implementation of reforms, while it had no discernible effect on the pace of reforms. There was no direct effect of initial structural factors on economic and social costs, but it was shown that the costs became the highest in cases where fast reforms were imposed on distorted countries which then were unable to sustain initial liberalization, deregulation and privatization coupled with institutional reforms. In these cases we found the most extreme cases of GDP-decline, high inflation and increase in poverty. Increase in inequality could be linked to neither institutional strategy nor initial conditions.

It was also shown that on the subjective level the effect of transition costs is filtered through initial egalitarianism and level of market support. Further, popular opposition channelled through elections is not a likely channel through which initial conditions (and in particular distortion) can be linked to institutional change. Over time support for economic reforms decreased in most countries in the wake of the general downturn in economic activity and increased social costs. But it was not possible to demonstrate a correlation of scope macro-social and macro-economic costs and popular support for market reforms. Nor was it possible to confirm Hirschman's tunnel-theory, as only Belarus reflects the expected pattern. Popular rejection of economic reforms in general bounced back at whatever government was in power, also because the choice of government did not seem to have much impact on the pace of reforms. This in particular affected the converted communist parties that, once back in power, did not slow down the pace of institutional reforms. In this context the dynamics of popular support for the market should rather be seen as a reflection of a general time factor measuring frustrated expectations and the effect of political circumstances. Alternatively, the negative relation between initial distortion and institutional change should be found in the asymmetrical power relations between the winners (society) and losers (huge corporations and bureaucracies). In this perspective primarily the elites concentrated in the incumbent industrial structures and associated state bureaucracies will restrain institutional change in distorted countries, supported by workers in enterprises and communities whose existence is jeopardized by emerging economic institutions and by the egalitarians of the incumbent system. This pattern explains why distorted economies do not block the adoption but the implementation of institutional reforms.

Whatever the routes of influence, the match between initial systemic conditions in terms of modernization and distortion, industrial structures, economic and social performance and institutional strategies is obviously not perfect. Some countries exceed our predictions of their ability to adopt and implement institutional strategies that induce growth and welfare. And still others do not meet our expectations concerning the association between initial conditions and institutional change. The next two chapters explain why some countries have adopted more far-reaching institutional strategies than we would expect based on the models developed in this chapter, and why others did not live up to our expectations.

NOTES

1. In this perspective I have previously argued that political science is to be seen as the 'science of democracy', because it has only flourished in democratic societies. Ole Nørgaard, *Political* honoris causa lecture. *Science and the Study of Post-Communist Regimes*, University of Latvia, 1994.

2. 'Modernity' in the normal Western understanding of the word comes as no surprise if we take into account that the highest ambition of Marx, Lenin and their successors always was to emulate and surpass the Western type of modernity – not to find a different path.

3. See below for data showing the association between distortion, egalitarianism and anti-market sentiments.

4. He mentions, for example, that while the Soviet Union in 1985 produced goods to stock amounting to 85 per cent of GDP, the equivalent figure for the USA was 31 per cent.

5. The paper also includes countries involved in wars and discusses the effect of political reforms.

6. He defines initial distortion as a percentage of GDP including measures of defence expenditures, industrial structure, trade openness and distortion. For a definition, see Popov (1998, p. 447).

7. It was expected that also initial level of wealth or welfare would have an effect on institutional strategies and outcome, because it could be hypothesized that greater wealth or welfare in a society would make it economically and politically easier to endure the hardships of transition. Hence, initial wealth or welfare would make it possible to choose an institutional strategy that, although efficient in terms of eventual outcomes, carries high economical, social and eventually political costs. However, when relative purchasing power parity (PPP 1987) is chosen as a proxy for initial wealth and welfare there are no significant links with either institutional strategies and outcomes (pace and scope94 and scope97) or social costs in terms of GDP-decline, inflation or increase in poverty and inequality.

8. The present (modest) attempt to conceptualize and measure the dimensions of post-socialist systems was originally inspired by Rummel's (1972, 1979) much more ambitious explorative analyses of 'The Dimensions of Nations'. For other attempts to employ factor analysis in political science, see Peters (1993) and Rummel (1995).

9. It would have been preferable to include variables reflecting popular values and mentalities as explicit variables and part of the two factors. Such cross country data are not, however, at present available. Available data from EastEurobarometer and World Value Studies on egalitarianism and market attitudes are presented elsewhere in this book. Jerschina and Górniak (1997) have made a comparative analysis of a range of countries also included in the present study that support the findings. Based on comprehensive surveys distinguishing dominating personality characteristics, they identify three groups of countries: A liberal-democracy oriented group consisting of the Czech Republic, Poland, Slovenia, Hungary and Estonia, all oriented towards activism and achievement in economy and democratic participation. A national-social oriented group with an opposition orientation based on anti-liberalism and political and economic passivism in response to the economic crises. This group comprises Russia, Belarus and Ukraine. Finally, an in-between group consisting of Latvia and Lithuania that waver between nationalism and liberalism. As seen, this distribution roughly corresponds to the picture obtained in the present analyses.

10. It should be observed that the plot contains the following inaccuracies: 1) Monopoly is coded differently for the Former Soviet Republics and the Central and East European countries, influencing slightly the relative position between the two group of countries on the distortion factor. 2) Separate figures for initial industrial structures in the Czech Rep. and Slovakia could not be obtained and the same value has been coded for both countries. However, according to all accounts, Slovakia has a significantly larger share of big enterprises. Consequently, Slovakia should be moved slightly to the right on the distortion factor. 3) No data were available for enterprise size in Albania. Interpreting secondary sources, monopoly was here coded with the same values as Bulgaria. Hence, the location of Albania on the distortion factor may be slightly imprecise. The four clusters were obtained through a K-means cluster analysis pre-specified with 4 clusters. The clusters were identified through three iterations.

11. It was decided not to include phasing (the distinct order of stabilization, structural changes and privatization) in the regressions, partly because of the low reliability of data on private sector share development and the equivocal character of privatization itself, making the real properties (nature of ownership) unclear. Instead privatization enters the analysis in the qualitative analyses in Chapter 7.

12. Taking the World Bank 1994 Cumulated Liberalization Index as the dependent variable produces an even better prediction with an extreme R-square of 0.96, because

the distortion variable increases the prediction by pace. In other words, the extremely high R-square is obtained because the distorted countries which launched early reforms were forced to slow down, and in effect increase the explanatory power of Equation 5.2.

13. As recalled from Chapter 4, we have only reliable data on poverty and inequality up to 1994.

14. This result contradicts the conclusions of others, for example De Melo and Gelb (1997); De Melo et al. (1997); and Sachs (1996b).

15. The core explanation of this association is of course that a suspension or even slow-down of institutional reforms indicates an underlying political and administrative instability or corruption (Mauro, 1995) detrimental to growth. Instability, for example measured through indicators based on country experts' perceptions of stability, trust and investment risks, impede domestic and foreign investments (Stern, 1997; Alesina, 1989; Haggard and Kaufman, 1994; Brunetti, 1997; Rose, 1995b). From this perspective it would be preferable to move ahead with slow institutional reforms that are democratically sustainable instead of fast reforms that risk being brought to a standstill – even if reforms at a given point in time would have moved further than slow reforms. The indicated political instability may also shorten the time horizons of politicians, and provide recurrent incentives to inflate, overvalue the currency and borrow (Moreno and Trehan, 1997, p. 277; Alesina and Perotti, 1994; Knack and Keefer, 1995).

16. See the final *Note on Data* for a description of the coverage and validity of the data.

17. In his 1959 article Lipset argued that 'Modernisation broaden men's outlook, enables them to understand the need for norms of tolerance (...) and increases their capacities to make rational electoral choices' (Lipset, 1959, p. 84).

18. The simple correlation between initial modernization (1987/88) and initial inequality and poverty is -0.64 and -0.77 respectively, (both significant at the 0.01 level).

19. We return to the connection between initial inequality and the political system below.

20. This has in particular been a problem in those countries where restitution to former owners has been an important mode of privatization.

21. They make this observation when comparing inequalities at the start of reforms in China and Russia. A high income inequality will generate capital leakage when high income groups buy foreign goods and export capital. China experienced a fall in the Gini quotient from 0.32 in 1980 to 0.26 in 1984, as opposed to the sharp increase in inequalities in Russia.

22. Average support calculated as the arithmetic average of market support for the years, where data from EastEuropebarometer have been available. See the final *Note on data*.

23. The simple bivariate correlation between the distortion factor and EQUINDEX is 0.54 (not significant). However, if the major outlier Hungary (more egalitarian than predicted) is removed, the correlation increases to 0.74 (significant at the 0.05 level).

24. The simple bivariate correlation between EQUINDEX and scope97 is -0.36. The small number of cases in combination with two major outliers (Hungary and Latvia) does not make the correlation significant.

25. For 1992–1996 the correlation is between -0.4 and -0.5. The simple correlation between average support for the market and EQUINDEX is -0.5. The small number of cases does not make the linkages significant.

26. Compare for example the analyses by Walton and Seddon (1994) in 'Free Markets & Food Riots'.

27. The analysis draws on the data in EastEurobarometer, 1991–1997 and consequently only include a limited number of countries. See the final *Note on data*.

28. Inflation is, as summarized by Asilis and Milesi-Ferretti (1994) on the basis of experiences from Latin America, '... a regressive tax, whose burden falls disproportional on lower income groups with limited access to hedging instruments'. In post-communist economies, the only hedging instrument available to normal citizens was (and is) foreign currencies, which are, however, of only minor importance because savings had been wiped out by the initial very high levels of inflation in most countries. For an extensive analysis of the social effect of inflation in Latin America, see Cardoso (1992).

29. The data are reproduced in Appendices A5.6 and A5.7.

30. Data from Central Europe also show that unemployment is an important parameter of support in countries where institutional changes have taken effect. Unemployment has not been included in this study because of the low reliability of employment figures in a number of countries. See further Gibson and Cielcecka (1995), Bell (1997), Pacek (1994) and Fish (1998a).

31. Hirschman's allegory compares the situation after the launching of radical institutional changes with a traffic jam in a tunnel. People in the inner lane will, for some time, accept their position even if they see that people in the outer lane start moving, because they see it as an indication that they will soon be able to move themselves. However, if they remain caught for long, they will begin to react against what they see as an unfair treatment of cars in the two lanes, and demand from the traffic police that they be given the privileges which so far have been reserved for cars in the outer lane. In a society undergoing rapid institutional changes this implies that people will, for some time, accept that some fare better than others, because it indicates that there are opportunities for everyone and that his or her chance may come. The patience, however, only works for some time, and ultimately people will lose belief in their own chances and demand that the 'police' (the state) interfere to provide a more fair (equal) distribution. This political dynamic only works in homogeneous societies, where there are no institutional barriers to individual mobility, as for example ethnic, regional or gender barriers.

32. Appendices A5.8 and A5.9 present the dynamic of popular support for market reforms in 15 of our cases.

33. Fish (1998a, p. 72) makes the same observation.

34. The year 1996 was chosen because this is the last year that the Survey included the non-Baltic post-Soviet republics at a time when the market reforms had taken effect.

35. See Chapter 8.

36. We return to the effect of the president–parliamentary relationship in Chapter 6.

37. The problem with this analysis is, however, that the measures of political performance applied by Stoner-Weiss become very conservative, and do not take into account that the solutions sought by these interests were very conservative and probably not economically sustainable in the long run.

38. On rent seeking in post-communist economies, see for example Schleifer and Vishny (1998).

APPENDIX 5

Table A 5.1. Components of modernization.

Country	Telephone lines per 1000 people 1994	Average years of schooling 1994	Televisions per 100 people 1994	Per cent of population urban 1989
Albania	12.00	6.20	9.00	36.00
Belarus	106.00	7.00	26.00	66.00
Bulgaria	95.00	7.00	26.00	68.00
Czech Rep.	212.00	9.20	38.00	76.00
Estonia	252.00	9.00	36.00	71.00
Hungary	269.00	9.80	52.00	62.00
Kazakhstan	117.00	5.00	26.00	57.00
Kyrgyzstan	73.00	5.00	24.00	38.00
Latvia	152.00	9.00	47.00	69.00
Lithuania	241.00	9.00	34.00	68.00
Moldova	126.00	6.00	28.00	47.00
Mongolia	29.00	7.20	6.30	57.00
Poland	131.00	8.20	30.00	62.00
Romania	123.00	7.10	20.00	53.00
Russia	162.00	9.00	38.00	73.00
Slovakia	187.00	9.20	28.00	56.00
Slovenia	287.00	9.90	30.00	59.00
Turkmenistan	76.00	5.00	22.00	45.00
Ukraine	157.00	6.00	23.00	67.00
Uzbekistan	69.00	5.00	18.00	41.00

Sources: Col. 1–4: Human Development Report 1997

Table A 5.2. Components of distortion.

Country	Components of the factor of distortion				
	Black market premium	Years under central planning	Share of trade within the CMEA area 1990	Repressed inflation 1987–1990	Monopoly in industry 1990 (% all union enterprises)
Albania	434.00	47	6.60	4.30	Approx.13.00
Belarus	1828.00	72	41.00	25.70	53.00
Bulgaria	921.00	43	16.10	18.00	13.00
Czech Rep.	185.00	42	6.00	–7.10	2.40
Estonia	1828.00	51	30.20	25.70	35.00
Hungary	46.70	42	13.70	–7.70	0.30
Kazakhstan	1828.00	71	20.80	25.70	50.00
Kyrgyzstan	1828.00	71	27.70	25.70	45.00
Latvia	1828.00	51	36.60	25.70	43.00
Lithuania	1828.00	51	40.90	25.70	42.00
Moldova	1828.00	51	28.90	25.70	36.00
Mongolia	1400.00	70	31.00	7.60	3.20
Poland	277.00	41	8.40	13.60	1.90
Romania	728.00	42	3.70	16.80	6.90
Russia	1828.00	74	11.10	25.70	69.00
Slovakia	185.00	42	6.00	-0.71	2.40
Slovenia	27.00	46	4.00	12.00	1.00
Turkmenistan	1828.00	71	33.00	25.70	30.00
Ukraine	1828.00	74	23.80	25.70	62.00
Uzbekistan	1828.00	71	25.00	25.70	35.00

Sources: Col. 1–4: de Melo et al. (1997), World Bank 1996, col. 5: **Bulgaria:** *Statisticeski Godisnik Balgaria, 1990,* **Slovakia and Czech Rep.:** *Statisticka Rocenka. Ceske a Slovenske Federativni Republiky, 1990, p. 215,* **Hungary:** *Hungarian Statistical Yearbook, 1990, p. 105,* **Mongolia:** *Länderbericht Mongolei, Statistischer Bundesamt, 1992,* **Poland:** *Rocznik Statystyczny, 1990, p. 293,* **Romania:** *Anuarul Statistic al Romanei, 1990, p. 428,* **Slovenia:** *Statisticki Godisnjak Jugoslavije, 1990, p. 265,* **The countries of the former USSR:** *Statistical Yearbook of the USSR, 1990 and Comecon Data, 1990, p. 351.*

Table A 5.3. Factor analysis for distortion and modernization.

Variables	Distortion Factor Loadings	Modernization
Years under central planning	.777	−.359
Black market premium	.971	−.139
Monopoly in industry	.923	5.599E − 02
Repressed inflation	.883	−.120
Trade dependence	.804	9.292E − 03
Eigenvalue	4.594	
% of variance	51	
N	20	

Modernization

Variables	Modernization Factor Loadings	Distortion
Telephone lines per 1000 people	.884	−.182
Televisions per 100 people	.889	1.198E − 02
Average years of schooling	.834	−.424
Level of urbanization	.842	8.360E − 02
Eigenvalue	2.592	
% of variance	28	
N	20	

Extraction method: Principal Component Analyses.

Rotation Method: Varimax with Kaiser Normalization.

Rotation converged in 3 iterations.

Table A 5.4. Indexes of initial conditions.

Country	Modernization	Distortion
Albania	−1.50	−.90
Belarus	−.07	1.09
Bulgaria	−.07	−.45
Czech Rep.	1.06	−1.34
Estonia	1.01	.45
Hungary	1.35	−1.29
Kazakhstan	−.51	.73
Kyrgyzstan	−1.10	.80
Latvia	.90	.62
Lithuania	.87	.68
Moldova	−.51	.44
Mongolia	−.93	.04
Poland	.18	−.95
Romania	−.41	−.79
Russia	.81	.79
Slovakia	.33	−1.23
Slovenia	.86	−1.04
Turkmenistan	−.99	.75
Ukraine	−.10	.93
Uzbekistan	−1.18	.67

Note: The indexes are based on the dimensions found in the factor analysis (see Appendix 4.3) and includes all the variables of this analysis. To obtain indexes I computed z-scores for all variables pertaining to each dimension and subsequently summed these scores and finally calculated the mean score resulting in an index score. Alpha values for Modernization index: 0.896 and for Distortion index: 0.972.

Table A 5.5. Equality index for selected countries, 1990.

Country	Equality index score
Belarus	41.90
Bulgaria	34.70
Czech Rep.	31.40
Estonia	32.10
Hungary	41.30
Latvia	46.50
Lithuania	38.30
Poland	33.10
Romania	35.80
Russia	40.00
Slovenia	32.30

Source: World Value Studies (1990).

Economic Institutions and Democratic Reform

Table A 5.6. GDP development and market support.

Country		1990	1991	1992	1993	1994	1995	1996	1997	Corre-lation
Albania	Support	na.	67.5	73.4	70	67.6	78.7	75.9	na.	0.57
	GDP	90.00	64.80	60.14	65.89	72.08	78.50	85.64	79.65	
Belarus	Support	na.	na.	33.8	30.5	28.3	32.8	35.1	na.	-0.09
	GDP	97.00	95.81	86.51	80.46	69.84	62.57	64.33	71.66	
Bulgaria	Support	46.4	61.8	56.3	52.1	39.7	40.3	45.8	52.3	-0.01
	GDP	90.90	80.26	74.41	73.29	74.60	76.18	67.89	63.20	
Czech Rep.	Support	58.1	61	55.4	51.8	48.6	43.7	44.9	29.8	-0.05
	GDP	99.59	83.76	76.64	77.07	79.15	84.22	87.50	88.38	
Estonia	Support		59	49.7	53.6	48.9	56	57	55.6	0.62
	GDP	91.90	84.63	66.32	60.88	59.78	62.35	64.85	72.24	
Hungary	Support	61.8	65.1	55.6	46.2	44.1	40.3	38.6	37.8	0.16
	GDP	96.50	85.03	82.42	81.95	84.32	85.62	86.77	90.74	
Kazakhstan	Support	na.	na.	na.	na.	28.2	32.1	33.2	na.	-0.97
	GDP	99.60	88.64	83.95	76.22	66.62	61.16	61.46	62.51	
Latvia	Support	na.	57.4	39.5	44.7	39.8	43.4	44.7	47.5	0.84
	GDP	102.90	91.48	59.28	49.72	50.77	50.94	52.62	56.04	
Lithuania	Support	na.	74.8	65.8	61.1	50.4	49.6	40.8	50.3	0.85
	GDP	95.00	89.59	70.50	59.08	53.31	55.06	57.66	61.17	
Poland	Support	61.1	56	55.7	57.3	51.6	64.2	63.4	66.3	0.76
	GDP	92.38	86.36	88.63	92.01	96.80	103.63	109.93	117.51	
Romania	Support	na.	35.3	66.1	51.1	71.9	71.5	80.3	69.1	0.35
	GDP	92.30	80.37	73.33	74.41	77.34	82.68	85.91	80.24	
Russia	Support	na.	46.7	40.6	30.7	23.2	19.9	24.6	na.	0.97
	GDP	96.00	91.20	77.98	71.19	62.22	59.67	57.58	58.04	
Slovakia	Support	58.1	61	51.3	42.1	43.6	39.8	42.4	36	0.16
	GDP	99.60	83.76	76.64	73.80	77.42	82.76	88.23	93.96	
Slovenia	Support	na.	na.	66.2	44.5	51.3	46.1	46.5	46.4	-0.60
	GDP	95.30	87.58	82.85	85.20	89.74	93.42	96.37	100.03	
Ukraine	Support	na.	na.	38.7	30.8	30	22.9	25.5	na.	0.92
	GDP	96.60	86.34	71.66	61.49	47.41	41.60	37.44	36.31	

Note: GDP is an index (1989=100) based on annual growth rates as reported in IMF World Economic Outlook 1999.

Support is defined as per cent positive answers among the respondents in the Eurobarometer Survey the listed years to the following question: Free Market Economy? Right/Wrong/Don't Know.

Table A 5.7: Inflation and market support.

Country		1990	1991	1992	1993	1994	1995	1996	1997	Corre-lation
Albania	Support	na.	67.5	73.4	70	67.6	78.7	75.9	na.	−0.40
	Inflation	na.	1.55	2.35	1.93	1.35	.89	1.10	1.52	
Belarus	Support	na.	na.	33.8	30.5	28.3	32.8	35.1	na.	−0.79
	Inflation	.97	1.92	2.99	3.07	3.34	2.85	1.72	1.81	
Bulgaria	Support	46.4	61.8	56.3	52.1	39.7	40.3	45.8	52.3	0.45
	Inflation	1.38	2.52	1.91	1.86	1.98	1.79	2.09	3.03	
Czech Rep.	Support	58.1	61	55.4	51.8	48.6	43.7	44.9	29.8	0.62
	Inflation	1.03	1.77	1.04	1.32	1.00	.96	.94	.92	
Estonia	Support	na.	59	49.7	53.6	48.9	56	57	55.6	−0.36
	Inflation	1.24	2.32	3.03	1.95	1.68	1.46	1.36	1.05	
Hungary	Support	61.8	65.1	55.6	46.2	44.1	40.3	38.6	37.8	0.68
	Inflation	1.46	1.54	1.36	1.35	1.27	1.45	1.37	1.26	
Kazakhstan	Support	na.	na.	na.	Na.	28.2	32.1	33.2	na.	−0.98
	Inflation	.75	1.96	3.18	3.22	3.27	2.25	1.59	1.24	
Latvia	Support	na.	57.4	39.5	44.7	39.8	43.4	44.7	47.5	−0.12
	Inflation	1.02	2.09	2.98	2.04	1.55	1.40	1.25	.92	
Lithuania	Support	na.	74.8	65.8	61.1	50.4	49.6	40.8	50.3	0.75
	Inflation	.89	2.35	3.01	2.61	1.86	1.60	1.39	.95	
Poland	Support	61.1	56	55.7	57.3	51.6	64.2	63.4	66.3	−0.17
	Inflation	2.77	1.85	1.63	1.55	1.51	1.45	1.30	1.18	
Romania	Support	na.	35.3	66.1	51.1	71.9	71.5	80.3	69.1	−0.58
	Inflation	2.11	2.21	2.32	2.41	2.14	1.51	1.59	2.19	
Russia	Support	na.	46.7	40.6	30.7	23.2	19.9	24.6	na.	0.18
	Inflation	.75	1.97	3.13	2.95	2.48	2.28	1.68	1.17	
Slovakia	Support	58.1	61	51.3	42.1	43.6	39.8	42.4	36	0.62
	Inflation	1.03	1.77	1.04	1.36	1.13	1.00	.76	.79	
Slovenia	Support	na.	na.	66.2	44.5	51.3	46.1	46.5	46.4	0.88
	Inflation	na.	na.	2.31	1.50	1.30	1.10	.99	.96	
Ukraine	Support	na.	na.	38.7	30.8	30	22.9	25.5	na.	0.56
	Inflation	.62	1.96	3.08	3.68	2.95	2.58	1.90	1.20	

Note: Inflation is the logarithm of annual inflation rates as reported in IMF World Economic Outlook 1999.

Support is defined as per cent positive answers among the respondents in the Eurobarometer Survey the listed years to the following question: Free Market Economy? Right/Wrong/Don't Know.

Economic Institutions and Democratic Reform

Table A 5.8. Evaluation of previous financial situation and market support.

Country		1990	1991	1992	1993	1994	1995	1996	Corre-lation
Albania	Support	na.	67.5	73.4	70	67.6	78.7	75.9	0.84
	Financial situation	na.	27.8	61.5	61.1	55.2	78.9	77.4	
Belarus	Support	na.	na.	33.8	30.5	28.3	32.8	35.1	0.90
	Financial situation	na.	na.	14.9	9.3	10.4	14.7	19.9	
Bulgaria	Support	46.4	61.8	56.3	52.1	39.7	40.3	45.8	0.04
	Financial situation	15.2	10.5	19.6	10.7	8.7	20.1	3.8	
Czech Rep.	Support	58.1	61	55.4	51.8	48.6	43.7	44.9	−0.85
	Financial situation	6.2	13.4	20.3	22.3	22.7	28.7	24.1	
Estonia	Support	na.	59	49.7	53.6	48.9	56	57	0.32
	Financial situation	na.	21.7	9.0	23.5	28.6	29.6	26.8	
Hungary	Support	61.8	65.1	55.6	46.2	44.1	40.3	38.6	0.61
	Financial situation	na.	8.8	6.0	7.7	8.1	5.2	5.3	
Kazakhstan	Support	na.	na.	na.	na.	28.2	32.1	33.2	0.19
	Financial situation	na.	na.	na.	na.	10.9	17.1	10.0	
Latvia	Support	na.	57.4	39.5	44.7	39.8	43.4	44.7	0.49
	Financial situation	na.	19.6	10.8	17.2	19.7	15.2	14.0	
Lithuania	Support	na.	74.8	65.8	61.1	50.4	49.6	40.8	0.30
	Financial situation	na.	24.5	10.8	11.6	16.4	18.9	14.1	
Poland	Support	61.1	56	55.7	57.3	51.6	64.2	63.4	0.89
	Financial situation	18.6	9.9	11.8	9.7	11.2	21.5	20.3	
Romania	Support	na.	35.3	66.1	51.1	71.9	71.5	80.3	0.11
	Financial situation	na.	26.4	27.6	10.6	23.5	22.8	22.3	
Russia	Support	na.	46.7	40.6	30.7	23.2	19.9	24.6	0.49
	Financial situation	na.	16.0	17.6	21.9	13.2	12.7	10.9	
Slovakia	Support	58.1	61	51.3	42.1	43.6	39.8	42.4	−0.64
	Financial situation	6.2	13.4	17.1	11.7	16.4	22.0	24.2	
Slovenia	Support	na.	na.	66.2	44.5	51.3	46.1	46.5	0.54
	Financial situation	na.	na.	17.9	13.3	19.8	17.0	13.9	
Ukraine	Support	na.	na.	38.7	30.8	30	22.9	25.5	0.57
	Financial situation	na.	na.	16.4	4.5	5.8	8.7	8.7	

Note: The evaluation of previous financial situation is the proportion of respondents stating that their financial situation got a lot or little better during the last 12 months from the year of the Eurobarometer survey

Support is defined as per cent positive answers among the respondents in the Eurobarometer Survey the listed years to the following question: Free Market Economy? Right/Wrong/Don't Know.

Table A 5.9. Evaluation of future financial situation and market support

Country		1990	1991	1992	1993	1994	1995	1996	Corre-lation
Albania	Support	na.	67.5	73.4	70	67.6	78.7	75.9	0.67
	Financial situation	na.	76.9	72.0	65.7	63.3	79.4	83.4	
Belarus	Support	na.	na.	33.8	30.5	28.3	32.8	35.1	0.16
	Financial situation	na.	na.	17.1	13.6	24.9	21.8	27.3	
Bulgaria	Support	46.4	61.8	56.3	52.1	39.7	40.3	45.8	0.35
	Financial situation	24.7	40.8	39.4	20.8	27.9	39.6	22.4	
Czech Rep.	Support	58.1	61	55.4	51.8	48.6	43.7	44.9	–0.52
	Financial situation	9.7	22.8	25.1	28.5	24.8	28.2	23.8	
Estonia	Support	na.	59	49.7	53.6	48.9	56	57	–0.35
	Financial situation	na.	25.3	26.8	33.1	34.8	31.0	32.4	
Hungary	Support	61.8	65.1	55.6	46.2	44.1	40.3	38.6	0.02
	Financial situation	6.0	22.3	14.5	18.5	17.0	11.3	15.5	
Kazakhstan	Support	na.	na.	na.	na.	28.2	32.1	33.2	0.21
	Financial situation	na.	na.	na.	na.	24.3	34.7	23.0	
Latvia	Support	na.	57.4	39.5	44.7	39.8	43.4	44.7	–0.07
	Financial situation	na.	23.1	22.5	29.6	25.1	22.3	21.1	
Lithuania	Support	na.	74.8	65.8	61.1	50.4	49.6	40.8	0.18
	Financial situation	na.	24.1	23.4	17.3	21.3	20.1	23.3	
Poland	Support	61.1	56	55.7	57.3	51.6	64.2	63.4	0.80
	Financial situation	30.5	20.7	22.1	29.9	18.4	31.1	26.4	
Romania	Support	na.	35.3	66.1	51.1	71.9	71.5	80.3	0.52
	Financial situation	na.	43.8	49.9	38.7	41.5	40.8	74.8	
Russia	Support	na.	46.7	40.6	30.7	23.2	19.9	24.6	0.20
	Financial situation	na.	18.7	24.8	27.0	18.2	21.9	15.2	
Slovakia	Support	58.1	61	51.3	42.1	43.6	39.8	42.4	–0.67
	Financial situation	9.7	22.8	20.5	25.3	24.0	25.6	25.1	
Slovenia	Support	na.	na.	66.2	44.5	51.3	46.1	46.5	0.82
	Financial situation	na.	na.	44.0	36.5	33.2	36.3	32.8	
Ukraine	Support	na.	na.	38.7	30.8	30	22.9	25.5	0.45
	Financial situation	na.	na.	29.8	13.6	16.8	19.3	23.9	

Note: The evaluation of future financial situation is the proportion of respondents stating that their financial situation will get a lot or little better during the next 12 months from the year of the Eurobarometer survey

Support is defined as per cent positive answers among the respondents in the Eurobarometer Survey the listed years to the following question: Free Market Economy? Right/Wrong/Don't Know.

6. Transcending the Structural Constraints of Socialism

> 'Mass dominated democracies promise more rapid economic advance through reforms attacking vested elite interests... (...) Democracies have transformative capacities ...' (Sørensen, 1993, p. 86).

In this chapter we approach the inner core of the matrioshka. Whereas previous chapters explained and predicted institutional change in terms of initial conditions and/or policy choices (Chapter 5), or as being endogenous to stabilization, growth and performance (Chapter 4), the present and following chapters dig one layer deeper. The ambition is to examine why some countries, but not others, have adopted policies that generate institutions conducive to economic success, while at the same time building democracy. Why some are overachievers and others underachievers in their capacity to adopt and implement efficient policies that transcend their initial structural conditions. As history has proven, a policy that changes institutions may be the key to economic miracles but also to economic disasters. An explanation requires that we examine the political feasibility and sustainability of institutional strategies in the search for a policy which is optimal with regard not only to economic outcomes. It should also be politically optimal in that it should 'reconcile the constraints of adjustment with social peace and political stability; political difficulties should not fundamentally threaten implementation of the program, and implementation, in turn, must not fundamentally change the initial political equilibrium by leading to greater repression or instability' (Haggard et al., 1995, p. 119). It must, in the context of this book, not threaten the survival of democracy.

In most cases the ideas and visions of future developments in the countries that initiated change of their economic institutions had very little to do with rational economic and political calculus or distinct social values. They rather tended to reflect imported ideologies or external pressures. As a result of the circumstances under which the old regimes were extricated, the reformers were, to varying degrees and during different periods, released from the social and political chains that constrain politicians in a democratic polity. However, as revolutionary excitement waned in the face of the social misfortunes of everyday life, political constraints reappeared and politicians were forced to realize that popular and group reactions must be integral parts of the design and implementation of sustainable reforms. As described in Chapter 5, such social and political constraints originate in the structures of the previous system and reflect the varying levels of distortion and modernization of the individual country. And as described in Chapter 4 we can conceive of three modes of democracy through which political grievances may be transformed into political action. One (not substantiated by the present data) focuses on popular reactions to reforms through the electoral channel. A second emphasizes elite competition and corporate power, while the third stresses the role of political institutions in structuring the access of competing interest to centres of power and influence. These alternative modes of democracy are not only placed in abstract systems reflecting the legacies of communism. They are also situated in concrete country settings where actors may mobilize around specific values or symbols formed by long-term historical trajectories. Consequently, no simple linear relationship exists between structural constraints and institutional strategies, as described in Chapter 5. Some countries mobilized and transcended the structural barriers that emerged from the communist era. Other countries moved more hesitantly than was to be expected, as described in Figure 6.1.

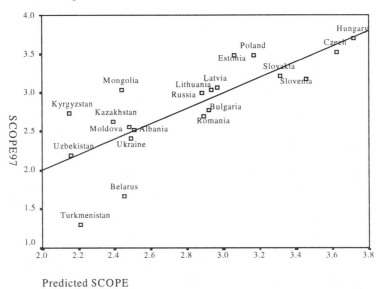

Figure 6.1. Predicted versus actual change of economic institutions.

Figure 6.1 illustrates the real compared to the predicted change of economic institutions. Five countries deviate significantly from the predicted position:[1] Turkmenistan and Belarus are underachievers in relation to both modernization and distortion. Estonia is an overachiever in relation to distortion but performs as predicted in relation to modernization. Kyrgyzstan is a slight overachiever on both dimensions. Poland performs better than predicted because it is relatively less modern, scoring relatively low on education, urbanization and infrastructural variables.

This chapter explains why some countries were granted better opportunities (or contrived fractures in the cohesiveness of the incumbent system) that enabled them to transcend the structural constraints of socialism, while others failed to avail themselves of opportunities provided by favourable initial conditions. The first section focuses on the dynamics and effects of civil society institutions and popular mobilization. The second section assesses the role of elite continuity and corporate power, originating in the way in which the incumbent system was extricated. Finally, the third section examines the role of political institutions, themselves subjects to change, for the change of economic institutions. The next chapter turns to the agents of change: the ideas, the persons and the external actors that exploit the opportunities described in this chapter, to change the economic institutions.

POPULAR MOBILIZATION AND INSTITUTIONS OF CIVIL SOCIETY

Chapter 2 introduced the concept of 'opportunity space', 'structural space' ,or what others have called 'the window of opportunity' or 'phase of extra-ordinary politics'. In this phase popular enthusiasm surges for any change that signals a radical break with the past and swift political changes produced by mounting popular fervour disarm a conservative elite with vested interests in the incumbent institutions. Is it this period of extraordinary politics and the length and depth of popular enthusiasm for reforms (though through more intricate elite-mass relationships than seen from electoral statistics) that determines the capacity available to reformers for adopting and implementing efficient institutional strategies? And what produced this period?

Initial support of (or enthusiasm for) change of economic institutions may be a reflection of positive identification with the symbols or expected outcomes associated with the new institutions, or it may be the resonance of a protest against the incumbent system. In concrete cases it may be impossible to disentangle exactly what caused the specific level and dynamics of support. Still, the incipient mobilization will provide the more or less fertile ground on which institutional change can occur.

The dynamics of market support reveals four groups of countries, as seen from Table 6.1. First, countries with high average and stable support for market institutions: Estonia and Poland. In the present context this preliminary classification would lead us to expect that potential overachievers were to be found in this group where there is very high and stable support for market institutions, possibly reflecting more deeply ingrained social values (in addition to political currents).[2]

A second group consist of countries with high but declining support for market institutions: The Czech Republic, Hungary, Lithuania, Latvia, Slovakia and Slovenia. Support seems to have stabilized in Latvia, Lithuania and Slovenia, probably reflecting expectations of EU accession. This second group reflects a more normal pattern where support decreases as initial expectations are frustrated and the economic and social consequences of the reforms become apparent. Hence, we would not expect overachievers in this group of countries.

Table 6.1. The dynamics of market support in 15 countries (per cent support).

Country	Support 1991	Support 1992	Support 1993	Support 1994	Support 1995	Support 1996	Support 1997	Average Support
Albania	67.5	73.4	70	67.6	78.7	75.9		72.2
Belarus		33.8	30.5	28.3	32.8	35.1		32.1
Bulgaria	61.8	56.3	52.1	39.7	40.3	45.8	52.3	49.8
Czech Rep.	61	55.4	51.8	48.6	43.7	44.9	29.8	47.9
Estonia	59	49.7	53.6	48.9	56	57	55.6	54.3
Hungary	65.1	55.6	46.2	44.1	40.3	38.6	37.8	46.8
Kazakhstan				28.2	32.1	33.2		31.2
Latvia	57.4	39.5	44.7	39.8	43.4	44.7	47.5	45.3
Lithuania	74.8	65.8	61.1	50.4	49.6	40.8	50.3	56.1
Poland	56	55.7	57.3	51.6	64.2	63.4	66.3	59.2
Romania	35.3	66.1	51.1	71.9	71.5	80.3	69.1	63.6
Russia	46.7	40.6	30.7	23.2	19.9	24.6		31.0
Slovakia	61	51.3	42.1	43.6	39.8	42.4	36	45.2
Slovenia		66.2	44.5	51.3	46.1	46.5	46.4	50.2
Ukraine		38.7	30.8	30	22.9	25.5		29.6

Source: EastEurobarometer, subsequent years.

A third group consist of countries with high but unstable support for market institutions, Albania, Bulgaria and Romania. They probably represent a case of negative support reflecting responses to political currents, rather than social values. The negative foundation of support makes it highly unlikely that overachievers are represented in this group.

The fourth group encompasses countries where market institutions, initially as well as in later stages, are conceived of as alien elements in the country specific context expressed in low average support: Belarus, Kazakhstan, Russia and Ukraine. As the introduction of market institutions in these countries (in addition to structural constraints) will most likely be met with popular suspicion, they are possible candidates for underachievership.

If we compare these observations with the prediction of institutional change in Figure 6.1, we can see that our expectation are partly fulfilled. The two countries with high and stable support, Estonia and Poland, are among the overachievers and Belarus, with low support for market institutions, is one of two significant underachievers. As our cases are, of course, too few in number for statistical analysis, we can only hypothesize about what produced these groups. The four groups are probably the combined result of at least three major components. First, they reflect the way in which the incumbent system was extricated.[3] The countries hosting extremely enthusiastic supporters of market institutions have all been characterized by radical ruptures with the previous systems, at some points involving violent confrontations. In this respect we are dealing with negative endorsement in that market institutions are perceived as a rejection of the previous system, rather than as support for them in their own right. This applies to the three first groups to various extent, but acquires special significance in the third group where political confrontations continue through most of the observed period. In contrast, in countries with a high level of support but without such preconditions we may expect a high degree of what could be termed initial 'market naivety' as to the real nature and consequences of the introduction of market institutions.

Second, previous experience of independent statehood which makes a change of economic system part of the national reconstruction (The Baltic States); previous experience with a modern market economy (The Baltic States, Czech Republic, Hungary, Slovakia and Poland), border (or just proximity) to non-communist state(s), and hence persistent exposure to alternative ideas and information (Czech Republic, Hungary, Poland and Estonia) and (especially in the later stages) prospective candidates for EU-membership (all countries except the non-Baltic former Soviet Republics),[4] will undoubtedly encourage support for market institutions.

Last but not least, especially in dealing with the fourth group of former Soviet Republics, we should include cultural explanations in the Weberian sense (Weber, 1992), as proposed by Fish (1998a, p. 40) and others.[5] In an attempt to test for the effect of cultural differences Fish tested for the effect of religion – Catholic, Protestant, Orthodox, Muslim/Buddhist (Mongolia), and he ended up with a dichotomy: Muslim/Buddhist/Orthodox countries have cultural barriers to the introduction of a market economy, whereas Catholic/Protestant countries do not. This cultural explanation places all former Soviet Republics (minus the Baltic States) in the reform opposing group.

In this context it can be hypothesized (following for example Pachomov, 1998), that for example the Russian animosity towards market institutions is partly based on cultural factors with longer historical precedents. All social movements in Russian history have been socialist and egalitarian, ranging back to the narodniki (agrarian socialists of the 19th century), esery (reformist socialists), anarchists and Bolsheviks. The ideology of these movements reflected more or less directly the egalitarian social system of the village community (the obshchina), a tradition framed by the huge distances and the despotic character of governments. Ideologically this tradition was underpinned by the Russian Orthodox church. The 'pravoslavie' religion is, in contrast to both Protestantism and Catholicism, profoundly anti-market, claiming that wealth is a religious offence, that commercial activities are sinful, that all material goods should be shared equally and, in particular, that land is given by God and cannot be turned into human property. In this perspective the Stalinist version of socialism is a special Russian phenomenon engendered by specific historical legacies.

These constraints first of all apply to Russia proper, whereas the other Slavic republics (Belarus and Ukraine) have been exposed to other types of ideologies when they at various times were part of other empires (Lithuania, Poland and – part of Ukraine – the Austro-Hungarian empire). In these countries, the Stalinist version of socialism is therefore more a consequence of external imposition than internal dynamics.[6] Ukraine in particular retains elements of participatory democracy ranging back to the Cossack tradition of independent peasantry, the Magdeburg legal tradition (in contrast to traditional Russian legal nihilism) and guild structures in some of the cities.

In this perspective historical and cultural factors (second order initial conditions) render some countries more receptive to the ideas of the market than others. While this explanation undoubtedly does form part of the picture, it is obviously not the whole explanation.

While the dynamics and level of support for market institutions provide one key to understanding what affords opportunities for changing economic institutions, initial conditions and popular attitudes obviously do not directly affect the change of institutions, as demonstrated in the previous chapter. To be transformed into policy (and change of institutions) these preconditions for change must be mediated by institutions in civil society. Hence, to proceed further in our understanding of what produced the over- and under-achievers, we must examine the effect of initial structures of civil society on institutional change. For the present purpose I will apply two dimensions of incipient civil society in our 20 countries: the level of political pluralism measured as the number of effective parties in parliament (n-seats)[7] and anti-systemic mobilization measured as percentage votes for post-communist parties at the first constituent election.

Society-based institutions are those that grow out of the dynamics and cleavages of civil society. They represent that part of the changes which are only partly under the control of incumbent elites whose ability to design state institutions that sustain their political power hangs on the uncertainty of electoral outcomes. In this process the core problem concerns the participation and inclusion of social interests as assets or liabilities in the changing of economic institutions. This is, of course, a classical discussion that refers back to Huntington (1968) and that has also been reproduced in the new context, for example by Bresser Peirera et al. (1993), who argue for the benefits of societal participation as a reaction to the top-down policy style of the 'radical' or 'big bang' style of the 'Washington Consensus'.[8] A first expectation is that political pluralism is positively related to level of modernization, whereas anti-systemic mobilization should be positively related to distortion and negatively related to modernization (Table 6.2).

These expectations are met by the data which demonstrate a weak (but significant) relationship between modernization and political pluralism and between anti-systemic mobilization and modernization (negative) and distortion (positive).

Table 6.2. Initial conditions and society centred institutions (beta coefficients).

	Adj. R^2	Modernization factor	Distortion factor
Political pluralism	0.23	0.54*	−0.10
Anti-system mobilization	0.76	−0.75*	0.33**

*Note: * significance at 0.05 the level; ** significance at the 0.01 level.*

A second question is whether political inclusion of a broad range of interests in political institutions, political participation and anti-systemic mobilization will hinder or advance the change of economic institutions. While this debate has followed the classical dictatorship–democracy dichotomy, more recent research within the democracy paradigm has stressed the need to distinguish between early and later stages of institutional changes. Early stages, goes the argument, involve the need for rapid decisions to cope with economic imbalances. In this phase it is an advantage if the population is not mobilized and the range of societal interests represented is relatively narrow. In later stages, however, when the need to cope with broader structural changes arises, the involvement of broader social and political forces is preferred (Haggard and Kaufman, 1992, pp. 312f.).[9] Does this logic also apply to post-communist systems?

To answer these questions, the two tables below look at proxies for pluralism and anti-systemic mobilization, respectively.

Table 6.3. Initial conditions, pluralism and institutional change.

	Adj. R^2	Modernization	Distortion	Pluralism
SCOPE(97)	0.29			0.58**
SCOPE(97)	0.58	0.55**	−0.44**	
SCOPE(97)	0.67	0.57**	−0.37**	0.18
SCOPE(97)	0.72	0.43**	−0.35**	0.35* (log)

*Note: * significance at the 0.05 level; ** significance at the 0.01 level.*

Table 6.4. Initial conditions, anti-systemic mobilization and institutional change.

	Adj. R^2	Anti-system mobilization	Modernization	Distortion
SCOPE(97)	0.70	−0.85**		
SCOPE(97)	0.58		0.55**	−0.44**
SCOPE(97)	0.71	−0.75**	n.a. (1)	−0.18

Note: (1) modernization excluded due to multi-coliniarity with anti-system mobilization;

* significance at 0.05 the level; ** significance at the 0.01 level.

Table 6.3 shows that the expected relations do not hold: in the early stages of reform (also involving drastic stabilization measures) the inclusion of broader political forces, here defined as number of effective political parties in parliament, actually increases the ability to explain eventual institutional changes in the economy by about 14 per cent.[10] It shows that increasing the number of effective parties to 5–6 (the log scale) raises the odds that comprehensive reforms will succeed.[11]

Table 6.4 reveals a relatively clear picture: the higher the initial level of mobilization against the incumbent regime, measured as the percentage of voters that did not vote for communist or successor-communist parties, the greater the chances that a country will implement comprehensive changes of economic institutions. Hence, in contrast to the experience of other emerging democracies, pluralism and anti-systemic mobilization are conducive to the change of economic institutions even when controlling for initial conditions. Participatory democracy does have a transformative capacity. In the context of the present chapter these findings imply that countries which at the beginning of the transformation had a relatively modern (differentiated) civil society and/or experienced initial high anti-system mobilization are more likely to transcend their initial structural conditions and implement institutional changes in their economy than countries without such characteristics. Generated by the dynamics of civil society, these were the very factors that produced the fracture in the structure of the incumbent system. In this group we find two of the overachievers, Estonia and Poland, while none of the underachievers had any of these attributes.

ELITE POSITIONS AND INSTITUTIONAL CHANGES

The second political mechanism that was suggested as a political explanation of delayed stabilization and institutional changes was degree of elite position and politics (cf. Chapter 4). Where incumbent political and administrative elites stayed on (in more or less mutated form) they hindered both the development of democracy (to which we shall return in the last chapter) and the development of market institutions. Chapter 5 further substantiated this thesis, in that we linked the strong position of conservative elites in distorted economies to late stabilization and absence of reforms. The mechanisms giving elites expanded opportunities to operate relatively independently in post-communist systems is described by Bartlet (1996), using the example of Hungary. In his analysis (ibid., p. 48) of stabilization in Hungary he notes that while communist rule hampered the possibilities for organized opposition to macroeconomics stabilization, 'it afforded local agents multiple institutional channels to negotiate individual exceptions to austerity policy'. Transition to democracy undermined these party/state channels for societal opposition to economic austerity that, under communism, enabled vulnerable actors to secure compensation. At the same time the Hungarian (and other post-communist countries) transition to democracy created a set of party and state institutions that bolstered the ability of governments to execute stabilization policies. However, this enhanced capacity for governance was not matched by a commensurate increase in representativeness (Sørensen, 1995), but was characterized by low membership of political parties and ineffective trade unions (ibid., p. 66). Hence, 'The demise of communism weakened the position of the societal actors most vulnerable to macro-economic stabilization: it unhinged the links to party/state institutions that formed the basis of individual bargaining while leaving local agents without the robust civil associations needed to mount collective political action.'

These patterns of increased elite autonomy provide the elite with large discretionary powers to decide on the institutional strategies.[12] However, only the incumbent elite has the network necessary to benefit from delayed stabilization. New governments without roots in the old system – or with only partial roots – do not have the network necessary for such a strategy. If this assumption holds we would expect elite continuity to be negatively associated with efficient stabilization policies. Analyses linking the degree of elite continuity to stabilization support that there is indeed a close association between elite continuity and average inflation, counting from year two after the initiation of reforms.[13] This confirms the initial assumption that it is first of all the incumbent nomenclature elite that has the motivation to either halt reforms or reap the benefits of inflation while they remain in positions of power. In these countries, in particular in most countries of the former Soviet Union, the old elite continued on in power and was able to halt reforms and exploit their positions to extract rent, and through privatization to reposition themselves as de jure owners of the assets they previously controlled de facto.

Hellman (1998, p. 204) pursues the same argument but broadens the perspective by including other 'new' elites, when he shows that short term winners have sought to stall the economy in partial reform equilibrium with high inflation which generates concentrated rents for themselves, while imposing high costs on the rest of society. Hence, the basic argument is that the major obstacles to reform in post-communist countries are not short term losers, but early winners who endeavour to stall reforms with high inflation, at great economic and social costs. He also demonstrates that 'intermediate' and 'inconsistent' reformers have the largest increase in inequality and concentration of wealth, an indication of the power and privileges of the new elite. In this perspective, when effective policies are chosen and pursued, it is because the decision makers do not have the inclination (or the opportunity) to collect rent because there is nothing more to collect, or – as argued by Treisman (1998, p. 266) in the case of Russia – by designing a policy that brings on board the benefactors of inflation. The commercial banks were given a vested interest in stabilization by granting them access to profitable business in state securities. The loss making enterprises were bought off by allowing payment arrears for energy. This sort of arrangement is not deliberate – rather 'the impression is more one of the parties stumbling into a mutually advantageous arrangement through trial and error, responses to crises, and bargaining at the margin' (ibid., p. 262).

In Chapter 4 I argued that early reforms (pace) tend to produce far reaching reforms (scope). And I substantiated the argument by a tentative causal model linking elite discontinuity to reform progress, an argument that was further substantiated when the distortion factor was introduced and discussed in Chapter 5. The connection between popular support for reforms, elections and institutional change should be seen in the same perspective. Elite continuity or discontinuity is reflected in the outcomes of the first elections, particularly in the percentage of votes cast for the incumbent communist party (or successor party). Little support to the incumbent elites or the successor communist party indicates a radical break with previous elite structures, which again opens the way for a continuation of reforms. In contrast, when we find stronger support for the communist or successor parties, it signals an elite continuity that impedes reform. These patterns are shown in Table 6.5, which presents the simple correlation between the communist share of votes at the first election after regime change, elite continuity and the three policy variables: pace, phasing and scope.

The table shows that the change of economic institutions is closely associated with the outcomes of the first elections; in which little support for post-communist parties indicates elite discontinuity which again paves the way for continued reforms.[14] The table also demonstrates that strong support for post-communist parties and elite continuity are associated with a privatization-first policy, an implicit postponement of stabilization.[15] This opens for the rent-seeking described previously, when the political and administrative elite can exploit the continued inflation, controlled foreign trade, or ultimately resort to semi-legal privatization practices.

Initial public support for the market which has little to do with the market as such, but should rather be seen as part of a general uprising against the previous system or as a structural variable, is again what produced the results at the first elections. And if we compare the outliers in Figure 6.1 a pattern emerges where positive outliers are characterized by low electoral support for post-communist parties (Estonia and Poland) and negative outliers by high

Table 6.5. Anti-system mobilization, elite continuity and institutional change. Pearson's R.

	Scope (EBRD-transition index 1997)	Structure of old regime elites	Post-communist share at first free election	Pace	Phasing
Scope (EBRD-transition index 1997)	1.000	0.738**	-0.846**	0.718**	-0.611*
Structure of old regime elites		1.000	-0.837**	0.524*	-0.643**
Post-communist share at first free election			1.000	-0.665**	0.484*
Pace				1.000	-0.335
Phasing					1.000

*Note: * significance at the 0.05 level; ** significance at the 0.01 level.*

support for post-communist parties (Belarus, Turkmenistan). Along similar lines, non-economic factors like nationalism, anti-Russian sentiments or a violent extrication process were the impetus for ousting the communist elite, thus paving the way for the change of economic institutions through a change of elite positions.

Hence, as described by Olson in another context, the first elections became the revolutions that 'weakened the power of vested interests' and increased the discretionary power of new elites who became the agents of change (Olson, 1987, p. 251). Some countries were able to proceed faster than predicted on the basis of initial conditions, not because they shielded the state from the grievances of the losers, but because they were able to shield the state from the winners (Hellman, 1998). Again, Poland and Estonia represent cases where high anti-system mobilization coalesced with a radical change of political elites. Turkmenistan and Belarus represent reverse cases.

THE EFFECT OF POLITICAL INSTITUTIONS

Under specific circumstances political institutions may overcome unfavourable initial structural conditions by altering the incentives of social actors (Bartlet and Hunter 1997, p. 88). Institutions do not alter the social preferences of social actors, at least in the short run.[16] But they affect their strategies and capacities and thereby also the likelihood that they will achieve their objectives. In this perspective, it does not make sense to speak of one set of institutional arrangements as more effective than others. To increase a government's capabilities to pursue a specific policy does, in effect, involve finding the best fit among three factors: the initial conditions that constrain policy choices, the type of policy actors want to pursue; and the set up of political institutions (Weaver and Rockman, 1993, p. 40). In this vein an analysis of the effects of political institutions provides us with a positive and analytical insight: positive because it helps us to understand the types of policies that are likely to emerge from specific institutional configurations; normative because that insight will help us design institutions that are conducive to achieving the desired changes (Asilis and Milesi-Ferretti, 1994). The potential impact of political institutions on policy formation is especially radical in post-communist transitional systems, where the totalitarian nature of the incumbent system and the interconnectedness and cohesiveness of all spheres of the social, economic and political system has produced an equally total transformation of societal institutions.

I have so far examined the role of initial conditions – 'distortion' and 'modernization' as though they were channelled directly from the preferences of social and political actors through civil society institutions to the change of economic institutions. That is obviously not the case. The power of political and social actors are defined by the formal and informal political institutions of the emerging democracies. If we want to pursue the dual goal of democratic consolidation and economic change, democratic institutions should be configured in such a way that a critical mass of interests in society find their way into the democratic institutions or find it worthwhile to process their demands through these institutions. If this is not the case, if major interests are permanently excluded from major decisions, they will either pursue other – extra-parliamentary – channels to process their demands or they will refrain from political engagement, and in that process also threaten democracy. In this context we might expect social and corporate interests to apply the bureaucratic resources described in the previous section. Hence, we find ourselves in an apparent catch-22 dilemma, where representation in democratic institutions seems to hinder any change of economic institutions, and where such change assumes that representative democracy is, at least temporarily, by-passed to allow for the decisions on economic change. Still, we see that in most cases the change of economic institutions has progressed in parallel with democratic development. Has the configuration of political institutions made it possible to reconcile the dual objectives of democratization and change of economic institutions? Democratic institutions are endogenous to the project of change and they are constrained by the same initial conditions that influenced the change of economic institutions. This produces a kind of three-dimensional game where even the rules are part of the game. This section examines the impact of two core aspects of democratic institutions on the change of economic institutions: 'democracy' measured as the scope of civil and political rights as measured by the Freedom House Index (Table A 6.2), and the presidential–parliamentary relationship as measured by the Index of Presidential Authority,[17] which measures the formal constitutional powers of presidents (Appendix 6).

The dictatorship–democracy dichotomy has been a major issue in the classical discourse on political institutions and economic development: is the isolation of political decision-makers conducive to adoption and implementation of socially costly structural reforms? Or is societal participation necessary in order to ensure the quality and long term sustainability of policies? (Alesina and Perotti, 1994; Przeworski, 1991.) The agenda has changed but the same issue dominates the contemporary debate on political institutions and economic development, now in the context of 'empirical institutionalism' (Peters, 1999, ch. 5). How much democracy is conducive to structural reforms – and at what stage of the reforms? And does the configuration of democratic institutions, and in particular the presidential–parliamentary relationship, have an impact on the effect of political institutions on economic development? (Lijphart, 1992, 1999; Nohlen and Fernández, 1991; Rasch, 1996; Stephan and Skach, 1993).

In order to answer these questions in the present context, I will follow Geddes (1995) and assume that during a period of rapid and comprehensive institutional change new institutions, whether political or economic, will be formed to serve the interests of those who have been provided access to take part in the drafting of the new regulations. The elites involved will, of course, refer to all kinds of other higher order principles – legal, historic, moral or the experiences of other countries – or, in most cases, a combination of them all. But at the core of the institutional conflict is the aspiration that the new institutions provide privileged access and power for the individual politician or the group or ideas he or she represents. In these constitutional battles, however, it is not merely a question of power and position. Timing is also important. As in the natural world where size may be a competitive advantage, already established individuals often have a competitive advantage over those that are trying to establish themselves. In nature this is the case for many plants and other sedentary organisms. In addition such mechanisms may even manipulate their immediate surroundings to hinder the establishment of other potential competitors.[18] In society this is matched by 'institutional engineering', when groups try to secure their positions by designing political institutions to secure their future position and privileged access to power and influence.

Proceeding from this observation we would expect that the same type of initial conditions that formed economic institutions would also control the formation of the institutions of an emerging democracy. That this is indeed so is shown in Table 6.6.

As seen from Table 6.6 there is a very strong correlation between level of democracy (as measured by the Freedom House Index) and the two initial factors, both with the expected signs: initial modernization is a strong positive predictor of democracy and distortion is a moderate negative predictor. Regarding presidential strength (Index of Presidential Authority), we see that this is moderately strongly predicted by initial distortion, whereas there is no significant connection to level of modernization.

Table 6.6. Democracy and presidential authority explained by initial conditions.

	Adj. R^2	Modernization factor	Distortion factor
Democracy	0.73	0.72**	− 0.44**
Presidential authority	0.30	0.28	0.47*

*Note: * significance at the 0.05 level; ** significance at the 0.01 level*

What are the causal models behind these linkages? Regarding the connection between modernization and democracy, this is not the place to enter the long-standing debate about how modernity influences democracy and about the causal direction between the two variables (Lipset, 1959; Diamond, 1997; Hadenius, 1992; Przeworski and Limongo, 1993). Regarding the impact of distortion on democratization, we should probably refer to the same type of explanations as in the previous section. The design of institutions reflects the narrow interests and survival strategies of the incumbent elites.[19] In the first stage of post-communist institutional changes all countries opted for relatively strong presidencies (and majoritarian electoral systems). However, it was only in those countries where the communist political and administrative elites survived (or partly survived) the changes, that strong presidencies withstood the changes. This is indicated, for example, by the strong connection between level of elite continuity and IPA.[20]

Based on these observations we would not expect political institutions to have a significant independent impact on the change of economic institutions, because they are basically the outcome of the same political processes that formed the scope of economic changes. These expectations are confirmed in Tables 6.7 and 6.8, which show that the inclusion of democratic institutions replaces the predictions of initial conditions, implying in effect that democracy is so strong a predictor of institutional changes that it leaves initial conditions without effect. As expected, IPA is negatively related to scope97, indicating that a strong parliament is an asset when pursuing economic change.[21]

Table 6.7. Initial conditions, democracy and change of economic institutions.

	Adj. R^2	Democracy	Modernization factor	Distortion factor
SCOPE(97)	0.80	0.90**		
SCOPE(97)	0.58		0.55**	−0.44**
SCOPE(97)	0.80	0.80**	0.03	−0.16

*Note: Significance at the 0.05 level; ** significance at the 0.01 level.*

Table 6.8. Initial conditions, presidential authority and change of economic institutions.

	Adj. R^2	Presidential authority	Modernization factor	Distortion factor
SCOPE(97)	0.17	– 0.46*		
SCOPE(97)	0.58		0.55**	– 0.44**
SCOPE(97)	0.55	0.05	0.55**	– 0.44**

*Note: * significance at the 0.05 level; ** significance at the 0.01 level.*

Hence, the evolution of political institutions in emerging post-communist democracies (democracy and IPA) were shown to reflect the same underlying political dynamics that also constrain and drive the change of economic institutions. In contrast, the society centred dynamics (pluralism and anti-systemic mobilization) make it possible for some countries to transcend their initial constraints. Hence, when elite continuity is broken it is reflected in the evolution of state centred political institutions, but it is caused by society centred institutions. Our causal model looks roughly like Figure 6.2.

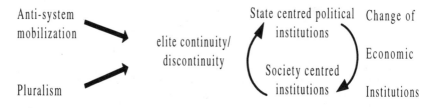

Figure 6.2. The virtuous and vicious circles of emerging institutions.

From this also follows that the political events at the beginning of the dual change of political and economic institutions are decisive, because they set the path for the consecutive change of economic and political institutions. In the cases where elite continuity was high we saw that powerful presidencies replaced the previous communist regimes and that these presidencies – where they remained in place – tended to hinder change of economic institutions, to provide privileged access for conservative interests and also to limit democracy. In other cases, where elite continuity was broken by mass mobilization and inclusion of a broader range of parties, the change of economic institutions progressed rapidly, as did democracy. Figure 6.3 shows the regional pattern of these linking degree of democracy to anti-system mobilization and the change of economic institutions.

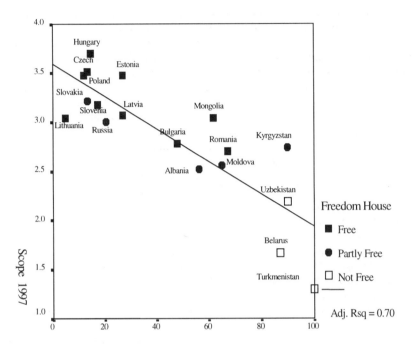

Post-communist share at first election

Note: Ukraine and Kazakhstan excluded due to absence of data on election outcomes.

Figure 6.3. Anti-system mobilization, democracy and change of economic institutions.

Figure 6.3 first of all shows the strong relation between democracy and change of economic institutions. Second, it shows that anti-system mobilization was especially strong in the institutionally most developed countries of Central Europe, the Baltic states and Russia, where all – except Russia and Slovakia – are categorized as 'Free' by the 'Nations in Transit' democracy measure of the Freedom House Organization (Karatnycky et al., 1997). South Eastern European Countries are in a middle category of democracy and institutional change. They also represent a middle category on anti-system mobilization and are split on the level of democracy. Finally, the countries which have developed their economic institutions the least are those of the former that have been characterized by low anti-system mobilization and little development of democracy.

From these arguments we can infer the existence of virtuous and vicious circles between political and economic institutions in emerging democracies, as illustrated in Figure 6.2. The virtuous circle appears when the initial events broke the bonds with the past and caused the establishment of democratic and inclusive political institutions. These institutions, in turn, produced the successful economic changes that again reinforced democracy, because they gave birth to new groups with vested interests in these institutions, and because their superior economic performance enhanced popular support for the political system that produced these results. Estonia is a good case in point. Here a parliament vested with strong powers became a firm institutional basis for the implementation of economic reforms.[22]

The vicious circle is described by the opposite logic. Here the development of political institutions provides privileged access for conservative or particularistic interests. The development in Russia is an illustrative case in point. The radical reform programme launched on 2nd January 1992 was designed by a group of relatively independent economic experts and supported by president Yeltsin, but without any specific social or political base. The reform programme was implemented by presidential decree, without parliament (Congress of People's Deputies) having had a say, a left-over from Soviet times dominated by industrial managers and agricultural leaders. Another cause of the initial passivism on the part of industrial managers was a degree of market naivety. They initially seemed to endorse price liberalization because this would give them an opportunity to fix prices, but they did not anticipate the possibility of decreasing demand, a behaviour best explained by the mental legacy of the incumbent system, characterized by shortages of goods and producer sovereignty. The forces opposing the changes rapidly realigned, however, and in the summer of 1992 a powerful anti-reform block had been formed representing the losers in the process, industrial managers, workers (trade unions) and agrarian leaders (Mau, 1996). The alliance preferred inflation to the bankruptcies and unemployment that was the inevitable corollary of the policies pursued by government. In this respect it was parliament that voiced society's concern over the economic and social effects of the radical economic policy, despite its non-democratic origin. The institutional battles between a presidency advocating a continuance of radical reforms and a parliament voicing social and economic concerns continued throughout 1992 and eventually reached its climax when the president attacked parliament in September 1993. This event was followed by the adoption of a new constitution which provided the presidency with almost unlimited powers vis-à-vis an impotent parliament (Duma). However, the political price the president had to pay was a transformation from laissez-faire to corporate capitalism (Kuz'min, 1998), providing privileged access first for exposed industrial groups attempting to escape hard budget constraints and foreign competition. At a later stage this structure also paved the way for the corrupting influence of the huge financial corporations (the oligarchs) who were audaciously enriching themselves at the cost of state and in the face of a powerless parliament and society (Pedersen, 1998). In this context, the decision about design of the political institutions of the Russian state and in particular the installation of a very strong presidency became a pivotal factor in the formulation of the disastrous economic policies. Hence, a clear causal relationship exists between the structure of state power and the path of economic transformation (McFaul, 1994).[23] Carlsen (1998) has demonstrated a similar logic reaching also to the local level in his analyses of modern social democracy in Russia.

Figure 6.2 represents an upstream analysis. The democratic institutions will eventually attain a life of their own and outlive the political circumstances that produced them. However, in the countries under discussion the first phase of institution building has yet to be completed. Constitutions and political institutions are still being changed. And the informal conventions that will eventually fill out the textual inaccuracies (and intended ambiguities) need time to evolve. Only when the political systems have found some kind of equilibrium shall we be able to answer the questions about the compatibility of alternative forms of political institutions with market institutions in a 'downstream' analysis.

CONCLUSIONS

The purpose of the present chapter was to search for capacities that increase the opportunities for post-communist countries to transcend the structural constraints embedded in their initial conditions. These resources were first found in the dynamics and level of popular support for market institutions. They were also found in the strength of civil society institutions who transferred this support to the political sphere. Both components ultimately reflect longer term historical trajectories (2nd order initial conditions). Second, it was shown that the less elite continuity, the greater the likelihood that economic institutions would change. Finally, it was shown that while political institutions are ultimately part of the same logic which generates change of economic institutions, democracy and strong parliaments are assets when fostering new economic institutions. Liberal and participatory democracy fosters economic change.

However, the observed capacities for change describe only opportunities for change. They are, so to speak, structural properties originating in second order initial conditions and capable of generating fractures in the structural cohesiveness of the incumbent system. As structural properties they do not initiate or direct the course of change, they only offer opportunities. To explain the source and direction of change we need agents. They are the subjects of the following chapter.

NOTES

1. Significance here defined as deviating more than one studentized standard deviation from the predicted position. Poland is the exception, but has been included despite not being quite on this level.

2. This is also supported by the level of egalitarianism as described in Figure 5.5.

3. See chapter 2. for a discussion of the impact of mode of extrication on transition outcomes.

4. De Melo et al. (1997) include previous statehood, market memory and border to a non-socialist system in regressions where they have a positive, significant effect of institutional changes. They do not, however, mention EU-candidacy, which is probably the most important although it overlaps other variables. In contrast to De Melo et al., I prefer the external factors to be a part of external agency, to be dealt with in Chapter 7.

5. For example Ágh (1998a: 180).

6. As shown in Chapter 7, the embeddedness of socialism in Belarus is a consequence of more recent developments and is in particular a legacy of World War Two.

7. While representation is, of course, ultimately produced by a combination of electoral provisions and cleavage structures, our focus here is on the consequence of these preconditions: the range of pluralism in parliament. For that purpose I apply the measure of the effective number of political parties as developed by Laakso and Taagepera (Taagepera and Shugart, 1989, ch. 8). Briefly stated, an effective party is one that in the given context has sufficient size to be an option in coalition building. As the number of effective parties increases, so does the number of parties needed to construct a majority coalition, and the less efficient the parliament. See Appendices.

8. In their approach which they term 'social democratic', they argue that '... the autocratic policy style characteristic of Washington-style reforms tends to undermine representative institutions, to personalize politics, and to generate a climate in which politics becomes reduced to fixes, to search for redemption. Even if neo-liberal reform packages make good economics, they are likely to generate voodoo politics' (Pereira et al., 1993, pp. 9–10).

9. See further Chapter 3 on the discussion of political inclusion and economic change.

10. The validity of this proxy can be disputed, because most parties in the emerging democracies of Central and Eastern Europe are catch-all parties with very vague (if any) social bases. Still, with that caveat in mind, for the following analysis it is assumed that more parties in parliament indicate greater inclusiveness than fewer parties. For a similar view, see Hellman (1998).

11. The theoretical argument for using a log scale is that there is a limit to how rapidly institutional reforms can proceed, irrespective of the number of parties. However, all countries with a score of above 3 on the EBRD scale have had more than two effective parties at the first election.

12. For a recent attempt to model rent-seeking in post-communist (and other) governments, see Andrei Schleifer and Robert W. Vishny (1998), *The Grabbing Hand. Government Pathologies and their Cures*. Cambridge, MA.: Harvard University Press.

13. The correlation is 0.6 (0.01 significance). The countries were coded into three categories of elite continuity. For the coding of countries, see Appendix A 6.3. For analyses of elite continuity in post-communist countries, see further Higley, Kullberg and Pakulski (1996); Clark and Soulsby (1996); Khrystanovskaya (1994); Wiatr (1994); Steen (1996); Easter (1997).

14. Similar results are reported by Fish (1998a).

15. Hellman (1998) demonstrates a clear association between elite continuity and institutional change. He also demonstrates that we find the highest increase in poverty and inequality in those countries that have the highest elite continuity. Hence, the enrichment of incumbent elites takes place at the expense of increasingly impoverished and polarized societies.

16. I here enter the essence of the discussion between alternate versions of New Institutionalism, where the rational choice position basically is that preferences are exogenous to institutions. In contrast the empirical and historical versions of new institutionalism argue that preferences are mutable by institutions: by participation in democratic institutions you become a democrat – or by participation in representative institutions you become sensitive to the values and demands of other groups. However, neither the time horizon nor the focus of this study make it feasible to test these propositions. For a discussion of alternative positions on the link between preferences and institutions, see Peters (1999).

17. The IPA measures the formal constitutional powers of a president by a summation and weighted average of his symbolic, appointive and political powers. The higher the score, the greater the formal powers of a presidential institution. For a description of how the IPA is constructed and the robustness of the measures, see Appendix 6.4.

18. I owe this observation to Freddy Bugge Christiansen, Department of Ecology and Genetics, University of Aarhus. It was developed in reaction to the following statement by Barbara Geddes (1995, p. 251): 'As in the natural world, survival and reproductive success belong not only to the fittest but also to the first. Those who manage to establish themselves initially have an advantage over competitors who arrive later because the pioneers control the design of new institutions and thus shape the political environment in ways that benefit themselves and erect barriers to the entry of potential competitors.' In this statement Geddes obfuscates ideas from evolutionary and ecological theory.

19. Higley, Kullberg and Pakulski (1996) describe elite continuity as a consequence of the institutional adaptation in individual countries in the post-Stalin era. The objective of elites in most communist systems has been to replace the personal insecurity under Stalinism with the institutional stability epitomized by the immobility of the Brezhnev era in the USSR and Central Europe. In some of these countries, however, emerging elites had been prepared to take advantage of the change of economic and political institutions (in particular in Central Europe). In these countries we saw a smooth transition to the market and to democracy. The parochialism and conservatism in less developed systems created a turn to nationalism, the only survival strategy for incumbent elites (southern Europe and most of the former Republics of the Soviet Union).

20. Using the present classification of elite continuity (Table A6.3), the simple correlation between elite continuity and IPA is 0.65 (0.01 sign.). The higher the level of elite continuity, the stronger the presidency.

21. Following the logic of analysis demonstrated by Hellman (1996) also shows that postponing constitutions (leaving room for the unconstrained actions of a strong executive) has no discernible effect on economic reforms. In contrast, stable constitutions that place constraints on the executive, and hence state power, appear to have a positive effect on the process of economic reform. The same can be shown if in the present context we examine the relationship between the presidencies and the national banks. The stronger the presidential control of national banks (contrasted to parliamentary control), the stronger the inflation in the period we are considering.

22. See further Chapter 7.

23. It is an irony of history that President Yeltsin's coup d'état, that eventually led to the destruction of the economic reforms and to corruption of the Russian state, was supported by a majority of Western leaders and opinion makers who naively believed

that an authoritarian implementation of radical economic reforms would eventually serve the cause of democracy. See for example Gowan (1995, pp. 450ff).

APPENDIX 6

Table A 6.1. Anti-system mobilization.

Country	% Post-communist votes at constituent election
Albania	56.20
Belarus	87.00
Bulgaria	47.90
Czech Rep.	13.20
Estonia	26.70
Hungary	14.60
Kazakhstan	.
Kyrgyzstan	90.00
Latvia	26.70
Lithuania	5.00
Moldova	65.20
Mongolia	61.70
Poland	12.00
Romania	67.30
Russia	20.30
Slovakia	13.30
Slovenia	17.30
Turkmenistan	100.00
Ukraine	.
Uzbekistan	90.00

Note: Figures for Ukraine and Kazakhstan are missing due to lack of reliable data.

Sources: Åslund, Boone and Johnson (1996), Rose and Chin (1998), The Electoral Websites, Copyright Wilfried Derksen.

Table A 6.2. Institutional variables.

	Nations in Transit index (reversed)	Index of Presidential Authority	Number of effective parties	Post-communist share of votes at first election (Year)	Electoral turn-out in % at first election (Year)
Albania	2.50	15.85	1.812	56.20	98.92 (91)
Belarus	1.12	45.98	..*	87.00 (95)	..
Bulgaria	3.19	45.10	2.521	47.90	90.80 (90)
Czech Rep.	5.62	13.62	4.804	14.00	96.70 (90)
Estonia	4.94	15.63	5.899	0.00	69.30 (92)
Hungary	5.56	21.00	3.788	14.50	69.50 (90)
Kazakhstan	1.75	62.50	2.124	..	80.73
Kyrgyzstan	2.25	46.88	..**	90.00 (90)	62.00 (95)
Latvia	4.94	10.25	5.115	0.00	89.90 (93)
Lithuania	4.94	37.95	2.172	0.00	75.20 (92)
Moldova	3.19	47.50	2.624	65.20	79.00 (94)
Mongolia	..***	35.00	2.609	61.70	..
Poland	5.56	49.11	10.855	12.00	43.20 (91)
Romania	3.12	42.50	2.196	69.00	86.20 (90)
Russia	3.25	57.50	8.643	20.30	54.80 (93)
Slovakia	3.19	17.41	3.186	13.60	95.30 (90)
Slovenia	5.12	19.20	8.184	22.70	83.10 (90)
Turkmenistan	0.06	40.63	1.000	100.00	99.77 (94)
Ukraine	3.12	46.88	3.666	..	74.80(94)
Uzbekistan	0.56	43.75	1.724	90.00 (90)	94.00 (95)

*Notes: * Parliament dissolved after elections. ** Parliament occupied by independent candidates from local regions. *** Mongolia is not included in the Freedom-house surveys*

Sources: Col 1: Nations in Transit 1997: Civil Society, Democracy and Markets in East Central Europe and the Newly Independent States by Adrian Karatnycky (Editor), Alexander Motyl (Editor), Boris Shor (Editor), Freedom House Org. Washington D.C. 1997, Cols 2, 3 & 4: Own data, *Col 5: Electoral studies, Vol 9, Elsevier Science Ltd, Great Britain, 1990, Electoral studies, Vol. 10, Elsevier Science Ltd, Great Britain, 1991, Electoral studies, Vol. 11, Elsevier Science Ltd, Great Britain, 1992, Electoral studies, Vol. 12, Elsevier Science Ltd, Great Britain, 1993, Electoral studies, Vol. 13, Elsevier Science Ltd, Great Britain, 1994, Electoral studies, Vol. 14, Elsevier Science Ltd, Great Britain, 1995, Electoral studies, Vol. 15, Elsevier Science Ltd, Great Britain, 1996, Electoral studies, Vol. 16, Elsevier Science Ltd, Great Britain, 1997, Wilfried Derksen's Electoral Website, URL: http://www.agora.stm.it/ elections/election.htm, 1998; Parline database 1998, InterParliamentary Union, URL: http://www.ipu.org, 1998*

Table A 6.3. Elite continuity.

Country	Elite Continuity	
Albania	2	Reformed
Belarus	2	Reformed
Bulgaria	2	Reformed
Czech Rep.	3	Dispersed
Estonia	3	Dispersed
Hungary	3	Dispersed
Kazakhstan	1	Consolidated
Kyrgyzstan	1	Consolidated
Latvia	3	Dispersed
Lithuania	2	Reformed
Moldova	2	Reformed
Mongolia	2	Reformed
Poland	3	Dispersed
Romania	2	Reformed
Russia	2	Reformed
Slovakia	3	Dispersed
Slovenia	3	Dispersed
Turkmenistan	1	Consolidated
Ukraine	2	Reformed
Uzbekistan	1	Consolidated

Sources: Easter (1997) offers a classification of post-communist systems according to elite continuity, consisting of three groups: high continuity (consolidated elites), medium continuity (reformed elites) and low continuity (dispersed elites). This table reproduces Easter's classification, but has recoded Lithuania to the medium (reformed) category. See also Steen, 1996.

THE INDEX OF PRESIDENTIAL AUTHORITY[1]

The Index of Presidential Authority (IPA) measures and compares Presidential Authority, based on constitutional provisions in individual countries. IPA is constructed with the help of three main constitutional power resources, (S) symbolic resources, (A) appointive resources and (P) political resources. In addition the IPA seek to account for the method of election to the presidency (E) (Direct election or elected by parliament) and the length of a presidential term (L). Each power resource is calculated on the basis of a number of powers. The president can either possess this power in full, in qualified form or not at all. In the first case the power counts 1, in qualified form ½ and if the president do not have the power no score is recorded.

A few examples may illustrate how scores are assigned and some of the problems. Among the appointive powers a president can possess is the power to appoint the Prime Minister. Irrespective that all countries (except Turkmenistan) in some form require that a government is eventually supported or approved by a majority in the parliament the coding here represents whether the president has the power to appoint the Prime Minister. In Russia the president appoints the Prime Minister and can do so without consultations with parliament or political parties.[2] Hence, in the Russian case the coding is 1. In contrast the Slovenian constitution stipulates that the president shall name the Prime Minister after consultation with the leaders of the various political groups in the parliament.[3] A similar procedure is set forth in the Moldovan constitution. Thus in these cases the item is coded as a qualified power (½). In Turkmenistan the president is the executive power and chairs the Cabinet of Ministers.[4] In this respect the constitutional system of Turkmenistan is the classical 'pure' presidential system. Since the president de facto is also the Prime Minister, we have chosen to code the Turkmen case as a full power. This may even be a understatement of the true power of the president, but to code it as missing or absent would underestimate presidential power in Turkmenistan even more.

The formula for IPA is:

$$IPA=1(\Sigma S_{1-7})+2(\Sigma A_{1-13})+3(\Sigma P_{1-17})*E*L=IS/336*100,$$

where IS is the index score in relation to the maximum possible value (336). Each power resource is weighted in the final calculation of IPA, thus S weights 1, A weights 2 and P weights 3. The election method multiplies 2, when the president is directly elected and the length of the term (L) is multiplied with 1.1 where l is the number of years in a term. If the president is elected for life L=2. The coding for each country is listed below.

Coding based on constitutional documents can be tricky, as we have attempted to apply a uniform coding procedure to documents written in different traditions. Furthermore, in some cases the provisions are unclear and/or may have given rise to later interpretations by the respective

Constitutional Courts. Moreover, we run the risk that parts of the constitution are not codified.[5] To reduce the error which may arise from these different traditions, language problems etc., we have first sought standardized translations, i.e. preferring to use the ICL standard, when possible. Second, we have made several pilot codings comparing independently made code sheets for the same country.[6]

With respect to the first question, we have presented the index questions to the members of the section for Comparative Politics and Political Science at the Department of Political Science, University of Aarhus and Jørgen Elklit, Department of Political Science, University of Aarhus for an extensive discussion concerning which question to include under each of the measures. Furthermore, we have consulted both McGregor (1994) and Frye's (1997) index questions to develop the framework. Compared to McGregor's index we omitted several symbolic powers, but maintained the idea of three composite measures. Compared to Frye's index we have included symbolic powers and made a distinction between the three sources of authority into symbolic, appointive and political powers.

Regarding the question of homogeneity of the IPA (correlation between the variables included in the index) it was examined through bivariate correlation between the main components of the index (see Table A 6.4). With respect to the question of the robustness of the IPA index (if it changes with different weights of the variables included) we tested it by several recalculations with different weightings for the measures and examining the consequences for the bivariate relationship between these 'shadow-indexes' and the IPA and as a further test compared these 'shadow-indexes' with alternative definition of the form of government (presidential, semi-presidential and parliamentary systems). For the three tests we raised the weighting of symbolic, appointive and political powers in turn with 50 per cent and in the fourth we reduced the weight of the method of election by 50 per cent. The results are reported in Table A 6.5.

The correlation between these alternative shadow-indexes and IPA is higher than 0.998. Further, using Scheffe's post-hoc test (Hays, 1974, pp. 605-612) we find that the mean difference, between parliamentary and semi-presidential and between parliamentary and presidential forms of government, is significant at the 0.05 level for all four shadow-indexes. We also find the expected pattern of increasing IPA when we move from parliamentarism to presidentialism (see Table A 6.6).

Finally, we changed the additive character of the index and standardized the three forms of power, by dividing the sum score of each form of power by number of variables in the category. The correlation between the original IPA and this new standardized index is 1.000. Our conclusion based upon these tests is that the IPA index is satisfactorily robust.

Table A 6.4. Correlation between the component parts of the IPA.

		L	M	S	A	P
L	Pearson	1.000	−.126	−.082	.244	−.282
	Sig. (2-tailed)	−	.597	.730	.300	.228
M	Pearson	−.126	1.000	.627	.369	.570
	Sig. (2-tailed)	.597	−	.003	.110	.009
S	Pearson	−.082	.627	1.000	.442	.772
	Sig. (2-tailed)	.730	.003	−	.051	.000
A	Pearson	.244	.369	.442	1.000	.533
	Sig. (2-tailed)	.300	.110	.051	−	.016
P	Pearson	−.282	.570	.772	.533	1.000
	Sig. (2-tailed)	.228	.009	.000	.016	−

Table A 6.5. Robustness: shadow-indexes and IPA.

		IPA
1. IPA (Symbolic raised by 50 per cent)	Pearson	1.000
	Sig. (2-tailed)	.000
2. IPA (Appointive raised by 50 per cent)	Pearson	.998
	Sig. (2-tailed)	.000
3. IPA (Political raised by 50 per cent)	Pearson	.999
	Sig. (2-tailed)	.000
4. IPA (Weight for method of election reduced 50 per cent)	Pearson	1.000
	Sig. (2-tailed)	.000

Table A 6.6. Means comparison of shadow-indexes and the form of government.

Form of government/Shadow-index	1	2	3	4
Parliamentary (N=7)	17.0	18.0	21.2	15.7
Semi-presidential (N=7)	46.1	48.7	58.1	32.7
Presidential (N=6)	52.9	56.6	67.0	37.8
Total (N=20)	37.9	40.3	47.8	28.2

NOTES

1. The IPA (and the present section) has been developed in cooperation with Lars Johannsen in connection with his separate project on the role of constitution in the democratization of the same range of countries included in this study.
2. The Constitution of the Russian Federation, Articles 83 (a) and 111 (4).
3. The Constitution of Slovenia, Article 111 (1).
4. The Constitution of the Republic of Turkmenistan, Articles 74 and 75.
5. For example: the principle of parliamentarism, i.e. that a government must resign following a vote of no confidence, is not codified in the Danish constitution.
6. Both Ole Hersted Hansen, Lars Johannsen and Ole Nørgaard have made separate coding, which we subsequently compared. Furthermore we have compared our coding, when possible, with McGregor's (1994) coding. Ole Hersted Hansen deserves credit, as he after the trial cases has made the actual codework.

INDEX OF PRESIDENTIAL AUTHORITY – TABLES

Table A 6.7. Index of presidential authority

Country	Presidential Authority
Albania	15.85
Belarus	46.88
Bulgaria	45.10
Czech Rep.	13.17
Estonia	15.63
Hungary	21.00
Kazakhstan	63.39
Kyrgyzstan	47.77
Latvia	10.64
Lithuania	38.84
Moldova	47.50
Mongolia	35.00
Poland	49.11
Romania	42.50
Russia	57.50
Slovakia	17.41
Slovenia	19.20
Turkmenistan	42.41
Ukraine	47.77
Uzbekistan	44.64

Source: Own estimate.

Table A 6.8. *Presidential election method and the length of a presidential term.*

	Albania	Belarus	Bulgaria	Czech Rep.	Estonia	Hungary	Kazakhstan	Kyrgyz Rep.	Latvia*	Lithuania	Moldova	Mongolia	Poland	Romania	Russia	Slovakia**	Slovenia	Turkmenistan	Ukraine	Uzbekistan
Length of Presidential term (years)	5	5	5	5	5	5	5	5	4	5	4	4	5	4	4	5	5	5	5	5
Method of election (I, D)	I	D	D	I	I	I	D	D	I	D	D	D	D	D	D	I	D	D	D	D

Legend: I = indirect election, D = direct election. As for the length of the electoral period for the presidency it is coded in number of years for one period. * The Saeima shall elect the President of State for a term of four years. (The December 4, 1997 amendment.) ** Constitution was amended in 1998 providing for a directly elected president.

Table A 6.9. Symbolic powers of the president.

	Albania	Belarus	Bulgaria	Czech Rep.	Estonia	Hungary	Kazakhstan	Kyrgyz Rep.	Latvia	Lithuania	Moldova	Mongolia	Poland	Romania	Russia	Slovakia	Slovenia	Turkmenistan	Ukraine	Uzbekistan
1. Awards decorations, titles, honours	1	1	1	½	1	1	1	1	1	1	1	1	1	1	1	1	1	1	1	1
2. Convenes constituent session of the parliament	1	0	1	1	1	1	1	0	0	1	1	1	1	1	1	1	1	0	0	0
3. Grants pardons and/or amnesties	1	1	1	½	1	½	1	1	1	1	1	1	1	1	1	1	1	1	1	1
4. Grants citizenship	1	1	1	0	0	½	1	1	0	½	1	1	1	0	1	0	0	1	1	1
5. Grants asylum	1	1	1	0	0	0	1	1	0	0	1	1	0	0	1	0	0	1	1	1
6. Signs and/or promulgate laws	½	1	1	½	1	1	1	1	1	1	1	½	1	1	1	½	1	1	1	1
7. Receives oaths of office	0	0	0	0	0	0	1	0	0	0	1	0	1	1	0	1	0	0	0	0
Sum of symbolic powers	5½	5	6	2½	4	4	7	5	2	4½	7	5½	6	5	6	4½	4	5	5	5

Notes: 1 = unqualified power, ½ = qualified power, 0 = a power the president does not have.

158

Table A 6.10. Appointive powers of the president.

	Albania	Belarus	Bulgaria	Czech Rep.	Estonia	Hungary	Kazakhstan	Kyrgyz Rep.	Latvia	Lithuania	Moldova	Mongolia	Poland	Romania	Russia	Slovakia	Slovenia	Turkmenistan	Ukraine	Uzbekistan
Prime Minister	1	1	1	½	1	1	1	1	1	1	½	½	1	1	1	1	½	1	1	1
Ministers	½	½	0	½	½	1	½	½	0	½	1	0	½	½	½	½	0	1	½	½
Caretaker government	0	0	1	0	0	0	0	0	0	1	1	0	0	1	0	.	0	0	0	0
Constitutional Court and/or Supreme Court	0	½	½	½	½	1	½	½	0	½	½	½	1	½	½	½	0	½	½	½
Electoral commission	0	0	0	0	0	0	½	0	0	0	0	0	0	0	0	0	0	0	½	0
Ombudsman	0	0	0	½	½	1	0	0	0	½	0	0	0	0	0	0	0	0	0	0
Judges	0	1	0	½	½	1	½	½	0	1	½	½	1	½	1	0	0	1	½	1
Prosecutor-general	0	0	½	0	0	1	½	½	0	0	½	½	0	½	½	½	0	½	½	½
Central Bank officials	0	½	0	1	½	½	½	½	0	½	0	0	½	0	½	0	0	0	½	½
Security Council	1	1	0	0	0	0	1	0	0	½	0	0	1	0	1	0	0	0	0	1
Senior civil servants	0	1	1	0	½	½	1	½	0	1	1	0	1	1	1	1	½	1	½	½
Senior commanders	0	.	½	½	½	½	1	1	0	½	0	0	1	1	1	0	0	1	½	1
Ambassadors	½	1	½	½	½	½	1	½	½	½	½	½	1	½	½	1	1	1	½	1
Sum of appointive powers	3	6½	5	4½	5	8	8	5½	1½	7½	5½	2½	8	6½	7½	4½	2	7	5½	7½

Legend: 1 = unqualified power, ½ = qualified power, 0 = a power the president does not have.

Source: IPA

Table A 6.11. The political powers of the president.

	Albania	Belarus	Bulgaria	Czech Rep.	Estonia	Hungary	Kazakhstan	Kyrgyz Rep.	Latvia	Lithuania
1. Commander in chief of the armed forces	1	1	1	.	1	1	1	1	½	1
2. Chairs the National Security Council	1	1	1	½	0	1	1	0	0	1
3. Remand laws for reconsideration	1	1	1	0	1	1	1	1	½	1
4. Sends law to Constitutional Court	0	1	1	1	1	1	1	1	0	1
5. Proposes legislation	1	1	0	0	0	0	1	1	1	1
6. Issues decrees in non-emergencies	½	1	½	0	0	0	1	1	½	1
7. Proposes amendments to constitution	1	½	1	0	1	0	1	1	0	0
8. Calls special sessions of parliament	1	0	1	0	1	1	1	1	1	½
9. Assumes special powers if parliament not in session or unable to convene	½	0	1	0	½	½	½	0	0	½
10. Assumes emergency powers at other times	0	½	1	0	1	0	½	½	0	½
11. Dissolves parliament and calls elections	½	0	1	½	½	½	1	1	½	½
12. Calls referendums	½	½	1	0	0	1	1	1	½	0
13. Participates in parliamentary sessions	0	1	0	1	0	.	1	1	1	0
14. May address or send messages to parliament	0	1	1	1	0	1	1	0	0	0
15. May convene cabinet sessions	0	1	0	0	0	0	1	0	1	0
16. Participates in cabinet sessions	0	1	0	.	0	0	1	1	1	0
17. May request reports from government	0	0	0	1	0	0	1	1	0	0
18. Sum of Political Powers	8	11½	11½	5	7	9	16	12½	7½	8

Notes: 1 = unqualified power, ½ = qualified power, 0 = a power the president does not have.

Source: IPA

	Moldova	Mongolia	Poland	Romania	Russia	Slovakia	Slovenia	Turkmenistan	Ukraine	Uzbekistan
1. Commander in chief of the armed forces	1	1	½	1	1	1	1	1	½	1
2. Chairs the National Security Council	0	1	0	1	1	0	0	0	½	0
3. Remand laws for reconsideration	1	1	1	1	1	½	0	1	1	1
4. Sends law to Constitutional Court	1	1	1	1	1	1	½	0	1	0
5. Proposes legislation	1	1	1	0	1	1	0	1	1	1
6. Issues decrees in non-emergencies	1	½	½	1	1	0	0	1	1	½
7. Proposes amendments to constitution	1	1	1	½	1	0	0	0	1	0
8. Calls special sessions of parliament	1	1	0	1	1	0	1	1	1	0
9. Assumes special powers if parliament not in session or unable to convene	0	½	½	½	0	0	½	0	½	½
10. Assumes emergency powers at other times	½	0	½	½	1	0	0	½	1	½
11. Dissolves parliament and calls elections	½	½	½	½	1	½	½	½	1	½
12. Calls referendums	1	0	½	½	1	½	0	½	1	0
13. Participates in parliamentary sessions	1	1	1	1	1	1	0	0	1	1
14. May address or send messages to parliament	1	1	1	1	1	1	1	1	1	1
15. May convene cabinet sessions	0	0	1	0	1	0	0	1	0	1
16. Participates in cabinet sessions	1	0	1	½	1	1	0	1	0	1
17. May request reports from government	1	0	0	0	1	1	0	0	0	1
18. Sum of Political Powers	13	10½	11	11	16	8½	4½	9½	12½	10

Legend: 1 = unqualified power, ½ = qualified power, 0 = a power the president does not have.
Source: IPA.

161

7. Agents of Institutional Change

'Ideas matter, and it is the combination of changes in relative prices filtered through the culturally conditioned ideas that are generated that accounts for evolving subjective models that shape choices in a society' (Douglas North, 1997).

The previous chapter demonstrated that democracy, pluralism and anti-system mobilization provided the framework for the 'opportunity space' that made the change of economic institutions possible. It was also shown that the corresponding construction of specific democratic institutions was anchored in the same pattern of political interests that generated the 'opportunity space'. But popular mobilization, pluralism and political institutions reflect only the opportunities for change. They do not explain who or what inspired and drove the changes in particular countries, why particular paths were chosen and why some countries, elites and societies turned out to be more receptive to ideas and agents of change than others.

The direction of change, the introduction of a market economy, is based on economic ideas but carried out by persons, institutions and organizations who become de facto agents of change. These institutions and persons carry ideas into societal and historical settings that are more or less receptive to these new ideas. But why were some societies more 'mutable' in the sense of being capable of 'radical, abrupt departures from existing social and cultural norms' (Dawisha and Turner, 1997, p. 401), and why were they more 'permeable' in the sense that elites and societies were willing and able to adopt new models and ideas? This is what has been termed 'Galton's problem', i.e. distinguishing diffusion of ideas from internal causes of variance in social systems (Peters, 1999, p. 42; Przeworski, 1987, p. 44; Galton, 1889, p. 272). The present chapter addresses these final questions by comparing the agents of institutional change in our 20 post-communist countries, focusing in particular on those that performed significantly better or worse than predicted based on initial conditions.

ECONOMIC IDEAS, AGENCY AND 2ND ORDER INITIAL CONDITIONS

The change of economic institutions is based on a set of economic ideas that reflect both the vision about a certain end stage and the means to get there. It also involves a set of beliefs about the means by which economic surplus (or deficit) should be distributed, and (implicitly) how great social and economic inequalities may be without becoming incompatible with a given social and political order (Reich, 1990). At the same time, new economic ideas never arise in an ideological or political vacuum. Hence the meaning and acceptance of new ideas is derived not only from the content but also from 'powerful symbolic issues, the nature of the political and ideological context into which new ideas they are introduced, the nature of who interprets or carries the idea (Sikkink, 1991, p. 252). As demonstrated by Peter Hall (1989), the acceptance, adaptation and eventual implementation of a new set of economic ideas also hinges on their economic, political and administrative viability: their capacity to solve the perceived economic problems, their ability to garner political support and state capacity to handle the concrete technical tasks required by the new policy. These observations, based on a study of developmentalism in Latin America and the diffusion of Keynesianism, also apply to the diffusion of market ideology into post-communist countries. As shown in previous chapters, the adoption of a democratic market economy was partly constrained, partly induced by the 1st order legacy of communism. In addition to the immediate legacies of the communist era, each country to a varying extent had another legacy, re-flecting deeper parameters of what was termed '2nd order initial conditions': the collective memories, foci of identification and values that outlived the communist era, reflecting long-term historical trajectories. These 2nd order initial conditions carried the symbols around which people could rally when mobilizing against the incumbent communist order and reflected the extent to which traditional values and patterns of behaviour would be compatible with the institutions of democratic capitalism.

The market ideology, the Washington consensus, was introduced into societies that found themselves on different levels of development and distortion. In comparison with the rise and diffusion of other economic ideas, Keynesianism in the 1930s and 1940s and developmentalism in the 1950s and 1960s, the ideology of the free market was nonetheless never really disputed in the reform process in Central and Eastern Europe. After some initial arguments about an alleged 'third way' that surfaced time and again in the political discourse under different synonyms, the market was, as a principle, agreed to by the dominating elites from Warsaw to Moscow and from Riga to Asgabad.[1] Future conflicts were to be over pace and phasing, not the virtues of the market as such. A number of factors contributed to the astounding adoption of the new set of economic ideas that were diametrically opposed to the communist system of economic governance. First, in many

countries the popular rejection of the communist system was combined with
the adoption of ideologically opposite systems within many fields: from the
sexual Puritanism under communism to the very liberal use of sex and sexual
symbols in advertising and politics, from totally controlled political systems
to the quest for libertarian democracy – and from a state controlled economy
to a free market ideology. Second, what Poznanski (1995) terms the 'concept
of inadjustment cycles'. Throughout history Eastern Europe has lagged
behind the development in the Western part of Europe. However, once
changes are initiated they very often assume radical and disruptive forms.
Also the inclination to think in ideological absolutes, a disposition that was
further reinforced by communist rule and way of thinking, can be seen as part
of the same trend. Finally, this trend towards totalitarian thinking and radical
rejection of the previous system was, in a majority of countries, combined
with virtual ignorance of what a free market system really was and what it
implied in terms of social and economic redistribution. Among the emerging
elites in many countries, this implied the absence of anyone who had the
technical or conceptual skills to conceive of alternatives to what soon became
the reigning economic ideas. In society (although not in all countries),[2] this
ignorance entailed a popular endorsement of policies of which the average
citizen himself would be the first victim.

The economic ideas which came to guide the transitions did not originate
within. They were the construct and ideology of the international community
and dominating international financial organizations at the time when the
change of institutions was initiated. In a broad international perspective the
set of economic ideas that came to guide the transformation of economic
institutions was an example of an 'economic regime' that reflected an
international power structure and probably also the interests of the core states
that formulate this ideology.[3] From the present perspective it is therefore
obvious that international actors, both more diffuse ideas (the zeitgeist) and
specific actors, have had a decisive impact on the choice of economic models
and on the means to achieve their implementation. When Gertrude Schroeder
(1997, p. 255) writes that 'The West has not attempted to impose on the new
states a particular model for a market economy or to prescribe the path to
achieve it. Each state, dictated by its own initial conditions and political
processes, has chosen its own model and rate of speed', it is an idealized
version. All stabilization programmes in the countries here described (except
Slovenia) have involved IMF financial and technical support. The
conditionality attached to many of the assistance programmes from the
international financial institutions, from the EU and from bilateral donors,
combined with the lack of knowledge about economics and the urgency of
the problems to be solved, have left most of the countries concerned without
much choice in the initial stage of transformation. In other more advanced
countries where domestic teams prepared the economic programmes, they
showed what Frenkel and O'Donnell (1979, p. 19) term 'convergence of
determination', that ideas and policies of external and internal actors con-

verged because of a common intellectual basis and because they all knew what was needed to obtain endorsement and support from the international financial community.

This takes us from economic ideas to agency. Building on Dawisha and Turner (1997), Sikkink (1991), Hall (1989) and Stalling (1992), we must, in order of importance, distinguish between external and internal agency. Concerning external agency we can adapt Dawisha and Turner's (1997, p. 405) classification of external agency for the present purpose.

Table 7.1. External agency and institutional change.

	Coercive	Voluntary	
External agency	Conditionality	Contagion	Consent
State-system level	International financial and political institutions	Diffusion of ideas, norms and models	Membership of international organizations
Sub-state level	Free market agents	Business and academic exchanges	Business and academic exchanges.

Source: Adapted from Dawisha and Turner, 1997: p. 405.

Figure 7.1 illustrates three conduits whereby external agents can influence domestic policy choices on two levels: on the state-system level and on the sub-state level.[4] On the state-system level countries can be compelled to adopt specific policies by the conditionality attached to loans and grants from international financial institutions, in particular the IMF. The limit on budget deficits especially will have obvious consequences for the fiscal policy that a country can realistically pursue. States are, however, also influenced by the diffusion of economic ideas to state officials and advisers and the adoption of foreign countries as models to emulate (contagion). Finally, membership of international organizations (consent) also constrain states in their policy choices. A radical example is here of course the obligation to adopt the acquis communautaire as a precondition for obtaining membership of the European Union. On the sub-state level conditionality occurs when free market agents, for instance multinational cooperation with substantial economic powers, compels states to adopt certain legislation as a precondition for badly needed investments. Contagion on this level of external agency results from exchanges taking place between non-state institutions, and from business and academic exchanges. Consent on this levels is a consequence of sub-state actors entering into obligatory contractual relationships.

The weight of external agency, however, differs between countries and depends on a number of factors, in particular their size, the urgency of problems and (in terms of 2nd order initial conditions) their permeability and mutability. The countries most susceptible to the new set of ideas proved to be those that I in Chapter 4 classified as 'modern societies'. In these countries local elites would have a broad international network that put their ideas on a par with prevailing global economic ideas. If circumstances were right they would be able to realize the new ideas. In such states the administrative capacities of the state to handle the technical intricacies of the new policy would be greater, as would the political support from a citizenry ostensibly well informed about the inevitable wealth of market economies. This pattern is seen in Table 7.2 which illustrates the close correspondence between the modernity index (as described in Chapter 5), aggregate resource flows and in particular foreign direct investment in the 20 countries.

Table 7.2 reveals the following patterns: First, the relatively greatest net resource flows and FDI per capita are directed towards the initially most modern countries, indicating the highest degree of foreign influence (permeability) and, consequently, that mutability and initial modernity are closely related. Second, the relative share of net resource flows and FDI per capita are largest in small and economically weak countries, indicating stronger foreign influence. Third, we find the relatively highest net aggregate resource flows as a per centage of GDP among the 'underdeveloped overachievers' (Mongolia and Kyrgyzstan) and in the smallest overachiever (Estonia), indicating that these countries have been the subject to strong foreign influence. The ratio of FDI to total resource flows, however, indicate that foreign donor influence has been the strongest in Mongolia and Kyrgyzstan, and more moderate in Estonia where FDI make up the largest share of flows. In general, it is this weakness of the link between initial conditions and institutional change in these countries that indicates the importance of external constraints on policy choices. In particular, the pattern shows that smaller countries with weak export sectors (in relation to GDP) have enjoyed a narrower array of policy options than larger ones.[5]

All indicators of external agency strength thus appear to be highly correlated with level of modernization, while obviously the lines of causation are blurred. Does this imply that we may in effect eliminate modernity as an explanation and replace it with the external agency explanation, a common argument? In my opinion it does not. While closely associated, it is important to distinguish analytically between the opportunity structure provided by internal level of modernization and the strength of external agency. While the former offers the opportunity for change, it is the second that drives and guides the process. It is where the two sets of factors are compatible that the changing of economic institutions proceeds the fastest. This happened first of all in the Central European and the Baltic countries, where the compatibility between 1st and 2nd order initial conditions and external agency was so strong that it significantly reduced the effect of domestic politics on economic policy choices for a major part of the 1990s.[6] Paradoxically, in this process it was primarily in the less modern and more distorted – but also less democratic – countries of the former Soviet Union that domestic politics came to have the most direct impact on economic policy making. Where democracy was the most developed it decided little, and where it was less developed it decided more. This has been the obscure political logic of globalization in democratizing post-communist systems.

This takes us to the role of internal agency. External agency will only have an effect on internal policy choices through internal agency. A policy will only become effective if it is advocated by internal actors and eventually becomes anchored in concrete institutions and – in the longer term – obtains a political basis.[7] In the short term, however, we have to look for more complex and ideographically generated patterns in order to identify internal agency. Internal agency is the mirror image of Figure 7.1. The institutions, organizations and individuals who are the objects of external agency become the internal agents of institutional change. This mirror image is reproduced in Table 7.3.

Table 7.2. Indices of external assistance to countries in transition.

Country	Moderni-zation	Net aggregate resource flow 1991–1996 (total per capita USD)	Foreign direct investment 1991–1996 (total per capita USD)	Net aggregate resource flow (share of total in 1996 GNP in per cent)	Foreign direct investment (share of total in 1996 GNP in per cent)	Ratio between total FDI and total net aggregate flow 1991–1996 in per cent
Albania	−1.50	535	87	64.8	10.5	16.3
Belarus	−0.07	198	8	9.3	0.4	4.0
Bulgaria	−0.07	264	56	23.9	5.1	21.4
Czech Rep.	1.06	1646	704	31.2	13.4	42.8
Estonia	1.01	1033	686	33.7	22.4	66.4
Hungary	1.35	1985	1267	46.7	29.8	63.9
Kazakhstan	−0.51	230	72	18.5	5.8	31.2
Kyrgyzstan	−1.10	230	50	62.2	13.5	21.7
Latvia	0.90	621	383	29.5	18.2	61.6
Lithuania	0.87	405	89	19.0	4.2	22.1
Moldova	−0.51	177	31	44.5	7.7	17.2
Mongolia	−0.93	280	12	75.8	3.1	4.1
Poland	0.18	691	329	19.9	9.5	47.6
Romania	−0.41	388	55	24.7	3.5	14.2
Russia	0.81	259	35	8.8	1.2	13.5
Slovakia	0.33	667	161	19.0	4.6	24.1
Slovenia	0.86	1719	447	18.1	4.7	26.0
Turkmenistan	−0.99	199	25	19.6	2.5	12.6
Ukraine	−0.10	90	18	10.3	2.0	19.7
Uzbekistan	−1.18	105	16	10.4	1.5	14.8
Correlation with modern-ization (Pearson's R)		0.68**	0.69**	− 0.33	0.45*	0.65**

Source: *Calculated from data in the World Bank,* Global Development Finance *(Washington, D.C. World Bank, 1998).*

*Note: *Significance at the 0.05 level; ** significance at the 0.01 level.*

Internal agency is concentrated in the formal state organizations that provide the legal basis for adopting and implementing policies. Where state organizations in the initial phase of transformation are relatively autonomous, the policies and capacities of state institutions will often be dependent on available experts or groups of policy experts, what Williamson calls 'technopols' or 'change teams' (Williamson and Haggard, 1994). It is these experts or groups of experts that will be the agents of internal change. Expert advisers will, however, only obtain political significance to the extent they have the support of political leaders. Expert advisers and political leadership are complementary categories, both of which are needed if ideas are to be turned into polices. Contagion of economic ideas may also turn NGOs, in particular universities and think tanks, into policy makers, as lobbyists, as politicians or as members of change teams. They may in particular become forceful internal actors if they are associated with international organizations with expertise and economic resources.

Table 7.3. Internal agency and institutional change.

Internal agency	Voluntary	Coercive	
	Contagion	Consent	Conditionality
State institutions	Change teams and technopols promoting policies	Implementation of international law and obligations	Implementation of policies adopted under external conditionality.
Non-state institutions and organizations	NGOs promoting specific policies	NGOs promoting specific policies	
Individuals	Experts, political leadership		

Finally, in emerging democracies where institutions and parties are weak, individuals gain greater importance as 'carriers' and 'interpreters' of new ideas. As summarized by Sikkink in her study of developmentalism in Latin America, 'individuals take on a symbolic role. They come to stand for the ideas themselves, and thus the interpretation of the idea is intertwined with the success and interpretation of the individuals and their political life' (Sikkink, 1991, p. 254). This applies both to skilful technocrats and strong politicians who provide the political clout behind the adoption of new policies. The relative autonomy of leadership may nevertheless have the opposite effect and open for the influence of idiosyncratic and conservative leaders that may gain decisive influence on the formation and implementation of policies. In both cases, the good and the bad, we must necessarily turn to 'individualistic' historical explanations if we are to understand the political basis of specific policies.

Internal agency does not operate in a societal vacuum. It exists in a concrete historical and institutional setting, constraining or reinforcing policy choices. In previous chapters I demonstrated a close causal link between 1st order initial conditions and institutional change. It has further been demonstrated that where these institutional constraints were transcended, it was in most cases due to a forceful popular democratic mobilization that allowed external and internal agency to set a path for the eventual change of institutions. These observations do not, however, explain why these popular anti-system mobilizations only occurred in some countries, rendering them permeable to new economic ideas and eventually gave impetus to change. And they do not explain why countries without such mobilization developed differently. Hence we cannot escape an analysis of the more murky (and certainly not quantifiable) sources of why some societies were more permeable to new ideas and eventually more mutable. Understanding the interface between internal and external agency and the nature of 2nd order initial conditions will take us the last part of the way to completing our study of the sources of institutional change in emerging democracies.

Through a focused comparison of the reform history of what became the significant outliers in our study – positive and negative – we will try to understand why they deviate from the general pattern identified by constraints and opportunities set by the initial conditions. Focusing on the relative role of external and internal agency, we will first compare the reform histories of those who became more successful than predicted: Kyrgyzstan, Estonia, Poland and Mongolia, followed by a comparison of the two major underachievers: Belarus and Turkmenistan.

THE OVERACHIEVERS: POLAND, ESTONIA, KYRGYZSTAN AND MONGOLIA

The four countries that performed better than one would have predicted based on their 1st order initial conditions are very different: Poland first entered the socialist path of development when she was occupied by the Soviet Union at the end of World War Two, and has since maintained a strong record of dissent and opposition but also a relatively high level of interaction with the West and openness to intellectual exchange. Also Estonia had the socialist system imposed upon it after World War Two but, in contrast to Poland, it became fully integrated into the Soviet economic and political circuit and was repeatedly exposed to a harsh repression that destroyed all opposition. For many years Estonia was also effectively cut off from intellectual contact with the West, although its linguistic and cultural bonds to Finland made it relatively more permeable than other former Soviet Republics. Kyrgyzstan, at that time an underdeveloped tribal society, was absorbed by the young Soviet state in 1924 and transformed into a formal Union Republic in 1936. Also Kyrgyzstan was effectively cut off from intellectual influence from the outside world. Last but not least, Mongolia represents an even more deviating case. A less developed country, it was caught between Russia and China for centuries. After the Russian supported socialist revolution in 1921 she was closely integrated in the Soviet Union and the other communist countries, politically and economically, through membership of CMEA. Yet, despite this diversity of origins and different initial conditions at independence, the four countries were all able to transcend the structural constraints of Soviet socialism. Why?

POLAND AND ESTONIA: CONTAGION AND 'CONVERGENCE OF DETERMINATION'

When *Poland* launched comprehensive economic reforms on 1 January 1990, it was the first example of a communist country attempting a radical change of economic institutions aimed at the establishment of a market economy.[8] The 'Balcerowics-programme', named after the deputy prime minister and minister of finance from 1989 to 1991 and major author of the programme, contained all the basic elements of the Washington consensus: an orthodox stabilization and liberalization of external and internal markets, a design for the institutions needed to promote and support a private sector and the eventual privatization of large state owned enterprises.[9]

While Poland shared the basic characteristics of a traditional socialist economy, history and previous attempts at reforms had left her with a somewhat different legacy. On the positive side it had a higher share of market regulation only paralleled by Hungary, agriculture was dominated by private (but inefficient) owners, a relatively large share of the population had rudimentary experience with the workings of a market economy through their involvement in the second economy, political development since the late 1960s had made intellectual and private exchanges with the West much more intense than was the case in other communist countries, some pre-war legal institutions were still in place and reform attempts during the 1980s had created marginally better management and human capital in the state owned enterprises. On the negative side, the country had compiled a huge foreign dept, the origin of which ranged back to the failed policies of Edward Gierek in the 1970s. A very strong and organized work force had been able to gain concessions from a weak government that had generated a huge monetary overhang and huge budget deficits, with an ensuing threat of hyperinflation. Despite these initial problems, and in particular the opposition that could be anticipated from workers and peasants, the Polish government was able to implement the basic features of the programme (except large scale privatization), before the parliamentary elections in September 1993 were won by moderately anti-reform parties who slowed down the pace of reform by halting large scale privatization and by reintroducing protection and subsidies in some fields to accommodate their worker and peasant constituencies. By

1997 Poland was still at the frontier of economic reconstruction, as seen from Figure 7.1 which illustrates the achievements as measured by the EBRD annual report.

As shown in Figure 7.1, three areas lag behind the general level of institutional development. One is restructuring of large scale industry where insider control has impeded privatization. Another area is competition and price policy where pressures from labour and management in the state sector and from peasant organizations has forced the government to maintain various subsidies and reintroduce protection in sensitive fields. Third, financial sector development remains a problem, as it does in other transition economies.

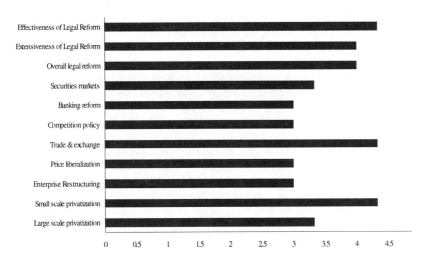

Source: EBRD Transition Report, 1998.

Figure 7.1. Change of economic institutions in Poland, 1997.

But the social costs have been high. Inflation spiralled in 1990 and continued at a relatively high level. The country experienced a radical drop in GDP, officially registered at 18 per cent,[10] but in reality somewhat lower with increased poverty from 1989 to 1994 from 6 to 20 per cent and in income inequality from a GINI-coefficient of 26 to 31. As in other countries the farmers and workers in the large state-owned enterprises have been the most exposed to critical declines in income and standards of living. The political effect of these costs generated the outcome of the September 1993 elections which produced the left–peasant government that can partly be seen as a rejection of the previous radical liberalization and pace of reforms. Apart from signalling a rejection of Walesa's personal style, Kwasniewski's victory in the 1995 presidential election was a result of his commitment to greater emphasis on welfare policies, in conjunction with his secularism, in a country where the secular–fundamentalist cleavage has remained salient.

Hence despite the organizational strength and political experience of organized labour, managers of state enterprises and peasants organizations, Poland was able to stay at the forefront of economic transformation. Part of the answer is to be found in the pattern observed in the previous chapter. The strong anti-system mobilization that preceded the drafting of economic reforms swept Solidarity into government after the voters had effectively rejected the negotiated transition which implied that the Polish United Workers Party (PUWP) would retain control of the Upper House, The Senate. It was the political victory and the ensuing political liberalization, preconditioned and reinforced by the ancient Polish tradition of opposition to foreign dominance and the whole history of dissent and rebellion against a system that was perceived as unjust and unfair that made Polish society mutable and led people to expect and accept radical initiatives. A readiness to tolerate hardship and a generally high level of support for the market in spite of economic decline, social costs and government changes is expressed in the continued high level of support for a continuance of reforms, as seen in Figure 7.2.

This initial high (structural) support became the basis of what Balcerowicz came to term 'the period of extraordinary politics', a time when there was a stronger than normal tendency to think and act in terms of the common good, where vested interests of the past were afraid to pursue their narrow interests and experts or groups of experts achieved an extraordinary influence. In the first stage of reforms this meant that the communist (and agrarian) parties in parliament were afraid to oppose reform legislation and supported it in order to gain legitimacy in the eyes of the population. It also meant that the old links between the major enterprises and the ministries were weakened as new ministers took over, and that the man in the street would support any initiative that he perceived as signalling a radical break with the past, as evidenced in the strong support for market reforms and the initial detachment of personal economic interests from the question of support. This phase lasted at least until the Biliecki government was defeated at the polls in December 1991 and Balcerowicz resigned as prime minister. It was the existence of this period that generated the opportunity for change in Poland. However, the fact that these opportunities, which were based on long historical trajectories (2nd order initial conditions) and recent political events, were exploited to launch reforms that proved both economically, administratively and (to a certain point) politically viable, was largely a matter of chance, of the history and actions of certain individuals and groups of individuals. But what distinguishes the Polish case is that, in spite of the economic and social costs, the demands from specific interest groups and change of governments that reflected these political currents, the general popular endorsement of the change of economic institutions remained high. From 1994 it even increased, as the approaching EU accession promised a type of democratic capitalism more in line with Polish values and tastes than the Anglo-Saxon model initially propagated by economic liberals.

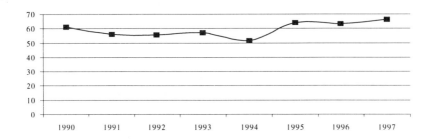

Source: EastEurobarometer. Successive years.

Figure 7.2. Support for economic reforms in Poland 1991–1997 (per cent support).

The 'Balcerowicz team', as it came to be known in the ministry of finance during the reform period, dated back to 1978, when Lescek Balcerowicz formed a group of 10 young economists to work on economic reform in Poland. The group continued to meet when martial law was imposed in December 1981. Partly because of the publicity surrounding the group until martial law was imposed and their continued activities during the 1980s, Balcerowicz was offered the job as minister of finance and deputy prime minister in Macowiecki's government. It was further accepted that Balcerowicz was free to chose his own team, which he brought into the ministry of finance. It was this closely knit team, bound together by 'the shared background, communality of purpose, similar age (around 40) and the common pressures created' (Balcerowicz, 1993, p. 170), that designed and carried the reforms through the political system. While foreign experts, the most well known being David Lipton and Jeffrey Sachs, did participate in the work that led up to the reforms; there is, however, no indication that they played a decisive role. Mostly they offered technical advice in the design of a policy which had already been decided upon, they played a certain role in gaining public support and they lent an air of internal and external credibility to the programme. Basically, however, the policy was homegrown and the new ideas were implanted into the Polish environment by a Polish economist who had had the chance to travel and learn abroad and to study foreign experience, rather than by foreign experts carrying the ideas into virgin territory. In this perspective the launching of reforms in Poland also came to reflect the traditional duality of Polish society, where an educated, modern – but also often insulated – elite would act unconstrained by the other Poland, the underdeveloped Poland concentrated in the rural areas of the southern and eastern parts of the country. While the 'Balcerowicz team' seems to have had quite a lot of leeway to form the economic programme according to their ideas and visions, it also, of course, depended on the support of the political leadership. Here the strong support that Balcerowicz and his team obtained from prime ministers Mazowiecki and in particular Biliecki became crucial. Especially Biliecki's support was decisive in the face of mounting protests during 1991. The strong political support was possible partly because of the allegedly non-partisan nature of the expert team, partly because of the great respect that surrounded Balcerowicz in both Poland and the West.

The three years of intensive reforms had institutionalized the idea of reform, destroyed the remnants of the old planning system and produced a path dependency that carried the reform process forward although the reformers themselves had left. First, a lot of policies were in practice impossible to turn back for economic and political reasons, for example small scale privatization, the rapidly growing private sector and the economic opening to the West, including the convertibility of the zloty. Secondly, Balcerowicz had at an early stage recognized that he had to concentrate on administration and oversight of the reform process in concrete institutions, because of political opposition and the technical ineptitude in the incumbent state administration. He chose to create new administrative units within the ministry of finance, in the ministry of privatization and in the deputy prime minister's office to oversee the implementation of the reform programme. The high standard of professionalism in these institutions became an important legacy that made it yet more difficult to return to economically non-viable policies, even when the political tide turned in 1991 and 1993.

Estonia was the first among the former Soviet republics to launch a comprehensive economic reform package, beginning with the introduction of a national currency in June 1992, less than a year after regaining independence from the Soviet Union.[11] Having been absorbed and integrated into the Soviet economic, political and economic system, Estonia shared a common legacy with the other Soviet republics. At independence from the USSR, the legacy of the Soviet system in the Estonian economy and society could be measured not only in terms of the systemic impact on organization, management, mentality and lack of efficiency. An equally disastrous legacy was an economic structure narrowly adapted to the Soviet system which did not reflect the comparative advantages of the Estonian state in the type of open market economy that it was now striving for. Like the other Baltic states Estonia had come to depend on raw materials and energy mainly from Russia, and they produced all the wrong goods. After independence, many of the former Soviet republics – and especially Russia – could buy many goods that they had once received from the Baltic states at a lower price and/or of better quality elsewhere. The Western markets and especially the EU-countries were closed to Baltic agricultural and industrial products. Their quality and design made them unsaleable in the West. It was from that perspective that Senik-Legoyne and Hughes (1992) calculated that the Baltic states had one of the highest shares of industries with a negative value added among the states of the former Soviet Union. Since ordinary export outlets for processed food products in the former Soviet Union were so chaotic that normal trade was becoming increasingly difficult, all three Baltic states found themselves in an almost hopeless economic situation. This situation was further aggravated by their close integration in the Soviet economy, where for example the USSR's share of Estonia's imports was about 85 per cent in 1985 and about 95 per cent of exports (Lainela and Sutela, 1997, p. 17).

Within this framework of the Soviet systemic economic legacy, there nevertheless were important differences between the former Soviet Republics, reflecting somewhat different initial conditions at independence. In this context, the most important feature was the relatively small share of heavy industries located in Estonia compared for example to the other two Baltic countries. Hence whereas heavy industry accounted for only 17 per cent of total industrial output in Estonia (Hansen and Sorsa, 1994, p. 27), the corresponding figure for the other countries was approximately 30 per cent (Sorsa, 1994a, p. 144; Sorsa, 1994b, p. 166). The same pattern was reflected in the relative weight of the huge, virtually monopolistic, Moscow-controlled all-union enterprises in each republic. In Estonia only 40 out of a total of 300 enterprises were of this type, while in Latvia and Lithuania they reached approximately respectively 140 out of 400 and 250 out of 600 industrial enterprises (Sorsa, 1994a, p. 144). Taking into account that it is generally easier for labour- and resource-intensive industries to adjust than for industries demanding large inputs of capital and energy, Estonia was in a relatively privileged position. Furthermore, Estonia had an obvious advantage because of its oil shale industry, which at that time produced enough electricity to meet half the country's needs, and its well developed transport infrastructure (the latter also true of Latvia). Both of these resources (energy and ports) proved to be important when the deteriorating terms of trade posed problems for the Baltic states after independence.

Hence from two perspectives Estonia was at independence in a relatively privileged position. From an economic perspective the relative costs and ensuing social consequences of the economic reforms could be expected to be less severe than in the two other countries. This starting point, however, also had a political aspect that made it comparatively easier for Estonia to adopt and implement sound policies. Yet even considering these fortuitous initial conditions Estonia has performed better than predicted, and by 1997 ranged among the most successful reformers, on a level with the most advanced countries in Central Europe. Estonia's development of economic institutions by 1997 is described in Figure 7.3.

As shown in Figure 7.3 Estonia is, despite its background as a Soviet republic, on a level with the most advanced reforms in Central Europe, reflecting that Estonia has steered a course very close to the recommendations in the Washington consensus. Price liberalization was initiated already in 1991 and by 1994 only a few public services remained under administrative control (Lindpere, 1994, p. 133). At the same time the most liberal foreign trade regime in the world was implemented, and from 1993 all goods could be imported and exported without tariffs. Also private sector development has

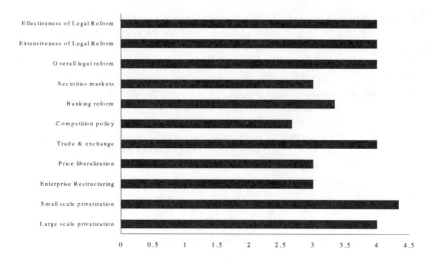

Source: EBRD Transition Report, 1998.

Figure 7.3. Change of economic institutions in Estonia, 1997.

proceeded rapidly, with the first legal initiatives ranging back to before independence. Small scale privatization proceeded rapidly, while the privatization
of the large state owned enterprises was initiated relatively late but then went
on rapidly. Only privatization in agriculture has so far proceeded slowly
because of legal conflict arising from strong emphasis on restitution to pre-
war owners. The fast-track reforms in a relatively distorted post-soviet
economy have, however, carried huge social costs. While inflation has been
kept down by a stringent monetary policy (implemented through the currency
board arrangement), growth resumed relatively early but was associated with
a great increase in poverty and inequality. Between 1987/88 and 1994 inequality increased by 17 Gini points and poverty from 1 to 33 per cent of the
population. Still the course and direction of reforms was maintained and only
marginally slowed down after the liberal Mart Laar government was defeated
at the polls in the elections of 1995 and replaced by the more moderate and
leftist government of Tiit Vähi.

How did Estonia manage to proceed with institutional reforms in the face
of the economic costs, opposition from an industry which feared being cut off
from the Russian market and the virtual destruction of agriculture when
Estonian farmers were singled out as the only farmers in the world able to
survive without subsidies or protection? One answer is the depth of the
period of extraordinary politics caused by the dual process of system transition and national reconstruction, and involving emotional orientation towards the West and Western institutions, in particular NATO and the EU. In

this phase the population maintained a remarkably high level of support for reforms despite mounting economic and social costs, as seen in Figure 7.4.

The introduction of the Kroon was perceived as a national symbol, and at the time people were willing to make sacrifices to help rebuild the national economy. The suspension of normal politics in Estonia also lasted quite a long time because of continued mobilization around first the withdrawal of Soviet troops and later the citizen issue and recurrent conflicts with Russia. It was this comprehensive and long lasting popular mobilization ignited by the national reconstruction that provided the political basis for the radical economic reform strategy. Institutionally the policy became anchored in a strong parliamentary system, in a situation where many of the previous economic elites and most socially exposed groups were deprived of citizenship and hence political influence under the new institutional set up.

The long and deep phase of extraordinary politics also made it possible for the first government, which was elected in 1992 on a wave of nationalistic fervour, to launch radical reforms in the state administration and replace the senior civil servants in Central ministries. The final outcome was one of the youngest administrations since the Bolshevik revolution in the early 1930s replaced the entire state apparatus in the newly established Soviet state. It was this institutional renewal and the entrenched position of reformers in particular institutions (especially the new Central Bank) that made the reforms administratively viable. These new and/or revitalized institutions then became the platforms from which the young Estonian technocrats in conjunction with foreign experts (some of whom came from the Estonian diaspora) designed and implemented the reform strategy. Also in the Estonian case, however, it appears that the reform strategy was basically home grown. Estonian economists were among the best in the former Soviet Union, although far from the level of their Polish counterparts. They nevertheless also reflected the 'market naivety' that characterized the majority of the broad

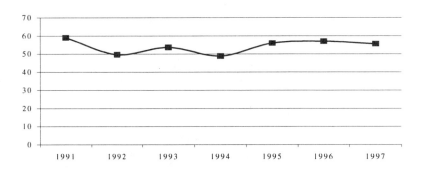

Source: EastEurobarometer. Successive years.

Figure 7.4. Support for reforms in Estonia 1991–1997 (per cent support).

population in the early 1990s. Already in 1987 the economists had begun to draw up plans for an independent Estonian economy. Hence also in Estonia it is more correct to speak of 'convergence of determination' rather than conditionality. It has in fact been reported that local authorities at times adopted more radical policies than recommended by international financial institutions. This happened, for example, when the Estonian government in mid-1992 launched its own currency, the Estonian Kroon, against the advice of IMF experts.[12] Also bilateral cooperation (assistance and training programmes) and massive sub-state diffusion of actors and ideas, in particular from the neighbouring Nordic countries and later on from the European Community, were important factors in the contagion of ideas into the previously isolated country.

Also in the Estonian case personal and accidental factors must be taken into account. The early preparation of national programmes by a small group of competent economists is one important factor. Another is the dedication of a few individuals to force through difficult reforms. Two of them were Rein Ottasson and Siim Kallas, the two first directors of the Central Bank. Finally, what Hansson (1994, p. 136), calls the 'accident of history' was important during the implementation of the economic reform strategy. With special reference to Estonia, Hansson calls attention to the rapid construction of connections to the West, the introduction of a currency board system and the choice of an undervalued fixed exchange rate as decisions made by narrow groups of individuals that had a decisive impact on subsequent developments. Similarly, the attempt by prime minister Edgar Savisaar to introduce an 'economic state of emergency' in the spring of 1992 was prevented by a very narrow margin. Had the state of emergency been instituted, it would have reintroduced strong state control over the economy and could thus have initiated a totally different path of development. Finally, the support of the top political leadership, in particular prime minister Mart Laar and president Lennart Meri, was of crucial importance.

When explaining Estonian performance and the mutability of Estonian society a set of 2nd order initial conditions must be considered. First, Estonia had a surviving (albeit obviously imperfect) collective memory of a previous market economy which made the social consequences of the market more acceptable because it was anticipated by the population. Second, exposure to Finnish TV (and Finnish tourists) and the limited economic experiments in the final years of the Soviet era had made the Estonian people somewhat more aware of and prepared for what the market would bring than was the case in other parts of the former Soviet Union. Third, and perhaps most important, the large influx of Russian emigrants into the industrial centres of Estonia had provoked strong national sentiments among titular Estonians, and this nationalism served to rally the independence movement and made the Estonian population ready to endure almost any hardship in the name of national independence.

In sum, Poland and Estonia were able to transcend the structural constraints of socialism for five reasons. First, 2nd order initial conditions associated with strong nationalism and opposition to foreign rule created a phase of extraordinary politics ('opportunity space') that was relatively longer and deeper than in comparable countries. Second, both countries retained a collective memory of a different social and economic system and were thus relatively mutable. Third, compared to the other countries examined in this book, both countries had to a larger extent been exposed to Western economic thinking, and the contagion of ideas at the sub-state level had also been relatively extensive.[13] Fourth, in both countries individuals and groups of individuals, 'change teams' or 'technopols', had been formed before reforms became politically possible. It was these teams that, with political backing, were able to launch and implement a critical mass of reforms, in effect making the reforms irreversible. Finally, at a later stage when the progress achieved meant that both countries had become first echelon applicants for EU-membership, the visions and conditionalities attached to membership became the driving force in the further reconstruction of market institutions that were now moulded to fit the West European model.

Kyrgyzstan and Mongolia: Leadership, conditionality and weak states.

Kyrgyzstan has been described as an island of democracy and economic progress in a Central Asian region where the successors to the former Soviet Republics have been plagued by slow economic reforms and authoritarian leadership.[14] While this image has been somewhat blurred by developments in the late 1990s, where especially increased presidential powers and the repression of the press has damaged the democratic image, Kyrgyzstan remains the most successful economic and political reformer among the five Central Asian republics. But it remains an open question why Kyrgyzstan, alone among the five Central Asian post-Soviet republics, was first to launch and to a major extent also implement simultaneous and comprehensive economic and democratic reforms.

At independence Kyrgyzstan had many features in common with the other Central Asian republics. There was no previous experience of independent statehood prior to it being absorbed into the young Soviet Union in the 1920s and elevated to the status of Union Republic in 1936. Nor did the society, which was dominated by traditional structures of clan and family ties, have a shared national identity. However, during the years of Soviet rule the artefacts of statehood did create an incipient nation state, although traditional ties continued to penetrate the formal state and party structures of the Soviet system. Economically the Kyrgyz republic was, as were the other Central Asian republics, by most indicators less developed and closely integrated into the Soviet economic circuit. The economy was basically agrarian, with more than 60 per cent of the economically active population working in agriculture, in particular traditional pastoral agriculture. Like the other less developed republics the country was also heavily subsidized by Moscow. These characteristics produced the extremely severe shocks that followed independence in August 1991, a stabilization programme in 1992 and the introduction of its own currency in May 1993. These were features that Kyrgyzstan shared with the other Central Asian states and yet it managed to change its economic institutions while sustaining an incipient democracy.

The causes of this relative success may be sought in four factors: history, geography, leadership and external agency. As summarized by Schmitt (1997), the nomadic egalitarian traditions of Kyrgyzstan have distilled the democratic rather than the theocratic (and hierarchical) aspect of Islam. Secondly, topography has effectively isolated the country from developments in Russia and the other Central Asian republics. The long border with China and the large Kyrgyz minority in the neighbouring Xinjiang province has influenced the economic reform strategy, and president Askar Akayev has copied much of Deng Xiaoping's agricultural privatization model. Third, the personal charisma and power of Askar Akayev, as a person who is able to bridge the North and South of the country, and hence ethnic conflicts, was also an important factor behind the reforms.

The process of change in Kyrgyzstan was initiated in October 1990 when the incumbent party leader Absamat Massalijev attempted to be elected president by parliament in accordance with the new Soviet constitution. He was rejected, partly due to his conservatism (he had remained opposed to the perestroika-process) and partly because of his handling of ethnic conflicts, and instead parliament chose the President of the Kyrgyz Academy of Sciences Askar Akayev as a compromise (and ostensibly controllable) candidate. This was done by a Soviet type parliament composed of party functionaries, regional bosses and factory managers. Akayev had no previous political experience and Kyrgyzstan was the first Central Asian republic where the president prior to the collapse of the USSR was not the head of the republican communist party. He immediately became the focal point of reform minded officials within the state and party administration and among intellectuals and nationalists. Akayev himself proved a much more determined reformer than anticipated by those who had elected him. However, the party organization remained a strong actor and for the next 11 months Kyrgyzstan had a dual power structure, the reformist administration of Askar Akayev opposed by the conservatives in the state and party administration.

This situation was radically changed when the attempted coup d'état in Moscow took place on 9 August 1991. Akayev here stood up as a firm supporter of President Gorbachev's reform course, while the communist leadership allied themselves with the insurgents and even attempted their own local 'mini-coup'. When the attempted coup had failed Akayev used the opportunity to thwart his political opponents and at the end of August the Communist party was banned. With the political opponents out of the way and independence declared, Akayev and his advisers had a free hand to proceed with economic and political reforms. Akayev's political basis was further strengthened when in October 1991 he won the presidential election with 95 per cent of the vote. Hence, whereas the failed coup d'état incited independence in other Soviet republics, in Kyrgyzstan it was used to power economic and political reforms. The reforms, however, very much remained an elitist affair, provoked initially by cleavages in the top political leadership and with negligible popular mobilization, although Kyrgyz social and political organizations proliferated much more than in the neighbouring republics. Using the prerogatives of the presidency, this popular passivity also permitted Akayev to proceed with an economic reform programme, very much in line with the Washington consensus. His ambition was by fast and comprehensive political and economic reforms to make the country attractive to foreign investors and international donor institutions. He was able to proceed with a voucher based privatization programme which had been prepared even before independence, and in mid 1992 he launched a stabilization programme, followed by the introduction of a national currency, the Som, in mid 1993. The economic reforms, the disruption of trade with the former Soviet republics and the termination of budget subsidies from Moscow, however, had dramatic economic consequences, with inflation remaining high, a decline in GDP surpassed only by Ukraine and the greatest increase in poverty of all transitionary economies, from 12 per cent of the population in 1987/88 to an extraordinary 76 per cent in 1993/94. The economic problems were further exacerbated when national sentiments provoked the exodus to Russia and Israel of a large number of Russians and Russian-speaking specialists and technicians that were sorely needed in the economy.

The economic reforms were implemented with substantial support and advice from foreign sources, which constitutes the fourth factor behind the Kyrgyz uniqueness. During a trip to the United States in 1992 Akayev made a very good case for his country, and was able to attract substantial financial support from international institutions and from bilateral, especially American, sources. The support of course also reflected that he abided closely by the advice provided by these international agencies, partly because of the desperate need for financial support, but also because of the absence of national expertise able to design the required policies. The heavy foreign presence also constrained the political choices of the political leadership and in particular halted the ever present inclination towards authoritarian solutions.

In 1997 the change of Kyrgyz economic institutions was still ahead of the other Central Asian republics and the former Soviet republics, only surpassed by Russia and the Baltic republics, as seen from Figure 7.5.

The figure reveals four remaining problem areas. First, the restructuring of enterprises is lagging behind because of insider control, lack of financial control, inter-firm arrears and ineffective implementation of bankruptcy legislation. Second, insufficient control with remaining monopolies and ensuing lack of competition. Third, financial markets are still underdeveloped. Fourth, problems with legal reforms reflecting the lack of specialization in

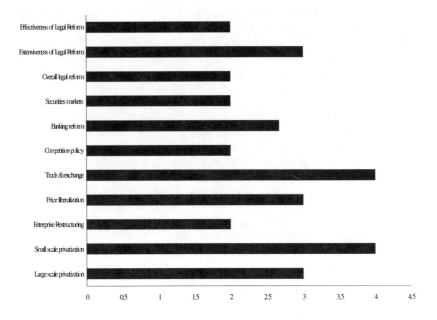

Source: EBRD Transition Report, 1998.

Figure 7.5. Change of economic institutions in Kyrgyzstan, 1997.

the legal system and insufficient transparency. Hence the basic problem remains institution-building, corporate governance and the creation of a legal framework for the market. All these items reflect the generally low level of effectiveness and capacity of the state administration.

This pattern also reflects that economic reform process proceeded without the benefit of a solid political and administrative basis. A 1993 survey showed that only 36.3 per cent of the population found the market economy 'much better' or 'better' than the planned economy, 27.7 per cent having the opposite opinion and 35.7 per cent that could not see any difference or had no opinion at all.[15] Nor were the reforms able to generate support among the economic and political elites outside the very narrow groups of presidential advisers and a small intellectual elite. The nationalistic groups, that had originally supported Akayev, also abandoned him when he tried to halt the Russian exodus by offering them special educational privileges. The party system remains weakly developed and unable to link civil society to the political sphere, which instead is penetrated by traditional structures where clan, kinship, patronage networks and family structures merge with nomenclatura networks. The traditional elites in the state administration and the managers of large enterprises therefore realigned to mount a counterattack at the parliamentary election in 1995. According to reports these elections were marred by serious irregularities (far from all favouring the president), and returned a parliament of bureaucrats and managers critical of the economic reforms. The outcome of the elections made Akayev increasingly wary about the problems of combining parliamentary democracy with economic change. His response was to call early presidential elections in December 1995 and by a popular referendum in early 1996 extend his powers substantially vis-à-vis parliament, granting him the right to appoint all top officials including the prime minister. Akayev also returned to an authoritarian style of government in other fields in order to curb the mounting opposition to his reforms. In particular, this new style of government became evident in the field of press freedom. Several opposition papers were closed and journalists sentenced for allegedly offending the president. The president also made an implicit alliance with regional administrative leaders (appointed by himself) to circumvent parliament. His argument was that the new parliament elected in 1995 was the outcome of manipulation by conservative and traditional elites who wanted to use their political powers for personal gain. That he was not completely off the point here was documented by the fact that 30 per cent of the deputies in parliament were under investigation by the state prosecutor's office for illegal financial dealings. Hence the 1995 elections finally demonstrated how traditional politics 'penetrated and distorted nominally democratic procedures' (Huskey, 1997, p. 259), and represented the 'criminalisation and regionalisation of politics in Kyrgizstan' (ibid, p. 265).

The Kyrgyzstan case is thus an example of institutional change by a leadership and external agency that, although increasingly insulated from society, was initially able to transcend the structural limits of socialism, but where reforms proceed without permeating society. It is also, however, an example of reforms that never became politically nor administratively viable, and the social costs also make their economic viability questionable. The fast and relatively comprehensive reform of economic institutions in Kyrgyzstan is also an example, replicated in many other former Soviet republics, of the corruption and fraud that easily results when formal institutions are imposed on a society where pre-modern bonds and dependencies (merged with elite networks of the incumbent Soviet system) continue to permeate formal economic and democratic institutions. In this perspective the seeming mutability of society is artificial because the formal (modern) institutions are colonized by the informal (traditional) institutions of pre-modern and post-communist societies. The return to a more authoritarian style with a strong executive (whether deemed benevolent or not) by a modern and Westernized leadership determined to proceed with reforms is one solution to this dilemma between reform of economic institutions and consolidation of an emerging democracy.

Mongolia[16] represents the perhaps most surprising positive overachiever. Being a small underdeveloped but extremely dependent economy, the expectation would be that this country would have to face the most difficult social and political obstacles when attempting to establish a market economy. But Mongolia has managed to go further towards the introduction of market economy institutions (and democracy) than any of the less developed previous Soviet Central Asian republics. In this perspective Mongolia, as commemorated by Fish (1998b, p. 139), 'represents the victory of voluntarism over determinism [...] the triumph of choice, will, leadership, agency, and contingency over structure, history, culture and geography'. Here the answer is hence to be found in a combination of history, initial conditions after the socialist era and leadership.

After the war of liberation in 1921 the Mongolian People's Republic was founded in 1924. Given the disunity of the Mongols and the lack of skilled domestic opposition, Mongolia very soon became deeply integrated into the Soviet political and economic system, first through the collectivization of agriculture and investments in the mineral industry and, second, via assimilation by means of prohibition of religion (and a purge of the large group of lamas), native script and compulsory education. In the course of time the Soviet influence produced a modernized infrastructure which made it possible to export national pastoral products and import the Soviet way of living. By the time shortly before independence in 1990, Mongolia had achieved a comparatively high level in terms of human development. The literacy rate was around 96 per cent and Mongolia also scored very high on other indicators of social modernization, for instance education and infant mortality rate, compared to other countries in the region. At independence, however, the disruption of links to the Soviet Union and the CMEA threw the Mongolian economy into total disarray. The subsidies from the Soviet Union which had amounted to about 30 per cent of the annual GDP ceased, and the external advisers from Russia and Central Europe, who practically managed the Mongolian economy for many years, left the country. In the late 1980s this group comprised about 50,000 workers and non-military specialists, making up 7.7 per cent of the workforce (Boone, 1994, p. 334). From 1991 Soviet aid was partly replaced by assistance from bilateral and multilateral donors. They also contributed experts who, although on a more modest scale, came to replace the Soviet advisers and transmitted new economic and political ideas into the local context.[17] In addition to the problems caused by the termination of Soviet aid and expertise, Mongolia was also subject to the dramatic effects of the collapsed CMEA trade, which in 1990 made up 90 per cent of all trade. Finally, the administrative capacities of the Mongolian state were very weak compared to other post-communist systems. In particular three factors made it possible for Mongolia to reform its economic structures and concurrently democratize its political system: leadership and especially the way the communist party (The Mongolian People's Revolutionary Party – MPRP) succeeded in reforming itself prior to independence, the role played by both external and internal actors in replacing the Russian financial assistance with aid and assistance from the world community and, finally, the weakness of the Mongolian state.

Inspired by events in the Soviet Union the Mongolian government, where a new generation of leaders had taken over after the death of Y. Tsedebal in

1984,[18] in 1988 officially criticized the former leadership and the repression of the past. This official recognition of past mistakes triggered a widespread discontent with the existing society among the populace, followed by student-led pro-democracy demonstrations in late 1989 (Rossabi, 1997, p. 5). In May 1990 this caused the government to amend the constitution, thus ending 70 years of one-party rule. Early elections were scheduled to be held in July 1990, making it difficult for the newly established opposition to organize. The MPRP won a clear majority in both the upper and lower houses, gaining much more than its share of the vote due to the first-past-the-post electoral law. In the election process the party had successfully detached itself from the old image of repression (Bruun and Odgaard (eds.), 1996, p. 29). That image was further reinforced when a coalition governmnent was formed which included 4 members from the opposition parties. The new government initiated a radical economic reform programme, the only country in the post-communist world where the post-communist party won the first elections and initiated a sweeping privatization programme. However, the government was internally divided, making the reform process erratic and more dependent on internal power constellations than on long range visions and strategies. As emphasized by Boone (1994), the lack of a clear direction of reform was also caused by the lack of a clear role model that, as in the case of the Central European countries, could anchor the end points of reforms. The difference between the MPRP and post-Soviet states where communist parties won the first election was that the MPRP did not entirely embark on the consolidation of power through patronage and legal changes in favour of the incumbent elite and, perhaps most important, there was no repression or illegal exclusion of opposition forces.

Having the absolute majority in the parliament also made it easier for the newly elected prime minister Dashiyn Byambasüren to grant concessions and administrative posts to the opposition. The economic reform programme that immediately followed the elections was in fact prepared by a group of young economists from the new National Progress Party headed by deputy prime minister Davaadorjiyn Ganbold (Korsun and Murrel, 1995, p. 1), supported by substantive (although inconclusive) advice and influence from foreign experts and international financial institutions. The economic reform pro-gramme had liberalization and privatization as its primary objectives. While stabilization and liberalization lagged behind, a comprehensive and wide-ranging privatization programme was adopted (ibid., p. 3). The ambition was to make it impossible for future governments to reverse the reforms and to attract foreign financial institutions and investors. The initial reform pro-gramme was not a success, however, first of all due to the withdrawal of Soviet subsidies and the collapse of CMEA in 1991 and internal divisions in the ruling party. There were also internal problems with the management of the reforms (Rossabi, 1997, p. 6) and with the sequence that put privatization ahead of liberalization, which in many cases increased economic inefficiency when inflation distorted price signals and private companies replaced state monopolies. The reform process was eventually slowed down at the close of the first parliamentary session in June 1991. The fact that several opposition parties were involved in financial scandals also increased popular resentment against reforms. The social consequences were harsh and product shortages arose, forcing the introduction of food rationing in the main cities.[19] At the same time, Mongolia was applying for membership of the IMF and the World Bank in the expectation of massive aid flows from bilateral and multilateral channels once they were admitted. On the positive side Mongolia already had a significant private sector, partly due to experiments with private ownership initiated before independence (Korsun and Murrel, 1995, p. 3), partly to the privatization programme that had been implemented during the intensive phase of reforms, and ultimately to the weak position of state institutions, which were unable to centrally control or direct the evolving private sector. In this perspective the Mongolian experience is a good example of what in Chapter 2 was described as the dual function of administrative capacity: a weak state administration may be an impediment to the launching of coherent and rapid reforms, but at the same time it does not constrain private sector development to same extent as strong states. As summarized by Boone (1994, p. 322) '... with the loss of control mechanisms, government agencies have been forced to abandon their policies. In effect, macro-economic liberalization has been led by microeconomic change.'

In terms of political reform the first task was to replace the already amended Soviet constitution. In many other post-communist states this process took several years to complete. In Mongolia, however, the parliament drafted the constitution as a compromise between all the parties during one year of marathon sessions in the Great Hural. The process was supported by the extensive presence of foreign advisers who gained substantial influence on the document. The foreign input in the drafting of the constitution was so strong that it was necessary to dampen the impression that it reflected the ideas of foreign advisers rather than Mongolian values and traditions. Still, the Mongolian constitution enacted in 1992 largely represented Western liberal values, and thus differs from other constitutions of the Central Asian republics that have strong presidencies, as demonstrated in the case of Kyrgyzstan. In contrast the Mongolian constitution is designed as a semi-presidential system with a strong parliament patterned on the French model, but with a stronger legislation. Another difference from the common pattern in the region is the rules of election which made it impossible to become a candidate without being nominated by a political party (Fish, 1998b, p. 5). In this way Mongolia avoided what was seen in many of the post-Soviet central Asian states where parliaments were filled up with locally elected candidates without visible party affiliation, thus paving the way for presidential politics.

At the time of the 1992 election there was widespread criticism of the economic reform programme that was blamed for the general economic re-cession. The MPRP campaigned for slower reforms and blamed the National Progress Party for the problems generated by the reforms hitherto instituted, and won 56 per cent of the popular vote, reaffirming its majority in the legislature. After the elections the government, now only consisting of the MPRP headed by Prime Minister Byambasüren, reforms were slowed down although without changing direction. The new government launched an external liberalization and export oriented strategy. An agreement with IMF which implied that Mongolia would be able to get access to credits from the World Bank and the Asian Development Bank was of major importance (Bruun and Odgaard, 1996, p. 244). In the period up to 1995 the total foreign aid implemented (grants and credit) totalled around USD 720 million (ibid., p. 238), a large amount considering that the GDP in 1994 was estimated at USD 700 million (JICA, 1997, p. 2). This combined with rising world market prices for the two primary Mongolian export products, copper and cashmere, helped the government in its efforts to stabilize the economy, although the domestic economy continued to decline. Still worse was the fact that imports increased more than exports, thereby eroding the gains from the price increases. Politically the government faced criticism because of the lack of administrative reform, which was plagued by corruption, scandals and inefficiency.

At the elections in June 1996 the MPRP lost the majority and was reduced from 71 to 25 seats in the parliament, primarily reflecting, however, a change of the electoral system, because they lost only 6 per cent of the votes. The elections were characterized by the strong presence and involvement of foreign NGOs who conducted effective campaigns to motivate people to vote and to unify the fragmented opposition,[20] a fragmentation that also reflects the regional and kin loyalties that still permeate Mongolian politics. The Democratic Union consisting of two major opposition parties (Mongolian National Democratic Party and Mongolian Social Democratic Party) and several minor parties won 50 of 76 seats (Fish, 1998b, p. 5). That the transition from communist rule in Mongolia was peaceful and democratic added further legitimacy to the process of democratization. The new government responded to the growing economic and administrative problems with radical reforms. In the economic sphere a total liberalization of prices and trade was implemented, making Mongolia one of the most liberalized trading regimes among the transition countries, which also paved the way for WTO membership in January 1997 (IMF 1997, p. 30). The privatization programme was completely revitalized after a long period of stagnation and a tax reform was finally implemented in 1997. By 1997 Mongolia had shown substantial progress in most spheres of economic transformation, the major problem areas being the privatization of large enterprises and the persistent weakness of the legal infrastructure and the state's administrative capacity (Figure 7.6).

Hence, the achievement of the two underdeveloped overachievers were based on three major factors: contagion of ideas, leadership and the mutability of societies and states. Foreign agencies and foreign advice played a major role in formulating economic and political choices in both countries. The role played by the foreign agencies, however, was only possible because

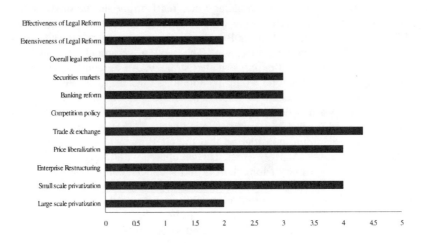

Source: EBRD Transition Report, 1998

Figure 7.6. Change of economic institutions in Mongolia by 1997.

of an internal leadership with the motivation, position and (in Kyrgyzstan) power to carry the changes through the political system. In Kyrgyzstan one charismatic and increasingly autocratic leader led the process. In Mongolia a rejuvenated communist leadership launched erratic reforms that eventually generated a dynamic private sector that could not be controlled by a weak central authority. Finally, the changes were probably also possible because of societal structures, and in particular an identical nomadic egalitarian tradition, that is broadly comparable to the ethos of political liberalism and market economy. In particular, it can be hypothesized that nomadic societies are more adaptable to pluralist democracy and decentralized market economy than traditional societies based on settled communities. First, nomadic societies are not subject to centralized power structures, like for example the Khanates in Turkmenistan or Uzbekistan. Here these traditional structures outlived the Soviet regime masked as the Communist Party, only to resurface as traditional institutions after independence. In these systems the Khan monopolized all political and economic relations. In contrast, nomadic cultures are based on values like power sharing, pluralism of ideas and opinions and economic bargaining. Further, because nomadic people move over great distances, they come into contact with various ideas and ideologies, thus bringing a pluralism into their mental universe, unlike traditional settled communities. We also know that nomadic Muslims are generally less orthodox (fundamentalist) than Muslims in settled communities. At the same time the endurance of these pre-modern social structures carried the obvious danger that they would permeate (and corrupt) the formal structures of the democratic market economy.

TURKMENISTAN AND BELARUS: ARRESTED DEVELOPMENT AND AUTOCRATIC LEADERSHIP

While it is possible although not unproblematic to identify causes that helped a country transcend given structural conditions when initiating a new policy, it is definitely more difficult to distinguish the causes of a development that has failed to occur. In practice we can only say that the country was unable to transcend the structural constraints and hence remained as it was. Still, the previous analysis has shown that the two major underachievers of the present study not only turned out to have been prevented from adopting new policies by the constraints imposed by 1st order initial conditions or the absence of opportunities provided by the same structures. They have actually performed even worse than predicted on the basis of these initial conditions. The present section makes an attempt to understand what caused the two major under-achievers – Turkmenistan and Belarus – to lag so far behind in the change of economic institutions, in particular the role of idiosyncratic leadership and 2nd order initial conditions.

Turkmenistan,[21] one of the five Soviet Central Asian republics, was the least developed and (next to Belarus) most distorted of the former Soviet republics. Hence from the outset we would expect reform prospects to be bleak. However, it actually performed worse than predicted, being the former Soviet republic that to the greatest extent has maintained a Soviet type economy, as shown in Figure 7.7.

As seen from the figure, Turkmenistan had hardly reformed at all by 1997. The privatization process is centred on small scale business and the level of foreign involvement is very low and only encouraged through joint ventures. Although bankruptcy legislation does exist only a few companies have been liquidated and inter-enterprise arrears are widespread. Price liberalization is under way but dual pricing still exists (state and free market). All trade is licensed, there are a few quota restrictions and duties are high. Turkmenistan did not subscribe to any international or bilateral customs union or trading agreements. The banking sector was dominated by state owned banks, accounting for some 83 per cent of credits, and there was no securities market. The failure to reform stands out especially in comparison with the institutional changes seen in Kyrgyzstan because they to a large extent share initial features. The failure to reform, however, is neither accidental nor entirely caused by structural factors. Rather it reflects a deliberate policy by the country's ruling elite and in particular the increasingly autocratic president Saparmurad Niyazov.

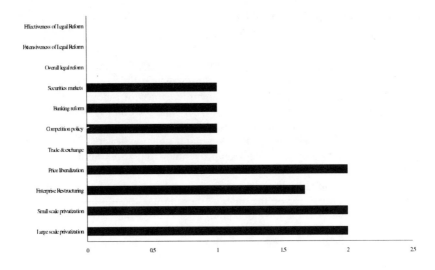

Source: EBRD Transition Report, 1998.

Figure 7.7. Change of economic institutions in Turkmenistan, 1997.

Like Kyrgyzstan, Turkmenistan experienced its first independence in 1991. Before the inclusion in the Russian and later Soviet system, where it obtained the status of Union Republic in 1936, the Turkmen had been a rural, mostly nomadic people divided into different tribes. Turkmenistan received independence hesitantly, and both the political leadership under party leader Saparmurat Niyazov since 1985 and the population supported the continuation of the Soviet Union. The perestroika process and democratic movements never gained a mass footing in the isolated and mostly rural country, and independence in 1991 was consequently the product of external developments rather than internal processes.

From the outset politics in independent Turkmenistan was dominated by the incumbent elites from the Communist party of Turkmenistan, now renamed The Democratic Party, and watched over by the same instruments of internal security that upheld the Soviet system. Despite paying lip service to the long range goals of pluralist democracy and market economy, the political leadership advocated an 'Eastern' and slow development, and maintained that applying Western models 'is fraught with serious cataclysms'.[22] In particular the president legitimized his leadership by overt comparisons with the ethnic strife in neighbouring republics, claiming that slow and conservative development in the political as well as economic sphere is the only way to prevent similar conflicts among different tribes. Still, with the uncertainty related to a country where independent reports of public opinion have yet to become available, researchers with insights into Turkmensitan probably have a case when they argue that the authoritarian regime is consistent with the mentalities of a society based on tribal and regional loyalties. In that respect Turkmenistan is an example of a traditional, centralized Muslim principality (Khanate), where the fundamental mode of governance and popular mentalities survived the Soviet epoch. This historical legacy has made it possible for the incumbent Communist regime to transform itself into a traditional centralized rule based on pre-Soviet values and structures. Similarly, it is likely that Niyazov enjoys broad popular support because he has managed to create the image that he is the Khan and thus above all clan interests, and protects the population from bureaucratic abuses and the bloody tribal conflicts that rage in neighbouring countries.[23] Instead the leadership has attempted to spur economic growth and development by increased exploitation of its abundant natural resources, in particular the huge reserves of natural gas, which in 1997 made the EBRD declare that 'Turkmenistan's natural gas deposits will almost certainly make it one of the key suppliers of energy to Europe and Asia in the 21st century'.[24]

This strategy, which supposedly would make the country as rich as Kuwait, has so far not been as successful as anticipated, partly because the unrest in neighbouring countries for some years has made it impossible to construct the pipelines that were to bring the gas to the world market. Nor has the slow pace of reforms with subsidized prices for basic foodstuffs, strictly controlled foreign trade, state control over basic industries (in particular energy resources) and only slow privatization of small enterprises spared the country from social and economic losses. Inflation has remained rampant and was in the three digit range throughout 1996, the relative decline in GDP is among the largest in the former Soviet Republics, and the absolute level as well as increase in poverty has been the highest among all transition countries. Partly as a response to these problems the government in 1995 launched minor reforms that spurred small scale privatization, liberalized a majority of domestic prices and made it easier to establish private enterprises.

In the political sphere developments have been equally slow, in some fields even regressive. The personal cult of president Niyazov has reached absurd levels reminiscent of Stalinist Russia, and Turkmenistan today is basically a one-man rule. This situation is also reflected in the quiescence of the rural population which, as in Kyrgyzstan, was never mobilized in support of independence or democratization. Simultaneously the harassment and persecution of the political opposition has been intensified. The only effective opposition to Niyazov's regime is currently located in Moscow. These political developments have impaired relations with Western governments and made it more difficult to obtain support from international financial institutions. The highly personal nature of government in Turkmenistan has also spurred considerable corruption in government, where the absence of control makes it possible for government elite to pocket the increasing revenues from the sale of gas and oil.

Hence both Kyrgyzstan and Turkmenistan represent cases of increasing authoritarianism where the role of an idiosyncratic leader seems to have been decisive in the absence of popular mobilization. However, whereas Kyrgyzstan represents an example of a virtuous circle with a president who uses his relative and increasing autonomy to force through institutional changes that activate and involve strong foreign agencies, Turkmenistan represents the opposite. Here the surviving nomenclatura elite in conjunction with the personal idiosyncrasies of an increasingly autocratic leader have so far produced a downward spiral, blocking internal change and impeding external involvement.

The same pattern of development can be observed in the other major underachiever, *Belarus*.[25] While ex ante we would expect that a peripheral and underdeveloped country like Turkmenistan, permeated by pre-modern structures, would have to face great difficulties when trying to adapt to imposed economic institutions, Belarus was in a completely different situation. When the country adopted independence in 1991, a status that was wanted neither by the population nor the dominating elite, it was one of the economically most advanced of the Soviet republics. The devastation of World War Two had provided the basis for major capital investments which made the Belarus industry one of the most advanced and modern in a Soviet context. Its industrial structure was dominated by machinery, electronics and chemicals, a combination which was similar to that which had helped give birth to the post-war German economic miracle. Being located in the Baltic–East European region was a further asset for development because of the potentials for trade and foreign investment and by reason of the proximity to the early political and economic reformers, first Poland and later the Baltic States. The Belarussian Socialist Soviet Republic also scored favourably on key indicators of social wellbeing, and on key points like education, infant mortality rates and life expectancy the comparison was favourable even with industrialized Western nations. Further, despite the presence of many nationalities, ethnic strife was never an issue in Belarussia where cohabitation with other nations was a part of the national history. During the late 1980s a number of political parties favouring a Western type democratic market economy and integration into Western institutions had sprung up. Still, at the end of 1997 the country that had previously been a showcase of what genuine Sovietization could accomplish, had turned into a showcase of perverted democratization and a disastrous economy resembling a museum of otherwise lost institutions and practices. Economic reforms were rudimentary (see Figure 7.8) and in the political sphere the tragi-comical presidency of Aleksandr Lukashenka was turning the country in a clown and pariah on the international scene.

At independence Belarus did initiate market oriented economic reforms, although at a very slow pace. But political events during 1994–1997 stalled and reversed the initial reform efforts. The privatization of enterprises lags behind in comparison with all the other post-communist countries, and the private sector only accounts for some 20 per cent of the total economy. This

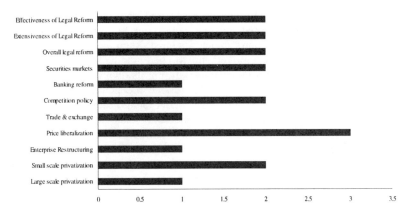

Source: EBRD Transition Report, 1998.

Figure 7.8. Change of economic institutions in Belarus, 1997.

is the cornerstone of the malaise besetting the Belarussian economy: the large, inefficient and heavily subsidized state owned sector. The minor privatization that has been carried out largely consists of manager/employee buyouts. The side effect of this slow pace of reforms has become politically self-perpetuating, because industry resists price liberalization, imports are controlled in order to protect the same industry and the state continues to intervene in the capital markets and banking sector because of the gap between official and informal prices/exchange rates.

One explanation why Belarus developed its economic institutions even less than predicted is to be found in the interface between long-term historical identities (2nd order initial conditions), the Soviet experience (1st order initial conditions) and the demands of specific individuals nurtured under these conditions. Despite the achievements in a Soviet economic context, the Soviet economic legacy was not all positive. The majority of Belarussian industries were not competitive on the international market, they were almost exclusively based on capital goods and constituted the largest share of military industry among the former Soviet republics. Industry was completely dependent on critical inputs (raw materials and energy) from Russia and on the markets in Russia and the other Soviet republics. The very size of the industrial enterprises also made changes politically difficult, because closures and reconstructions would affect entire regions or cities. Close integration into the Soviet military industrial complex made part of the industry obsolete after independence, exacerbated by the down-sizing of post-Soviet armies. Secondly, the national legacy was also closely connected to the Soviet experience. Belarus had never developed a strong historically defined national identity, caught as it has always been between major empires. On this background the partisan warfare of World War Two that involved an underground army of more than 100,000 troops became a formative period for the national identity.

It was an identity that became closely associated with the Soviet system of government that had sustained the war effort. For the next generation the institutions of the Belarussian Soviet Socialist Republic were staffed by former leaders of the partisan movement who had obtained semi-independent status vis-à-vis Moscow. But rather than defining its own national identity as did Yugoslavia and Central Europe, Belarussian independence was used to develop a system that came closer to the Soviet ideal of developed socialism than seen anywhere else in the Union, including Russia. And the average Belarussian citizen came as close as we are ever likely to get to the ideal-type of 'sovietskij chelovek' (Soviet Man). One indicator of this mentality was the very low level of support for market institutions that dominated the Belarussian population from the very start, in sharp contrast to Poland and the Baltic States (Figure 7.9).

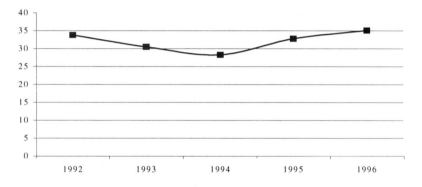

Figure 7.9. Support for the market in Belarus (per cent positive).

This historical background entailed that the perestroika and democracy movements never gained strong political footholds in Belarus. The mobilization that took place after the Chernobyl catastrophe and the revelation of the Kurapaty massacre[26] was a protest against the authorities' secrecy and irresponsible handling of the affairs, not the system as such. The fact that the Belarussian Popular Front (BPF) never succeeded in gaining support from core groups in the intelligentsia deprived the movement of mass appeal. In that context it is illustrative that the only public upheaval up to independence was a mass protest against an increase of canteen prices. The lack of popular support finally became clear when the BPF only won 7.5 per cent of the vote at the election to the republican Supreme Soviet in 1990, while the Communist party won 86 per cent. It was this background that made it possible for the traditional communist elite to continue on in power until 1994 when Belarus, following the example of Russia, introduced a strong presidency. In that period Belarus conducted an economic policy of very gradual reforms of a so-called 'social economy', combined with a rapprochement with Russia that postponed the massive drop in production seen in other republics. This boosted the legitimacy of a leadership who could use the recessions in neighbouring countries to glorify their own achievements. However, the lack of reforms eventually produced the recession and economic decline that characterize Belarus today.

The presidential elections in 1994 carried a newcomer, a former Kolkhos director Aleksandr Lukashenka, to a landslide victory by 82 per cent of the vote. Although the presidency had been designed for the incumbent communist prime minister Vyachaslau Kebich, the populist appeal of Lukashenka, who ran his campaign on a law-and-order and anti-corruption agenda, was more appealing to a population yearning not for democracy, market economy or independence but a return to the relative prosperity and stability of the Soviet past. It was also a protest against the economic and social decline which began during the perestroika-period and was accelerated by the incipient market reforms that were instituted following independence. It was the combined effect of the Soviet legacy and the absence of a non-Soviet national identity that brought Lukashenka to power. In 1995 he obstructed the parliamentary elections and in November 1996 he staged a semi-legal (or illegal) referendum that vastly increased his powers and effectively abolished parliamentary democracy and installed a presidential dictatorship. At that point Belarus had already turned down the road towards the reinstatement of an authoritarian state, or what an OSCE report terms 'a system of totalitarian government' (Eggleston, 1997). However, while initial conditions provided a fertile ground for this development, the ensuing development cannot be explained without accounting for the personal traits of Lukashenka. As phrased by the present leader of the BPF, he is 'a curious ideological hybrid construed of communism. Nostalgic yearning for the Soviet Union and anti-western orthodox Russian chauvinism.'[27] In other words he is one of those 'accidental politicians, brought to power during the time of problems and difficulties, and susceptible to turn toward authoritarian methods at any time' (Marples, 1996, pp. 98, 124).[28] It would nevertheless be wrong to dismiss Lukashenka as an autocrat using the traditional instruments of Soviet power to control a democratizing population. By all accounts the president is still the most popular politician in Belarus. Fairly reliable polls show that he has the support of about 45 per cent of the electorate and that his principal political basis is in the rural constituencies, among the elderly, the military and the secret police. Hence Belarus represents an almost perfect example of political constraints on economic reforms in a country where a distorted industrial structure merges with anti-market mentalities, reinforced by the absence of a national identity that could serve as a vehicle for change.

Hence our two underachievers represent two initially very different societies in terms of 1st and 2nd order initial conditions, neither had a clear national identity that could have served as a focal point for an anti-system mobilization that could have effectuated a break in elite structures. And in both cases, it was the power of idiosyncratic and increasingly authoritarian individuals that prevented the institutional developments seen in other systems.

CONCLUSIONS

The comparison of four overachievers and two major underachievers illustrated by examples demonstrates why some countries have been able to change their economic institutions more than predicted from the initial institutions, while others have not. We found that specific combinations of external and internal agencies, and in particular personal factors, formed the outliers, and that the relative weight of the factors was linked to the level of development.

Table 7.4 summarizes the major components of 2nd order initial conditions that have produced the outliers – countries that performed either better or worse than predicted from 1st order initial conditions.

Table 7.4. Outliers and 2nd order initial conditions.

	Overachievers	Underachievers
More developed countries		
Previous statehood	Yes	No
Close neighbour	Yes	No
Change team	Yes	No
EU candidacy	Yes	No
Strong leadership	No	Yes
Less developed countries		
A small country	Yes	No
Weak state capacity	Yes	Yes
Pastoral, nomadic culture	Yes	No
Strong leadership	Yes	Yes

The limited number of countries in the subset of outliers obviously limits the level of generalization. Yet, with this reservation in mind, Table 7.4 summarizes the most important 2nd order initial conditions that seem to have produced the 6 outliers. First, the table illustrates that in the more developed countries (Poland and Estonia), it was a combination of previous statehood (that generated nationalism), contagion of ideas from a close neighbour, the existence of a change team of competent economists and, eventually, the vision of EU membership, that made it possible for these countries to transcend the structural constraints of socialism. A strong leadership was a liability in these countries, and the only country that we may place in this group that produced a strong leader (Belarus) became a significant underachiever. Less developed countries seem more difficult to differentiate with the regard to factors that created over- and underachievers. Smallness (in terms of GDP) was seemingly an important predictor of overachievement because it was likely to open the door to direct influence from international organizations. (We here assume that Turkmenistan is 'larger' in politico-economic terms because of its prospective incomes from gas and oil extraction.) Weak capacities of state in the less developed countries may either become an asset because of less opposition from the administration (as we saw in Mongolia), or it may turn into a liability because it is embedded in conservative societal structures and is exposed to corruption. We may also hypothesize that a pastoral, nomadic culture may become an asset for economic (and political) transformation, as in Kyrgyzstan and Mongolia, because of its compatibility with market (and democratic) values. Finally, in less developed countries, strong leadership may become either an asset or a liability, reflecting the importance of the idiosyncrasies of individual politicians. It might, as in Kyrgyzstan, be an increasingly autocratic ruler who, in conjunction with foreign agencies, implemented reforms in the face of a reluctant society. It could also, however, be individuals or groups of individuals that, nurtured by initial conditions and the popular support they could generate as a result thereof, used personalized power to block the reform process, as we saw in Belarus and in Turkmenistan. In both cases they represented a more or less personal (or group) choice that helped tip the balance in a process that could have taken a different direction.

However, in both cases – where the reform process has been blocked and where reforms have been imposed by an increasingly authoritarian ruler – we face an unstable situation. In the former case, the inefficiencies associated with the incumbent system will persist and the legitimacy of the system will further erode. In the latter the imposition of market institutions by an increasingly authoritarian ruler may easily jeopardize the long term political and administrative viability of the institutional changes (and therefore also the economic viability) when the perseverance of traditional institutions give way to pervasive corruption and perversion of formal institutions. The same danger applies to the cases where weak administrative capacities makes the state unable to monitor and regulate private sector development. This precarious balance becomes starkly obvious if the institutions and their capacities are strained by external events. We shall return to these questions in the concluding chapter.

NOTES

1. I still recall how the dream of the 'third way' was still alive among incumbent elites in the Baltic states after the collapse of the Soviet Union. During the winter of 1991–1992 some Swedish colleagues and I had arranged the first conference between Nordic and Baltic social scientists. It took place in an ice-cold Soviet style hotel in the Estonia city of Pärno. For reasons that remain unknown, on the last day of the seminar the president of the World Association of Peace Studies suddenly arrived directly from Hawaii to deliver the final speech, which appeared to be about the acute crisis of American style capitalism. After the speech the president was surrounded by a large group of incumbent communists trying to find support for their hope that there was still a rationale for not changing the system too radically. The proceedings from the seminar were eventually published in Dellenbrant, Nørgaard and Willumsen (eds.), *The politics of transition in the Baltic States*. Collection of papers from the Pärnu Seminar 16–19 January 1992. Department of Political Science, University of Aarhus, 1992.
2. As seen in Table 6.1 the market ideology was rejected by a majority of the populations in the Slavic and Central Asian republics from the very start.
3. This is not the place to examine the rise of neo-liberalism (The Washington consensus) as the governing ideology of the core capitalist states. For a theoretical framework see Ruggie (1982).
4. Dawisha and Turner have a fourth category, 'control', where the external actor by force (military) or coercion (economic sanction) compels countries to adopt specific policies. While obviously important in other policy fields, and for the relation between Russia and the former Soviet Republics, it has no relevant application in the present context. For an analysis of the 'control' mechanisms imposed by the Western powers on the defeated countries after World War Two, see articles in Herz (ed.) (1984).
5. On this issue, see also Remmer (1993). Focusing on the link between regime form and policy choice in Latin America, she concludes that longitudinal analyses suggest that large countries – particularly those with dynamic export sectors – have enjoyed a broader range of policy options than smaller countries with weak export sectors.
6. I owe this observation to Greskovits (1998, ch. 4) who also offers a vivid description of the mechanisms through which the international community influenced policy making in the region: conditionality attached to financial support, economic advice and expertise (change teams).
7. Ruggie (1982) claims that the adoption of new economic ideas is related to the rise of new classes. This is obviously not the case in post-communist countries. As already emphasized, there were no groups or classes with transformative interests in the post-communist countries.
8. The present account is based on descriptions and analyses in Balcerowicz (1993, 1994, 1995, 1997), Balcerowicz et al. (1997), Johnson and Kowalska (1994), Sanford (1999), Zubek (1997), Saxonberg (1998).
9. It also had or acquired additional features reflecting the specificity of the Polish situation, for example a wage tax intended to curb the power of organized labour.
10. As in other countries the initial drop in GDP reported was probably too high. Whereas offical reports registered a drop in GDP 1990–91 of 18 per cent, the Main Statistical Office later reduced the estimated decline to 5–10 per cent (Blejer and Coricelli, 1995, p. 112).
11. This section is based on Nørgaard and Johannsen (1999, ch. 4).
12. This observation later became the subject of some controversy. See further Lainela and Sutela (1997, pp. 40ff).

13. In relative terms, of course. Estonia's exposure to Western ideas was extensive in a Soviet context, not in comparison to Central European countries.

14. This section is based on Huskey (1997), Hyman (1994) and Reinecke (1995). I am also indebted to Lone Bøge Jensen, former UNDP representative in Mongolia (now in the Danish Ministry of Foreign Affairs) for insightful comments to this section.

15. Kyrgyzskaja Respublika: Peremeny v processe transformacii obshchestva. Sociologicheskaja informatea. Pervey vypusk. Kyrgyz Sociologdor Koomu, Bishek 1994, p. 80. Here after Reinecke (1995, p. 31).

16. This chapter is based on Anderson (1998), BBC News July 24, 1998, Bruun and Odgaard (1996), Fish (1998a, b), Freedom House (1999), Ginsburg (1997), UNDP Human Development Report, Mongolia 1997, IMF (1997, 1999), JICA (1997), Korsun and Murrel (1995), Poole (1998) and Rossabi (1997).

17. Griffith (1995) reports that by 1995 there were 24 bilateral donors and 14 multilateral organizations working in Mongolia.

18. Y. Tsedebal had ruled the MPRP from 1952 to 1984.

19. For a thorough examination of the social repercussions of economic reform in Mongolia, see Griffith (1995).

20. In particular, the German 'Conrad Adenauer Stifftung' and the American 'International Republican Institute' were active during the campaign.

21. Based on Ochs (1997), Freitag-Wirminghaus (1998a, 1998b).

22. Statement by President Niyazov in October 1994. Here quoted after Ochs (1997, p. 32).

23. Freitag-Wirminghaus (1998a, p. 158).

24. Quoted after RFE/RL, 16 April, 1997.

25. The account is based on Zaprudnik and Urban (1997), Mihalisko (1997), Eggleston (1997) and Marples (1996).

26. In 1988 excavation of mass graves in the Kurapaty forests outside Minsk revealed that Stalin's secret police in the late 1930s had executed large numbers of Belarussians (and other nationalities). The official figures stated that at least 30,000 were found buried, but unofficial figures put it as high as 250,000.

27. Quoted in Jan de Weydenthal, 'Dealing with Belarus' Lukashenko', Radio Free Europe (rferl.org/nca/features/1996/07/F.RU.96071164653838/html).

28. Le Figaro, quoted in Radio Free Europe (rferl.org/nca/features/1996/07/F.RU.96071164653838/html).

8. Emerging Markets – and Democracy

'... policy makers have to consider three different rates: interest rate, exchange rate and the tax rate, but above all, respect a fourth rate: the electorate' (Grzegorz W. Kolodko, 1998).[1]

This book has been about change of economic institutions in 20 new democracies in the post-communist world. It placed the post-communist transition in a comparative perspective by arguing that these countries reflect extreme cases of the dilemmas and needs for trade-offs that we have seen in other countries and regions. The lessons drawn from the post-communist experience suggest that the economic and social costs generated by (1st order) initial conditions in conjunction with institutional strategies constrain the actors' choice of institutional strategies. While fast and comprehensive reforms ultimately produce superior results in terms of growth and alleviation of poverty, this (radical) strategy is only superior if it is democratically viable. The countries that are worst off are those who launched radical reforms and then stopped half-way because of political costs or administrative obstruction. A few countries have been able to successfully transcend the social and political constraints of 1st order initial conditions when building new economic institutions. This was observed in cases where initial anti-systemic popular mobilizations around the symbols of 2nd order initial conditions broke the power of elite interests embedded in the incumbent system, and when this mobilization produced an opportunity space in which reform minded elites were able to launch reforms of economic and political institutions. Hence the experiences of the 20 post-communists show that liberal, participatory democracy has a transformative capacity which has not been recognized by those who argue in favour of authoritarian or elite guided solutions to the difficulties of economic change. In other cases countries were able to transcend constraints without popular mobilization, but through the impetus of international organizations in conjunction with endogenous reform minded elites sustained by strong presidential executives. In these cases we saw that new institutions were often colonized by traditional structures, producing corruption, crime and ultimately a return to a more authoritarian style of government.

This final chapter takes the relationship between emerging democracies and the market back into the broader theoretical and geographical context of Chapter 3. The first section addresses the flip side of the issue: how do the alternative strategies for transition to the market and the social and political effects influence the consolidation of democracy? We may then finally ask how the consolidation of democracy feeds back into sustainable market reforms. The second section discusses the applicability of these findings to other regions and transitions. Finally, the third section discusses outstanding issues that were either not addressed or left unanswered (or insufficiently answered) in this study, and what issues are next on the research agenda if we are to improve our understanding of how to combine the dynamics of the market with the fairness and legitimacy of democracy.

DEMOCRACY AND THE MARKET

This book began by describing how the call for freedom and democracy, in many cases also nurtured by aspirations for national independence, in some countries generated the opportunities for changing economic institutions.[2] In other countries such changes were launched by local elites in conjunction with external agencies. In most cases the changes were welcomed by a majority of the population, although the initial enthusiasm for the market was less pronounced in especially the Slavic and Central Asian republics of the former Soviet Union. Nevertheless, a majority of the populations in the emerging post-communist democracies initially greeted the new economic institutions as part of the general change of the old regime. In that respect they were initially subject to the reverse illusion of what had misled Western leaders (and populations at large) at the beginning of the changes. Whereas the latter expected the consolidation of democracy to proceed more or less spontaneously from the introduction (or imposition) of market institutions, the populations of the emerging popular democracies suffered from the opposite illusion: that the efficiency and welfare of the market would follow more or less spontaneously once democracy had been installed.

As demonstrated throughout this book, these expectations were not and could not be met. The radical changes of economic governance from plan to the market inevitably led to a temporary decrease in efficiency and welfare, while the institutional changes took effect. Another consequence was that greater shares of the population slid into poverty, thus increasing inequality. It was shown that the political effect of these costs feeds back into the political process and the strength of support for a continuation of reforms and specific policies as filtered through perceptions formed by different historical legacies and evolving political institutions. It were also these perceptions that would decide if people would and could dissociate the outcome of the political system from institutions as such. In other words, as long as the populations of post-communist countries were guided by the illusion that the benefits of developed market economies would automatically follow from adherence and support for democratic principles and democratic institutions, democracy itself would be in danger when people discovered that democracy and welfare capitalism, the images of which they were increasingly exposed to, were not one and the same thing. In the perspective of this book, it was only when people became able to disassociate the two – democracy and what it produced for society in terms of individual and public welfare – that democracy could be normatively consolidated in the minds and actions of people and strategic elites.[3] They would thus enjoy the benefits of democracy either because they valued the democratic process for its own sake, or because they could see their own strategic interest in a system designed to allow them a fair chance to influence decisions or take over government at a later stage.[4]

However, up to the point when democracy became valued for its own sake, there were two channels through which the costs of economic change could jeopardize the legitimacy of the principles and institutions of democracy: the social and economic effects of economic policies on the system, government credibility and popularity and the breakdown of the structures that used to link the government and the people. If these repercussion of the market on democracy make people turn down democracy or break the links between people and government, this in turn jeopardized the effect of market reforms because they would either be halted by grudging elites or populations, or they led to an instability that in any system is detrimental to growth and prosperity. Was democracy then endangered, by the more or less synonymous introduction of market institutions?

The costs of economic transformation and satisfaction with democracy

Looking first into the level and character of popular satisfaction with democracy, the data reveal that we are also here probably dealing with a structural variable. It can of course be argued that the level of democratic support reflects popular satisfaction with a concrete regime and the performance of the politicians in power. This certainly is correct in the later stages of democratic government, where we see that the notoriously corrupt and incompetent regimes have used up what they had of initial political capital. This explanation does not, however, carry the same weight in the initial changes of political changes, where democracy (then in unspecified variants) was set up as a common goal. This implies that the level (but not the development) of democracy satisfaction and the initial legitimacy of the new system of government reflect the extent to which the new system is perceived as a return to a preferable past and as a radical break with the incumbent system – or as an unknown, maybe even alien type of institution imposed by foreign powers. If this is the case, we would expect to find a correlation between the level of positive attitudes to the market and democracy, as it has previously been argued (Evans and Whitefield, 1995). It may also be that attitudes towards the political system were being influenced when the evolving power structure provided illegitimate groups with disproportional privileges. This was obviously the case in for example Russia, where the criminalization of the state structures have left scant belief in the existing democratic institutions.

A survey of 490 citizens in the Kon'yakovo Okrug in Moscow in January 1996, on whom they believed controlled political power, gave the following results:[5] mafia–corruption groups – 50 per cent; a political elite – 25 per cent; administrative apparatus – 20 per cent; entrepreneurial groups – 6 per cent. Twenty-nine per cent responded that nobody has real power today. Less than 8 per cent answered that real power lies with the president. Not one single repondent answered that the power rested with the people or with the deputies in parliament (Smol'kov, 1999, p. 43).

Whatever the causes, Figure 8.1 illustrates on a country basis the high association between average support for the market and average satisfaction with democracy for the years where data are available (the simple correlation is 0.85, significance 0.01).

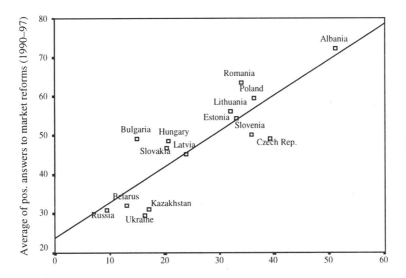

Average satisfation with democratic development 1992–97

Source: EastEurobarometer, subsequent years.

Figure 8.1. Market support and satisfaction with democracy.

The pattern in the figure is roughly similar to the pattern we found in Chapters 5 and 6 when we examined support for market institutions. Also here we can identify three groups of countries: a first group consisting of one outlier (Albania) that demonstrates extreme market support and democracy satisfaction, in all likelihood due the turbulent nature of the break with the previous very repressive system; a second group (or two subgroups) consisting of the Central European and the Baltic countries with medium market support and democracy satisfaction and a third group consisting of the non-Baltic former Soviet republics which have low scores on both dimensions. The figure also shows that market support is consistently greater than satisfaction with democracy, indicating that the latter contains a large element of regime performance assessment which in this context is inseparable from system satisfaction. That we are in fact measuring different aspects of people's satisfaction with institutional changes is also indicated by the relatively low individual level correlation between market support and satisfaction with democracy, for most countries fluctuating between 0.20 and 0.30 (see Appendix 8). Most country cases also demonstrate an increasing correlation between market support and democracy satisfaction, probably reflecting that people increasingly associate both with regime performance rather than system satisfaction. This is the case of the Czech Republic, where the correlation between democracy satisfaction and market support during the economic crisis in 1997 reached 0.49. The major exceptions to this growing association between attitudes to democracy and the market are Belarus which has not seen much progress in either the market or democracy; Slovakia under the rule of the semi-authoritarian Meciar government, and Poland, where we may assume that the prospect for EU membership increased support on both scores.

That satisfaction with democracy so far appears to measure regime performance rather than systemic satisfaction is further supported by the clear association between macro-economic development (GDP-index and inflation), social costs (increased inequality and poverty) and satisfaction with democracy, as seen in Table 8.1.

Table 8.1. Correlation between satisfaction with democratic development and economic and social indicators.

	GDP-index 1996 (1989=100)	Inflation 1996 (log)	Poverty headcount 1994	Gini 1995
Satisfaction with democracy development 1995	0.641*	– 0.634*	– 0.292	– 0.261

*Note: * significance at 0.05 level; ** significance at the 0.01 level.*

Source: EastEurobarometer, subsequent years.

The countries where satisfaction with democracy is the lowest (in 1995) also experienced the largest decline in GDP, the highest inflation and (less clear) the steepest increase in poverty and inequality. Yet, the association is not so strong as to exclude that the structurally determined average level of satisfaction with democracy, understood as a filter through which subsequent developments will be perceived and assessed, varies between different groups of countries.

We would here expect the association between economic and social development and satisfaction with democracy to assume a bell shape. In the first stage of reforms, during the 'opportunity space' when aspirations and hopes are driven by political concerns and while the general economic development proceeds, one's personal financial position becomes secondary. In the second stage of reforms when the revolutionary excitement has faded, we would expect people to start looking for the concrete benefits offered by the new system of government, and that performance can be expected to be important to individual satisfaction with democracy. It is only in the third stage involving the 'gradual dissociation between the evaluation of the economic situation and of political institutions' (Pereira et al., 1993, p. 206), that normative democratic consolidation is actually proceeding. Table 8.2 shows the simple correlation between estimation of past financial situation, future financial expectation and satisfaction with democracy.

Table 8.2. Satisfaction with democracy correlated with evaluation of economic situation.

	1992	1993	1994	1995	1996
Past	0.27**	0.30**	0.36**	0.35**	0.39**
Future	0.30**	0.33**	0.33**	0.35**	0.40**

*Note: ** significance at the 0.01 level.*

Source: EastEurobarometer, subsequent years.

Table 8.2 shows that in the 15 countries for which data (of maximum coverage) are available, the correlation between personal finances, past or future, increases over time. The association is strongest for past financial situation and weakest for the non-Baltic countries of the former Soviet Union, indicating that high expectations in emerging democracies in Central Europe also breed the greatest disappointments. Nevertheless, if we consider the response to 'satisfaction with democracy' a valid proxy for systemic satisfaction and legitimacy, then we are in the second phase of democratic consolidation. If we prefer to see it as an assessment of government performance and legitimacy, it implies that one's personal financial situation is taking on increasing salience as a basis of judgement.

The market and popular engagement in governance

Popular participation and engagement in governance in post-communist systems show a pattern that is partially in contrast with what has been argued to be the optimal pattern recommended on the basis of experiences with previous transitions.[6] During the first stage of transformation in the most successful countries, we saw that high popular mobilizations signal great expectations to political decision-makers. This also became manifest during the first elections which showed a very high turnout rate. At later stages, however, where organized interests ought to play a more prominent role in decision-making, mobilization and participation (where it had occurred) there were drastic declines. Instead the political field was left to parties controlled by elites that had a shallow popular base and to the conservative industrial interests portrayed in Chapter 5. When the transformed communist parties, initially perceived as defenders of a minimum level of social security, proved to be as compliant with the demands of international financial institutions as other parties, the popular reaction was increased political alienation and loss of faith in the effectiveness of political participation. The clearest sign of this development was the decrease in turnout in subsequent elections, as seen in Table 8.3.

Table 8.3. Turn-out at parliamentary elections 1990–1998.

Country	1st election	2nd election	3rd election	4th election
Albania	98.92 (04.1991)	90.35 (03.1992)	89.00 (05.1996)	72.56 (1997)
Belarus	n.a.	n.a.	n.a.	n.a.
Bulgaria	90.8 (06.1990)	83.9 (10.1991)	75.2 (12.1994)	58.86 (04.1997)
Czech Rep.	96.7 (06.1990)	83.9 (06.1992)	76.4 (06.1996)	74.0 (06.1998)
Estonia	69.3 (09.1992)	69.55 (03.1995)		
Hungary	69.5 (03.1990)	68.1 (05.1994)	56.26 (05.1998)	
Kazakhstan	80.7 (12.1995)			
Kyrgyzstan	62.0 (02.1995)			
Latvia	89.9 (06.1993)	71.9 (10.1995)	71.9 (10.1998)	
Lithuania	75.2 (10.1992)	52.92 (11.1996)		
Moldova	79.0 (02.1994)	72.3 (03.1998)		
Mongolia	95.0 (1990)	95.6 (1992)	92.2 (1996)	88.38 (06.1998)
Poland[7]	62.23 (1989)	43.2 (1991)	52.1 (1993)	47.9 (1997)
Romania	86.2 (05.1990)	76.1 (09.1992)	76.0 (11.1996)	
Russia	54.8 (12.1993)	64.4 (12.1995)		
Slovakia	95.3 (06.1990)	82.0 (06.1992)	75.6 (09.1994)	84.2 (09.1998)
Slovenia	83.1 (04.1990)	85.7 (12.1992)	73.7 (11.1996)	
Turkmenistan	99.77 (12.1994)			
Ukraine	74.8 (04.1994)	70.0 (03.1998)		
Uzbekistan	94.0 (1995)			

Sources: Electoral studies *Vols. 9, 10, 11, 12, 13, 14, 15* and *16, Elsevier Science Ltd, Great Britain, 1990–1997; Wilfried Derksen's Electoral Website, URL: http://www.agora. stm.it/elections/election.htm, 1998; Parline database 1998, Inter-Parliamentary Union, URL: http://www.ipu.org, 1998; Rose et al. (1998), Attila Ágh (1998a).*

As seen from the table, the countries of Central Europe especially show a pattern of increasing abstention at parliamentary elections. Only countries with continued political mobilization (Mongolia and Slovakia) and countries where turnout rates are least reliable (Central Asian Republics) maintain a relatively high level. In particular the transformation of the initially mass based post-communist parties of central Europe pose a danger to democracy, because they have deduced people to believe that their votes mattered in the formulation of economic policies. The consequence was that an increasing number of people were alienated from the institutions of the new democracies and – in a few cases – risk being pushed into the hands of populist parties nurtured by the social decay and benefiting from an exclusive nationalism, as we have seen in particular in the war torn republics of the former Yugoslavia and in some republics of the former Soviet Union, but on a smaller scale also in the support for right wing parties in Central Europe.[8] It is here important to recognize the democratic potential of the common man (or the proletariat if such a group can be identified). As it was the proletariat that carried the introduction of participatory democracy in Western Europe (Sørensen, 1997), it was the democratic commitment of ordinary people (rather than elites) that carried economic and political reforms forward in the post-communist countries. The radical decrease in political participation (as exemplified by the decrease in electoral turnout) therefore not only threatens democracy by weakening the link between the institutions of decision making and ordinary citizens. It also threatens democracy because it weakens the role of those groups that initially have shown the strongest commitment to democratic principles, illustrated by the low success rate of undemocratic radical rightist parties among the losers of transition.

Modes of institutional change – and of capitalism

In Chapter 3 we summarized three alternative strategies of institutional change in post-communist systems: first, the radical 'Washington consensus' approach based on neo-classical economic theory and on the assumption that new institutions are formed on a tabula rasa and that the new set of incentives of these institutions would change behaviour rather easily, emphasizing comprehensiveness, pace and a top-down political approach which limits popular involvement and emphasizes the virtues of a strong executive able to overcome opposition from embedded elites and popular dissatisfaction. Implicitly, this approach envisages the Anglo-Saxon version of democratic capitalism combining a free market with liberal democracy but with less social solidarity. Second, we described a gradualist alternative that, underpinned by different theoretical premises (historical institutionalism, evolutionary economic theory and conservative political theory) emphasized the virtues of slow and gradual changes and maintaining institutional capital while strengthening participatory democratic institutions. This approach carries the seed of what we termed 'West European capitalism' which combines participatory democracy with a regulated market and social solidarity. Third, we defined an Asian variant that, while also gradualist in its approach to change of economic institutions, has historically pursued economic reforms before democracy and limited societal participation in corporatist structures linking government to huge industrial corporations. What has the present study taught us about the accomplishments of these alternative approaches to pursuing the dual goal of economic change and democratic consolidation in post-communist systems?

A general observation is that the basic neo-liberal approach (and the basic assumptions of rational choice approaches) fare poorly when measured against the development of political and economic institutions of the post-communist world. They did not act under tabula rasa conditions and behaviour did not adapt painlessly to the incentives of the new institutions. Neither were people's political responses in most cases economically 'rational' in response to macro or individual level economic developments. In contrast we saw that similar institutions and institutional strategies produced widely different outcomes, reflecting the different orders of historical legacies and the endurance of traditional institutions. This in particular became clear in those cases where the new institutions were imposed by foreign institutions in association with more or less insulated domestic elites. In these cases the new institutions were colonized by surviving elites and moulded by traditional patterns of behaviour. The rationale of the neo-liberal 'shock therapy' and the preference for strong executive presidencies was that this political strategy would transfer power from legislatures to executives, where insulated 'change teams' could enact reforms unopposed by particularistic and short-term popular protests. The Washington consensus, and the Anglo-Saxon version of democratic capitalism, has the advantage of simplicity because it does not assume the existence of a state capable of designing and implementing sophisticated policies. But the tacit lack of social solidarity leading to radical increases in inequality is anathema to societies that for decades were nurtured by a socialist communitarian propaganda. Further, the perception of strong presidents as the benevolent dictators is an illusion of economic theory. As demonstrated throughout this book, a strong presidency can be part of the problem rather than the solution when he imposes economic reforms for which there is no political or administrative basis in society. It was in exactly these cases, as exemplified by Russia, that the most dramatic social and economic costs arose, contributing to continued social and economic decay and political instability. Further, in the countries included in this study presidents have proved even more susceptible to particularistic interests than parliaments, in particular by enfranchising elite groups with exclusive connections to the presidental office. In particular, the evidence presented in Chapters 4 and 5 indicated that extensive concentration of powers in an executive president (as measured by the IPA), has produced extraordinary opportunities for conservative interests embedded in outdated industrial structures to block the implementation of economic reforms. It also provided extraordinary opportunities for rent seeking and reforms being stopped halfway after external and internal liberalization had been carried out, but before sufficient institutional capacity to constrain the pursuit of personal gain at the expense of social interests was developed.

In particular, this trend was observed when market institutions were imposed by a strong presidential executive in conjunction with the agents of international financial institutions, but not carried by popular mobilization. Here the trappings of Western democracy and markets were penetrated or colonized by traditional and/or criminal structures. Under such circumstances the loss of economic efficiency is evident when transaction costs are aggravated by crime and political instability. However, democracy is also endangered by the imposition of political and administratively unsustainable economic reforms, when the constitutional system provides the president with extensive decree powers, effectively undermining the authority and influence of parliaments. In these 'delegative democracies' (O'Donnell, 1996) the president is accountable to the public only at elections, but between elections he may effectively circumvent other democratic institutions as courts, parliament and political parties and organizations. In this scenario the privileges attributed to traditional interests – or rent-seeking elites – will effectively de-legitimize the fragile institutions of the new democracies when presidential cronies prove able to bypass the laws and norms of democracy. This does not, however, imply that parliaments by necessity induce slow and gradual reforms. In some cases where the changes were carried by strong popular mobilization it was this mobilization institutionalized in strong parliaments that instigated a rapid change of economic institutions against conservative, corporative interests. Estonia is a good case in point. But the broad popular base in conjunction with the very existence of a vocal and influential parliament has imbued the process with greater legitimacy and probably also quality, when subsequent elections have moderated the course and taken popular protests into account. Parliaments are not above particularistic interests. But parliaments turn the secluded lobbying of a privileged elite under a strong president into a transparent, multi-player game, whereas strong presidents with extensive decree powers tend to undermine and de-legitimize the construction of effective democratic institutions (Orenstein, 1998).

This general conclusion is nevertheless complicated by cases where the process of systemic transformation (correcting distortion) is accompanied by the traditional problems of socio-economic underdevelopment and state building. Huntington's (1965) classic dictum, that you have to concentrate political power before you can distribute it, obviously also applies to post-communist countries trying to combine the dual challenges of democracy and the market with state building. In some cases, as for example Kyrgyzstan, it is difficult to see how the reform minded President Akayev in a short-term perspective could have acted any differently than he did by increasing his powers at the expense of a parliament penetrated by traditional, conservative and partly criminal structures. Also here the trappings of Western liberalism failed to break the link between European republicanism, electoral competition and authoritarian clientism, described by Fox in nineteenth century Latin America (Fox, 1994). Also in Turkmenistan it is understandable that President Niyazov prefers to maintain the vestiges of a strong, although not

democratic statehood in order to maintain the support of a traditional population, in particular in view of the civil wars raging in neighbouring republics.

But a strong president is no guarantee that viable and feasible political and
economic reforms will proceed. In Kyrgyzstan the reforms could proceed
only at the expense of democracy. In Russia it was the decay produced by ex-
cessively rapid economic reforms without political or administrative basis
that gave rise to the social and economic decay that in view of later events
proved to leave the presidency even more exposed to particularistic interests
and in opposition to rational economic changes and insulated from the
broader society. And in Turkmenistan the maintenance of a strong statehood
hindered almost any change of economic institutions while the lack of
democratic controls provided vast opportunities for corrupt bureaucrats,
formed more by the legacy of the Soviet system than by the morality of
Islam. And then there is of course Belarus where the idiosyncrasies of one
particular person nurtured by the peculiar environment that fostered him
exemplifies all the dangers inherent in a strong executive beyond democratic
control. The success stories were those where reformers took advantage of
the initial popular mobilization to launch comprehensive reforms. However,
here also the social effects of reforms have reverberated, resulting in political
alienation when initial popular engagement and mobilization was frustrated
by institutions disassociating themselves from the society in which they
should rightfully be based.

Where does this take us in the pursuit of institutional strategies that combine the efficiency of a market economy with the fairness of pluralist
democracy in post-communist countries? First, the evidence provided in this
book indicates that the initial advantages enjoyed by radical economic strategies when abandoning a planned economy are in most cases outbalanced by
their negative impact on democracy, when the need for strong executives
undermine the development of democratic institutions. In later stages the
political instability or illegitimacy nurtured by an undemocratic development
will impede the construction of strong and legitimate political and administrative institutions, which this study has demonstrated as being closely
associated with economic growth and welfare. This strategy would also
present a danger to the new born democracies, when the neo-liberal strategy
as a response to these complications emphasized speed. Second, although
parliamentary democracies in some – but far from all – cases can slow down
the process of economic transformation, it will also make the contest of interests transparent and thus educate populations in the practices of democracy.
In this perspective the West European type of democratic capitalism which
emphasizes participatory democracy and social solidarity is more in tune with
the prevailing social values and mentalities of the post-communist system,
than are the inequality and implicitly elitist democracies associated with the
Anglo-Saxon version. However, the (alleged) slower capacity for growth and
the financial constraints of all post-communist states make this model contingent upon sufficient external finance, something that is only available to

the fortunate few that were allowed into the first echelon of EU applicants. And all the new democracies lack the institutional preconditions for the corporatist/consocial mode of democracy that traditionally underpin this type of capitalism, making a continued democratization contingent upon a conscious effort to reconstruct the structures of civil society.

However, the solution is not strong presidencies. That only seems justifiable in less developed countries where state building is uncompleted, political powers diffuse and the need for strong national symbols persists. But also here the danger of corruption and weakening exist as a legacy of the Soviet system. A reproduction of the East Asian path of development with economic reforms ahead of democracy, is not very likely to provide similar results in the less developed post-Soviet republics where the arguments for strong executives and bonds on democracy are the strongest. Despite the lack of democracy East Asia had strong institutions providing economic agents with clear legal and economic framework conditions, and the state institutions were 'embedded' in society through traditional intimate links to major industrial actors.[9] In post-communist systems the large enterprises (or financial groups) are, as shown in this study, part of the problem rather than the solution because of their inability to compete on world market terms. In this context the weakness of law-based institutions becomes a central part of the problem that can only be solved by imbuing them with democratic legitimacy – not by the decrees of presidents that enjoy even less authority than the party secretaries of the past. Hence any institutional strategy that weakens democracy will also weaken the prospect for the strong institutions that are a precondition for sustainable economic change. Where strong presidencies are instituted they should be accompanied by conscious efforts to strengthen democratic institutions by providing for solid legal guarantees that protect the integrity and independence of such institutions: parliaments, courts and political parties and organizations and by reinforcing their administrative capacities. The sort of 'autogolpe' that we saw in Belarus, Kyrgyzstan and Turkmenistan only weakens the prospect that democratic institutions will ever gain the legitimacy and strength necessary to sustain the economic development (Cameron, 1998). It is only through free and transparent democratic processes which in some cases may involve provisions for a strong and authoritative presidency, that it will be possible to abandon the corrupt practices that in most of these systems persist as a legacy of the communist system and/or traditional structures. It is no coincidence that the fastest growing post-communist economies are those where state institutions and the rule of law is most advanced.[10] Thus, post-communist developments confirm Max Weber's classical insight that rule of law is a basic precondition for economic and social development. So, yes, in post-communist systems in general good things – (parliamentary) democracy and the market – go together.

THE LESSONS OF POST-COMMUNIST INSTITUTIONAL CHANGE

In Chapters 2 and 3 the experience of other emerging markets – and democracies – were taken as points of departure for generating the hypothesis that guided this study. And in the world of real politics, the post-communist countries have incessantly looked to the experiences of other countries for guidance and advice that would help them solve their own problems. But is there a wider aspect of this process in which the experiences of post-communist countries of combining introduction of market principles with the consolidation of democracy have broader applicability to other countries and regions? To answer this question we must first recall that the post-communist systems in Chapter 2 were defined as a sub-set of emerging democracies and markets, distinguished by path-dependencies associated with the (totalitarian) communist mode of political and economic governance and international framework conditions, including influence from international organizations (IMF, the European Union). The expectation was that the dilemmas and trade-offs between democratization and change of economic institutions could teach us something about how to deal with similar processes in other countries and regions.

A core issue concerns the comparability of post-communist systems and other emerging democracies and markets in view of the findings of this study. The 1st order initial conditions defined the legacies of the ex-communist path of modernization, providing societies with the dual structural qualities of modernity and distortion. Modernity addresses the classical questions of socio-economic development and the challenges facing the post-communist countries are similar to those faced by other less developed countries. Distortion, in contrast, reflects a structural factor specific to post-communism, linking together economic and political structures, trade patterns, policy variables, mentalities and social values into a cohesive system. Whereas other countries may be burdened with some of the components of distortion, it is the totality and structural interconnectedness of components in all societal spheres that distinguishes democracies and markets emerging from totalitarian communist systems (with varying degree of completeness) from democracies and markets emerging from authoritarian systems. While the former in their extreme forms embody stable, basically self-reproductive systems, the latter often have incipient civil societies, are ruled by coalitions of different political forces and do not have legitimizing totalitarian ideologies. This difference implies that the lessons to be learned from markets and democracies emerging from communism can be only partially useful, and we must at all points consider the inter-connectedness that is specific to post-totalitarian systems.

With this reservation in mind, one of the basic lessons of the present study is the importance of what was termed '2nd order initial conditions' in fostering the change of totalitarian institutions. It was these longer term historical trajectories, distilled into national identities and the permeability of societies to new ideas, that explained the capacities for change. The mobilization of national identities made it possible for people in some distorted economies to accept and overcome the social costs and social and ideological upheavals of economic and political transformation. In some cases it produced virtuous circles, where mobilization, when it created 'opportunity spaces', was transformed into incipient liberal democracies and growing market economies. In other cases mobilization around ethnic identities produced vicious circles, generating 'illiberal democracies' (Fareed, 1997), where populist politicians have been elected on the basis of illiberal policies based on ethnic or cultural exclusion, as we have seen in Serbia and, at an early stages, in Latvia and Estonia. Or their victories may be based on a xenophobia that halts any institutional change as we saw in Belarus. These cases all emphasize the important role of the international community in insisting that political liberalism and participatory democracy are basic preconditions if the pursuit of economic progress shall succeed.

These examples clarify both the dangers and opportunities associated with popular mobilization during the extrication of an incumbent system. The experiences from our 20 post-communist countries show that anti-system mobilization and elite discontinuity were major factors behind future political and economic successes. This observation contradicts, as it will be recalled, experiences from other democratizing systems which saw elite negotiations and pacts and not popular mobilization as the best 'mode of extrication' before introducing democracy. In post-communist systems the totalitarian nature of the incumbent system produces a different logic where a (more) radical break with the past is a precondition for future change. The same logic is also expressed in the transformative role of strong parliaments, as opposed to the conservatism of strong executive presidencies. The experiences of post-communist countries thus become a strong case in support of the positive role of popular based parliaments, as opposed to presidencies that are susceptible to conservative and particularistic interests. In this perspective developments in the 20 post-communist countries provide a strong case for participatory democracy, where people at all levels are involved in the formulation of policies that affect their lives. This is also a lesson that applies to the 'remote control imperialism' by the European Union vis-à-vis the large groups aspiring for membership. It is likely that the West European brand of capitalism is more applicable to the social and political landscape than is Anglo-Saxon laissez-faire capitalism. But as long as the aquis communitaire is imposed on governments over the heads of populations, there is a danger that it may prove counterproductive and lead to either political cynicism or the erosion of those democratic values that have so far characterized the region.

This finally takes us to the basic question of institutional strategies, of whether fast and comprehensive institutional strategies are superior to gradual and partial strategies. As shown in this study, there is no general answer to this question. Any answer should take into consideration the initial societal context in which institutional changes are launched, and in particular the level of modernity and level of distortion. In the relatively modern and less distorted countries of Central Europe the evidence of this study has shown that fast and comprehensive reforms are preferable, in particular when they are backed up by substantial financial and political resources from foreign agencies. Under these circumstances fast and comprehensive institutional reforms produce superior results in terms of growth and welfare. In the less modern societies of Central Asia, fast and comprehensive reforms may be in danger of being colonized by traditional structures, giving rise to fraud and corruption which can ultimately de-legitimize the entire reform process. A similar danger threatens fast and comprehensive reforms in the more distorted countries where the economic and social costs can simply be so high that they are incompatible with liberal democracy, producing different versions of delegative democracies. The latter argument is supported by those cases where we saw that the imposition of foreign models by intrinsically undemocratic methods proved counterproductive, either because political opposition halted the changes half way, or because the trappings of Western political or economic institutions were colonized by traditional interests or corrupt structures, increasing economic insecurity and undermining popular confidence in democracy.

These arguments obviously do not imply that gradual and stepwise change of economic institutions is without dangers. All the hazards spelled out by the proponents of fast and radical changes of economic institutions do exist. This applies to the political dangers as well as to the absence of administrative capacities to carry out any policy. But if it is maintained that we should pursue the dual goal of democracy and the market we must necessarily consider the country-specific effect on democracy of economic reforms in each case – and vice versa. This is the major general lesson of this study.

THE NEED FOR FUTURE RESEARCH

The present study has been limited in its objective: to explain the different capacities of the post-communist systems to transform their economic systems without jeopardizing emerging democratic systems. While the type of variables included to explain the differences have been fairly broad, the focus has been on the interaction between different layers of initial and external conditions, political institutions and alternative institutional strategies. This implies that I have omitted other factors that might have influenced the capacity for institutional change, as indicated in Figure 1.1 in the introduction. These 'other factors' are next on the research agenda.

The dependent variables are far from completely explained by the factors included in this study. This applies in particular to GDP-development, to increase in poverty and, to a lesser extent, policy. GDP-development is not only (or even mainly) the result of change in economic institutions. As shown in Chapter 4 institutional strategy only explains about 30 per cent of GDP-development and is only under specific assumptions linked to poverty. Increase in inequality appears to be a consequence of factors not included in this study. Here we should ideally also consider the impact of factors like geographical location in order to account for the importance of proximity to markets as has been documented in other research.[11] We should also consider the effect on political and economic change and growth of large natural resource endowments, which in the coming years will be of particular importance in a number of Central Asian states and – on the most general level – all the other components that are included in the economists' growth equations.

Regarding systemic capacity to adopt and implement specific institutional strategies and hence the applicability of alternative modes of capitalism it is, in a long term perspective, the ingrained social values or more precisely the readiness of the population to accept and endure a certain level of inequality and poverty as generated by communist and pre-communist history that will allow or restrain the adoption and implementation of concrete institutional strategies. The data for the 11 countries included in the *World Value Survey, 1990* showed that countries most dominated by egalitarian values are least likely to adopt policies implying a steep increase in inequality. Further research is now needed to study how ingrained these egalitarian attitudes are, if they are the result of long historian trajectories or of communist socialization, or whether they are changeable in the short term. In this respect, it is particularly necessary to substantiate the theoretical distortion factor with additional components that reflect social values and mentalities.

When studying the preconditions for long term growth and democracy we should further consider that the initial structures of civil society may have a longer term impact on performance. Pioneered by Robert Putnam's research on the economic effect of civic traditions in Italy (Putnam, 1993), recent and ongoing research points to a similar influence in other regions of the world (Inglehart, 1996; Whitely, 1998), including the former communist countries (Rose, 1997). As summarized by Whitely (p. 17), social capital (civic values), defined as interpersonal trust, influences economic performance by reducing transaction costs in a market economy, by minimizing the dead weight burdens of enforcing and policing agreements, and by holding down the diseconomies of fraud and theft. While complete data are not at present available, preliminary data from the *World Value Survey* covering 11 of the countries included in this study, do not indicate that social capital correlate with economic growth.[12] However, the data are still inconclusive, both because they only cover 11 countries, and because the time lag since the systemic changes is too short. Hence further research along this dimension is needed.[13]

This finally takes us to the central role of the state and administrative capacities in the simultaneous development of markets and democracy. Lack of data and previous research has made this the weakest point of this study, despite the obvious implications for the technical and ultimately political feasibility of alternative institutional strategies. It has been a basic observation that countries that have been able to sustain economic liberalization with institutional reforms and the rule of law have been the most successful, both in terms of economic growth and of democratic consolidation. We have also seen that administrative capacity and absence of corruption varies between countries. It was indicated that one factor behind the strength of institutions was the applicability of an institutional strategy (and ultimately mode of capitalism) to local conditions. But we have little knowledge about what other factors influence the strength or weakness of state institutions in new democracies: courts, parliaments, administrations and political parties and organizations. If we further adhere to the argument that a version of participatory democracy (the West European version of capitalism) or a socially embedded developmental state of the Asian type (Evans, 1995) is most applicable to the social and political landscape of post-communist systems, we will in particular need to find out how to create the bonds between structures of civil society and the state institutions that are preconditions for institutional capacity and strength in a democratic polity. The last question especially should have priority, because the answers we come up with will not only be relevant to the internal development of emerging post-communist democracies and markets – but also help us determine how Western countries should prioritize their assistance to political and economic development of distorted and/or less modernized post-communist countries.

NOTES

1. 'Economic liberalism became almost irrelevant', interview with Gregorz W. Kolodgo, *Transition*, The World Bank, Washington, DC, **9** (3), 1998, Pb.

2. It is of course complicated to determine if democratization is ultimately caused by value changes in the broad public and among the political elite or because it was perceived as the only way in which a new balance of power between leading interest groups and strategic elites could be achieved (Braguinsky, 1998). In all countries it was to a certain extent a result of both, although it may be hypothesized that the lower the initial support for democracy, the greater the importance of elite interaction.

3. I do not intend to engage in formal definitions of democracy or discussions about 'the best' taxonomy of stages of democratization transformations. Basically I here follow Larry Diamond (1999, p. 18) in his conception of democracy (and democratization) as 'a developmental phenomenon'. In this understanding the institutions, structures and values that uphold any democracy – young and old – remains in a permanent process of change and consolidation at all three levels, responding to changes in the environment but without ever reaching an ideal type stage of 'consolidation' (Gunter, Diamandiuros and Puhl, 1995; p. 153). Further support for this implicit critique of the more closed definitions of democratic consolidation is found in the 'concept stretching', obtained by adding adjectives to it (Rose and Chin, 1998, p. 5).

4. This is not the place to enter the discussion about how the correct design of political institutions may make democracy attractive even in cases where the expected benefits do not occur. For an introduction to this discussion on the role of institutions versus values in the consolidation of democracy, see Przeworski (1991, ch. 2).

5. The respondents were asked to state their level of satisfaction with democratic development in the following categories. 1 Very satisfied; 2 Fairly satisfied; 3 Not very satisfied; 4 Not at all satisfied; 5 Don't know; 6 No answer. Satisfaction has been coded as the percentage who stated that they were very or fairly satisfied with democracy development in their own country. Categories 5 and 6 were excluded from the samples.

6. See Chapter 3.

7. The picture of Poland represented in the table is not quite fair, as the high mobilization took place around the election before the systemic change, in 1989, as a follow-up to the round table talks. Hence the 1991 election pictures a situation where the fatigue has already set in.

8. Greskovits argues that the support for populists in Eastern Europe is a response to real problems – hence more like leftist – propagating national interests in the face of international capital.

9. Evans (1995, 1996), Evans and Rauch (1995).

10. That it ultimately is not the type of institutions that is decisive for economic progress, but rather the capacity of institutions to generate political stability and administrative predictability, is indicated in a number of recent studies that have examined investment and growth in post-communist countries (Brunetti, Kisunko and Weder, 1997). The proxy for stability has in some cases been the various 'confidence' measures (Clarke, 1995; Knack and Keefer, 1995).

11. As Argued by Moreno and Bhadura 'a country's growth rate is closely linked to that of nearby countries'.

12. 'Trust in own countrymen' is negatively correlated with growth while there is a weak positive correlation between 'trust in own family' and growth.

13. The relevant countries will be covered by The International Social Survey Program (ISSP) in 2001.

APPENDIX 8

Table A 8.1. Correlation between satisfaction with democracy development and support for the market (country level)

	1992	1993	1994	1995	1996	1997
Correlation	0.876**	0.782**	0.714**	0.856**	0.854**	0.600

*Note: ** significance at the 0.01 level.*

Table A 8.2. Correlation between satisfaction with democracy development and support for the market, country specific (individual level).

Country	1992	1993	1994	1995	1996	1997
Albania	0.25**	0.21**	0.27**	0.43**	0.41**	–
Belarus	0.20**	0.19**	0.13**	0.10**	0.04	–
Bulgaria	0.41**	0.31**	0.33**	0.32**	0.19**	0.49**
Czech Rep.	0.36**	0.34**	0.34**	0.43**	0.40**	0.44**
Estonia	0.30**	0.27**	0.31**	0.35**	0.27**	0.36**
Hungary	0.15**	0.15**	0.15**	0.17**	0.25**	0.36**
Kazakhstan	–	–	0.26**	0.32**	0.34**	–
Latvia	0.24**	0.22**	0.17**	0.23**	0.34**	0.23**
Lithuania	0.23**	0.06	0.20**	0.27**	0.27**	0.32**
Poland	0.36**	0.28**	0.22**	0.16**	0.30**	0.31**
Romania	0.14**	0.21**	0.16**	0.20**	0.24**	0.34**
Russia	0.41**	0.34**	0.27**	0.27**	0.39**	–
Slovakia	0.30**	0.21**	0.21**	0.12**	0.17**	0.24**
Slovenia	0.15**	0.19**	0.17**	0.19**	0.17**	0.21**
Ukraine	0.32**	0.23**	0.15**	0.23**	0.29**	–

*Note: **significance at the 0.01 level.*

Source: EastEurobarometer, subsequent years.

A Note on Data

When the study of the communist world proceeded under the heading 'Soviet Studies' hard data were scarce, and insights often based more on informed speculation than systematic research. Economic data were notoriously unreliable (Pockney, 1991; Bartholdy, 1997), and serious empirical sociology limited to a few of the more liberal countries. This situation changed fundamentally when the old systems collapsed. Since the beginning of transition the field has been brimming with hard data flowing from international financial institutions, from in-country sociological research and from innumerable surveys of public attitudes and political culture, the latter developing into a virtual industry, keeping alive local research centres and jump-starting academic careers in the West. However, the present abundance of hard data present opportunities as well as dangers. They offer new opportunities because we are obviously on firmer ground when we are able to base our research on empirical data than when we had to base our conclusions on casual observation and more or less manipulated data which served the interests of local politicians rather than independent research. The new opportunities, however, also present new problems related to the structural change in these societies, change in statistical methods – and the survival of old problems. Below I briefly summarize the major hazards that are associated with the major categories of quantitative data included in this study. For an in depth critical analysis of the problems related to the various types of data please refer to the cited literature. The hazards apply to a various extent to the types of data applied: national accounts – estimates of GDP development and inflation; living standards and social welfare – poverty and inequality; quantitative survey methods – attitude to market reforms and democracy. Institutional change – estimates of change in economic and political institutions – was dealt with in Chapters 4, 5 and 6 and will not be repeated here. Nor will I engage in the wide-ranging discussion about the validity of alternative measurements of liberal democracy. In the present study I have used The Freedom House Index and its special survey of transitional countries, 'Nations in Transit' (Karatnycky et al., 1997), applying a slightly different methodology compared to the standard Freedom House Indexes. For a survey of the methodological discussion about measurements of democracy, see Shin (1994, pp. 146–150). Nevertheless, all the data are beset with problems and biases to varying extents which should be taken into account when making a prudent assessment of the conclusions, and in particular of the level of exactness that (falsely) appears when applying quantitative methodology. Still, with all these caveats in mind, it is my belief that the analyses of available data represent the correct trends and (largely) the relative ranking of the individual cases (countries), but not (necessarily) their precise position as reflected in the use of interval scales.

ESTIMATION OF NATIONAL ACCOUNTS IN TRANSITION ECONOMIES

A large number of authors have observed that the output statistics produced by local agencies – and to a lesser extent by international organizations – have tended to exaggerate the contraction in output that has occurred since the beginning of the economic transition (Hellman, 1998; Bartholdy, 1997; Holzmann and Winkler, 1995; EBRD, 1994, chapter 11), adding to the reliability problems that historically besieged national account statistics in planned economies (Grossman, 1950; Pockney, 1991). First of all, the estimates had a built-in bias because of the shrinking state sector (with large enterprises) has produced more reliable data than the emerging and growing private sector comprising predominantly small enterprises. Secondly, the introduction of market prices and attempts to adopt the UN System of National Accounts (SNA) improve the validity of GDP figures, but also increases the observed contraction when assessed against the traditional Material Product System (MPS) that excluded many types of services of what in socialist parlance was known as the 'non-material sphere'. At the same time evidence of economic growth may in some instances be exaggerated, as it reflects the entry into official statistics of activities that were previously not included or simply went unrecorded (the black economy). The level of inflation may have been overstated too because of problems with the choice of base year, deflation mechanisms and indexing formulas. Similarly, the exclusion of black market trading, where prices have been negatively affected by price liberalization, has further exaggerated inflation because of the inability to take the increase in quality of output into account.

A number of factors further complicate the picture when national account estimates are used as a proxy for welfare measurements. Especially the exclusion of the unofficial economy, side payments, the shadow economy, informal trade or even home grown vegetables exaggerates the implication of economic aggregates for individual welfare (Rose and McAllister, 1996; Rose, 1992, 1995a, b). Nor do the aggregates reflect the shift in output from heavy and military industry towards goods and services that satisfy consumer demands, the benefits engendered by the abolition of queues and improvement in the quality of consumer goods. Finally, the discontinuation of Russian subsidies to the former Union republics (in the form of cheap energy, raw materials and direct transfers) add to the welfare of Russian citizens but make things even worse than registered in the national accounts for citizens of the new independent states.

Although the hazards associated with national accounts in countries of transition should of course be considered, there is no reason to believe that there are any systematic biases in the sources and directions of the hazards described. It can at most be hypothesized that the more peripheral the country, the less developed its statistical agencies, and the greater the difficulties of registering new activities as unregistered activities become more extensive. This implies that the recession in most of the newly independent states of the former Soviet Union has been more exaggerated than in the core countries of Central Europe and of Russia proper.

ESTIMATES OF INEQUALITY AND POVERTY

A second group of variables in the study attempt to estimate the social costs of the change of economic transformation. While the social decay incurred in these countries covers a broad range of fields – from unemployment and divorce rates to alcoholism and mortality rates – the present study applies increase in inequality and poverty as general proxies in estimating the relative costs in each of the 20 countries. It was further decided to use the GINI quotient to represent the increase in inequality, because the use of the alternative decile ratios are severely constrained by the systematic underreporting of high incomes in transition economies. While it will of course be subject to infinite discussions, it was – for practical reasons – decided to use a poverty line of $120 per month per capita in 1990 international prices (a critical discussion of alternative poverty lines is found in the 1997 World Development Report, pp. 251ff). The data used in this study was compiled and revised by World Bank researcher Branko Milanovic (1995; 1998a, b). Most of the East European data are based on surveys conducted by the national statistical offices, while the studies of most republics of the former Soviet Union were of such low quality that they were either profoundly revised or replaced by new surveys. Most estimates are based on disposable income (gross income minus payroll and direct personal income taxes). Where possible, more reliable expenditure-based estimates were applied. Because of the pre-transition quality of surveys and processes related to the transition process, the data are vitiated by a number of biases (Atkinson and Micklewright, 1992, chapter 3). First, pre-transition surveys in the former Soviet Union were flawed and systematically excluded the poorest segments of the population, thus underestimating real poverty and inequality. Secondly, the coverage of wages and social transfer incomes has deteriorated and probably given rise to an upward bias in the lowest incomes. Thirdly, refusal rates in recent surveys have been very high in the highest income brackets, thus underestimating inequality and increase in poverty. Fourthly, the growth of the informal economy creates an upward bias in the lowest incomes, leading to overestimates of the growth in poverty because people have a portfolio of different non-monetary means of income (Rose, 1995b). Fifth, the transition from non-monetary fringe benefits in the old system to monetarized inequality overestimates the actual increase in inequality. The bottom line of these biases probably overestimates increase in poverty and inequality. As summarized by Milanovic (1998a, p. 155), this especially applies to countries where the quality of recent surveys has increased, and where present data are therefore compared with old data with a downward bias in both poverty and inequality assessments: The Baltic States, Russia, Belarus and Ukraine, Kyrgyzstan and Romania.

PUBLIC OPINION SURVEYS

If you ask a person who has spent all his or her life in a non-democratic and non-market environment impregnated with decades of anti-market and anti-pluralist and anti-liberal propaganda, if he or she support market reforms or is satisfied with democracy, interpreting the answers obtained is obviously no straight forward matter. People may support any change that signals a radical break with the incumbent system without thereby signalling any firm commitment. This is for example the case when Denisovsky et al. (1993) argue that support for market economy is overstated. Through an analysis of a broader array of indicators they show that only 12 per cent of respondents supported the market on the basis of a clear understanding of the concept and its implications. They may associate the concepts with a foreign and idealized life style, like the images that were brought to distant parts of the Soviet Union when soap operas made their way into Soviet media in the late 1980s. Capitalism was associated with supermarkets (contrasted to the local empty stores) and democracy with the fair and uncorrupted policeman or politician, so very different from the local corrupt party officials. Or people may imbue Western concepts of market and democracy with local meanings, as when for example Reisinger et al. (1994, p. 215), observe that in many post-Soviet states the desire for a strong leader is positively correlated with support for democratic values. The problem is that we simply do not know how the respondents understand the concepts. And all we can do is to do the best we can to understand each individual society, its history and experiences, and from there infer how concrete concepts are interpreted. To these conceptual travails is further added the psychological disorder, or what Eckstein (1988, p. 796) terms 'cultural formlessness', which arises when a population 'loses its cohesiveness and become disoriented; in a representation of Durkheim's anomie, individuals are unable to use their past cultural base to make sense of their new surrounding' (Alexander, 1997, p. 109). The conceptual ambivalence and the formlessness produced by a rapidly changing context explains the contradictory results that have been obtained by different researchers. In the present study I have chosen to use data from only one source, the

EastEurobarometer, produced by the European Commission, which covers an increasing number of transition countries from 1991 to 1997, as shown in Table N1.

While the data are far from perfect, an attempt was made to use the same questions when surveying representative groups of citizens. By using only one source, I try as far as possible to avoid the ambiguities associated with different phrasing of questions and varying survey procedures. I use only two sets of answers: level of support for the market and satisfaction with democracy, in conjunction with a number of background variables. Rather than insightful assessments of abstract economic and political systems, I see these attitudes as formed by a mixture of concrete experiences, idealized stereotypes and local conceptual traditions. The initial or average level of support or satisfaction will at most tell us something about the compatibility between the market, a Western type democracy – and local traditions and values. The last argument implies that the further we move from Western Europe, or the more distorted the country, the more cautious we must be in the interpretation of answers to questions that carry concepts which originate in the Western hemisphere. In this connection I still believe that people will increasingly support the market for what it offers in economic and social terms. And people's satisfaction with democracy will increasingly reflect the virtues or misconduct of successive democratic governments.

Table N1. Countries in the East European Barometer Survey 1990–1997.

	1990	1991	1992	1993	1994	1995	1996	1997
Albania		*	*	*	*	*	*	
Belarus		*	*	*	*	*		
Bulgaria	*	*	*	*	*	*	*	*
Czech Rep.	*	*	*	*	*	*	*	*
Estonia		*	*	*	*	*	*	*
Hungary	*	*	*	*	*	*	*	*
Kazakhstan					*	*	*	
Latvia		*	*	*	*	*	*	*
Lithuania		*	*	*	*	*	*	*
Poland	*	*	*	*	*	*	*	*
Romania		*	*	*	*	*	*	*
Russia	*	*	*	*	*	*	*	
Slovakia	*	*	*	*	*	*	*	*
Slovenia			*	*	*	*	*	*
Ukraine		*	*	*	*	*		

SIGNIFICANCE TESTING

Throughout this study I have chosen to report significance in correlation and regression analyses despite working with a population or universe comprising all post-communist countries not beset by war or natural disasters. As significance testing normally assumes the existence of a sample, and significance measures make inferences about the probability that the sample represents a 'true' picture of the total universe, this might seem self-contradictory. However, I am first of all following a practice that has been applied in virtually all other research that has dealt with the same group of countries – or with similar numbers of countries or regions. Substantially it can be argued that although we are dealing with a universe of all countries included in the category, it is in another sense not a universe but a sample of all future regimes that will become organized along similar patterns and want to engage in economic and political transformation. Or it can be seen as a sample of countries that in the course of history might have entered the path of communist modernization, but where the 20 countries (and about 9 more that have not been included) entered this path. For further discussion of significance testing of non-samples, see Risbjerg Thomsen (1997).

References

Aage, Hans (1994), 'Sustainable Transition', Chapter 2, pp. 15–41 in R. W. Campell (ed.), *The Postcommunist Economic Transformation*, Essays in Honour of Gregory Grossman, Boulder, CO: Westview Press, 1994.

Ágh, Attila (1998a), *Emerging Democracies in East Central Europe and the Balkans*, Cheltenham: Edward Elgar.

Ágh, Attila (1998b), *The Politics of Central Europe*, London: Sage Publications.

Ágh, Attila and Gabrielle Houdki (eds.) (1996), *Parliaments and Organized Interests: The Second Steps*, Budapest: Hungarian Centre for Democracy Studies.

Albert, M. (1993), *Capitalism against Capitalism*, London: Whur Publishers.

Alesina, Alberto (1989), 'Politics and Business Cycles in Industrial Democracies', in *Economic Policy* **April**.

Alesina, Alberto and Roberto Perotti (1994), 'The Political Economy of Growth: A Critical Survey of Recent Litterature', in *The World Bank Economic Review*, **8** (3).

Alexander, James (1997), 'Surveying Attitudes in Russia. A Representation of Formlessness', in *Communist and Post-Communist Studies*, **30** (2).

Amsden, Alice H., Jacek Kochanovicz and Lance Taylor (1994), *The Market Meets Its Match*, Cambridge, MA.: Harvard University Press.

Anderson, James H. (1998),'The Size, Origins, and Character of Mongolia's Informal Sector during the Transition', World Bank, *Policy Research Working Paper* 1916, World Bank, Washington DC.

Andrei Shleifer and Robert W. Vishny (1998), *The Grabbing Hand. Government Pathologies and their Cures*, Cambridge, MA: Harvard University Press.

Arato, Andrew (1990), *Revolution, Civil Society, and Democracy*, New York: New School for Social Research (unpublished).

Armijo, Leslie Eliot, Thomas J. Bresstecker and Abraham Lowenthal (1994), 'The Problems of Simultaneous Transition', *Journal of Democracy*, **5** (4), pp. 161–175.

Asher, Herbert B. (1976), 'Causal Modeling', in *Quantitative applications in the social sciences*, Sage University Press, London.

Asilis, M. and Gian Maria Milesi-Ferretti (1994), *On the Political Sustainability of Economic Reform*, IMF Paper on Policy Analysis and Assessment, IMF, Washington, DC.

Åslund, Anders (1994), 'Lessons of the First Four Years of Systemic Change in Eastern Europe', *Journal of Comparative Economics*, **19**, pp. 22–38.

Åslund, Anders, Peter Boone and Simon Johnson (1996), *How to Stabilize: Lessons from Post-communist Countries*, Brookings Papers on Economic Activity, Brookings Institution, Washington, DC.

Atkinson, Anthony B. and John Micklewright (1992), *Economic Transformation in Eastern Europe and the Distribution of Income*, Cambridge: Cambridge University Press.

Balcerowicz, Leszek (1993), 'Poland', pp. 153–177 in J. Williamson (ed.), *The Political Economy of Policy Reform*, Washington, DC: Institute for International Economics.

Balcerowicz, Leszek (1994), 'Understanding Postcommunist Transitions', *Journal of Democracy*, **5** (4), pp. 75–89.

Balcerowicz, Leszek (1995), *Socialism, Capitalism, Transformation*, Budapest: Central European University Press.

Balcerowicz, Leszek (1997), 'The Interplay between Economic and Political Transition', pp. 153–167 in Salvatore Zeccini (ed.), *Lessons of Economic Transition*, London: Kluwer Academic Press.

Balcerowicz, Leszek, B. Blaszczyk and M. Dabrowski (1997), 'The Polish Way to the Market Economy 1989–1995', in Woo, Parker and Sachs (eds.), *Economics in Transition*, Cambridge, MA: The MIT Press.

Barry, B. (1989), 'Claims of Common Citizenship', *Times Literary Supplement*.

Bartholdy, Kasper (1997), 'Old and New Problems in the Estimation of National Accounts in Transition Economies', in *Economics of Transition*, **5** (1), pp. 131–146.

Bartlet, David (1996), 'Democracy, Institutional Change, and Stabilisation Policy in Hungary', in *Europe–Asia Studies*, **48** (1).

Bartlet, David and Wendy Hunter (1997), 'Market Structures, Political Institutions, and Democratization: the Latin American and East European Experiences', in *Review of International Political Economy*, **4** (1).

Bates, Robert H. and Anne O. Krueger (1994), *Political and Economic Interactions in Economic Policy Reform*, Cambridge, MA: Basil Blackwell.

BBC news, 'Mongolian Government Resigns', BBC News, Asia–Pacific, July 24, 1998, news2.thdo.bbc.co.uk/hi/english/world/asia–pacific/mongoliangovernmentresigns.htm

Bell, Janice (1997), 'Unemployment Matters: Voting patterns during the Economic Transition in Poland, 1990–95', in *Europe–Asia Studies*, **49** (7).

Berend, Ivan T. (1995), 'Alternatives of Transition? Choices and Determinants: East Central Europe in the 1990s', pp. 130–150 in B. Crawford (ed.), *Markets, States and Democracy: The Political Economy of Post-Communist Transformation*, Boulder, CO: Westview Press.

Blejer, Mario O. and Fabrizio Coricelli (1995), *The Making of Economic Reform in Eastern Europe*, Aldershot: Edward Elgar.

Bofinger, Peter (1995), *The Political Economy of Eastern Enlargement of the EU*, London: Centre for Economic Policy Research, discussion paper series no. 1234.

Bondarenko, Valerij (1995), 'Institutional'naja ekonomicheskaja teorija: nekotorye osnovnye voprosy', in *Mirovaja Ekonomika i Mezhdunarodnye otnoshenija*, **11**, pp. 15–30.

Boone, Peter (1994), 'Grassroot Macroeconomic Reform in Mongolia', in *Journal of Comparative Economics*, **18**, pp. 329–356.

Brada, Josef C. (1993), 'The Transformation from Communism to Capitalism: How Far? How Fast?', *Post Soviet Affairs*, **9**, April-June, pp. 87–110.

Brada, Josef C. (1995), 'A Critique of the Evolutionary Approach to the Economic Transition from Communism to Capitalism', pp. 183–209 in Kazimierz Z. Poznanski (ed.), *The Evolutionary Transition to Capitalism*, Boulder, CO: Westview Press.

Braguinsky, Serguey (1998), 'Democracy and economic reform: Theory and some Evidence from the Russian Case', in *Contemporary Economic Policy*, Long Beach, CA: Western Economic Association International.

Bräutigam, Deborah (1997), 'Institutions, economic reform, and democratic consolidation in Mauritius', in *Comparative Politics*, **30** (1), pp. 45–62.

Bruckner, Scott A. (1995), 'Beyond Soviet Studies: The New Institutional Alternative', pp. 198–221 in David Orlovsky (ed.), *Beyond Soviet Studies*. Baltimore, MA: The Johns Hopkins University Press.

Brunetti, Aymo (1997), 'Political variables in cross-country growth analyses', in *Journal of economic surveys*, **11** (2).

Brunetti, A., G. Kisunko and B. Weder (1997), 'Institutions in transition. Reliability of Rules and Economic Performance in Former Socialist Countries', *Research Working Paper Nr. 1809*, Washington, DC: The World Bank.

Bruszt, L. (1992), 'Transformation Politics in East Central Europe', in *East European Politics and Societies*, **6** (1), pp. 52–70.

Bruun, Ole and Ole Odgaard (eds.) (1996), *Mongolia in Transition, Old Patterns, New Challenges*, Nordic Institute of Asian Studies, **22**, Richmond, Surrey.

Bunce, Valerie (1983), 'The political economy of the Brezhnev era: The rise and fall of corporatism', in *British Journal of Political Science*, **13**, pp. 129–158.

Bunce, Valerie (1995a), 'Comparing East and South', in *Journal of Democracy*, **6** (3), pp. 87–100.

Bunce, Valerie (1995b), 'Should Transitologists Be Grounded?', in *Slavic Review*, **54** (1), pp. 111–127.

Bunce, Valerie and John M. Echols (1988), 'Soviet Politics in the Brezhnev Era: "Pluralism" or "Corporatism"', in Donald R. Kelly (ed.), *Soviet Politics in the Brezhnev Era*, New York: Praeger.

Cameron, Maxwell A. (1998), 'Self Coups: Peru, Guatamala and Russia', in *Journal of Democracy*, **9** (1).

Cardoso, Eliana (1992), *Inflation and poverty*, NBER working paper 4006.

Carlsen, Axel Vladimir (1998), *Socialdemokratismens muligheder og begrænsninger i det postsovjetiske Rusland.* Aarhus: Department of Political Science, University of Aarhus, Ph.D. thesis.

Carr, E.H. (1950), *The Bolshevik Revolution*, London: Penguin Books.

Castles, F.G. and D. Michells (1993), 'Worlds of Welfare and Families of Nations', in F.G. Castles (ed.), *Families of Nations: Pattern of Public Policies in Western Nations*, Aldershot: Dartmouth.

Chirot, Daniel (ed.) (1989), *The origins of backwardness in Eastern Europe*, Berkeley, CA: University of California Press.

Citrin, Daniel A. and Ashok K. Lahri (eds.) (1995), 'Policy Experiences and Issues in the Baltics, Russia, and Other Countries of the Former Soviet Union', *Occasional paper 133*, Washington, DC: IMF.

Clark, Ed and Anna Soulsby (1996), 'The reformation of the managerial elite in the Czech Republic', in *Europe–Asia Studies*, **48** (2), pp. 536–560.

Clarke, George R.G. (1995), 'More evidence on income distribution and growth', in *Journal of Development Economics*, **45**, pp. 405–443.

Collier, David (1991), 'New Perspective on the Comparative Method', pp. 7–31 in Rankwort A. Rustow and Kenneth Paul Erickson (eds.), *Comparative Political Dynamics*, Global Research Perspectives, New York: Harper Collins.

Collier, R.B. and D. Collier (1991), *Shaping the political arena: Critical junctures, the labor movement, and regime dynamics in Latin America*, Princeton, NJ: Princeton University Press.

Coppedge, M. (1999), 'Thickening thin concepts and theories – Combining large N and small n in comparative politics', in *Comparative Politics*, **31** (4), pp. 465–488.

Coricelli, Fabrizio (1997), *Economic Performance and Liberalization in Transition Economies: the Role of Reforms and the Weight of the Past.* Unpublished paper, Universitá di Siena: Central European University.

Cornea, Andrea Giovanni, Richard Jolly and Frances Stuart (1987), *Adjustment with a Human Face.* London: Clarendon Press.

Crawford, Beverly (1995), 'Post-Communist Political Economy: A Framework for the Analyses of Reform', in B. Crawford (ed.) *Markets, States and Democracy*, Boulder, CO: Westview Press.

Dabrowski, Marek (1996), 'Different Strategies of Transition to a Market Economy', *Policy Research Working Paper* 1579, Washington, DC: The World Bank.

Dahl, Robert A. (1989), *Democracy and Its Critics*, New Haven, CT: Yale University Press.

Dawisha, Karen and Michael Turner (1997) 'The Interaction Between Internal and External Agency in Post-communist Transitions', in K. Dawisha (ed.) *The International Dimension of Post-communist Transitions in Russia and the new States of Eurasia*, Aremonk, NY: M.E. Sharpe.

De Melo, Martha and Alan Gelb (1996), *Transition to Date: A Comparative Overview*, The World Bank, 1996, unpublished manuscript, 32 pp.

De Melo, Martha and Alan Gelb (1997), 'Transition to Date: A Comparative Overview', in S. Zeccini (ed.), *Lessons of Economic Transition*, London: Kluwer Academic Publishers.

De Melo, Martha, C. Denizer, A. Gelb and S. Tenev (1997), *'Circumstance and Choice: The Role of Initial Conditions and Policies in Transition Economies'*, Mimeo, Washington, DC: The World Bank, International Finance Corporation.

Deininger, Klaus and Lyn Squire (1997), *Economic Growth and Income Inequality: Reexamining the Links*, Washington, DC: The World Bank.

Deleeck, H. and K. Van den Bosch (1992), 'Poverty and Adequacy of Social Security in Europe: A Comparative Analysis', in *Journal of European Social Policy*, **2** (2).

Denisova, E. (1994), 'Ot finansovoj stabilizatsii k ekonomicheskomu rostu: nekotorye uroki razvivjushchixhsja stran', in *Mirovaja ekonomika i mezhdunarodnye otnoshenija*, **8–9**, pp. 115–118.

Denisovsky, G., P. Kozyreva and M. Matskovsky (1993), 'The Twelve Percent of Hope: Economic Consciousness and a Market Economy', pp. 224–238 in A. Miller, W. Reisinger and V. Hesli (eds.), *Public Opinion and Regime Change,* Boulder, CO: Westview Press.

Diamond, Larry (1997), 'Democracy and Economic Reform: Tensions, Compatibilities and Strategies of Reconciliation', in E. Lazear (ed.), *Economic Transition in Eastern Europe and Russia: tensions, compatibilities*, Stanford, CA: Hoover Institute Press.

Diamond, Larry (1999), *Developing Democracy. Toward consolidation*, Baltimore, MD: The Johns Hopkins University Press.

Dornbush, Rüdiger and Sebastian Edwards (1991), *The Macroeconomics of Populism in Latin America*, Chicago: University of Chicago Press.

Easter, Gerald M. (1997), 'Preference for Presidentialism. Postcommunist Regime change in Russia and the NIS', in *World Politics*, **49**.

Eatwell, John, et al. (1995), *Transformation and Integration. Shaping the Future of Central and Eastern Europe*, London: Institute for Public Policy Research.

EBRD (European Bank of Reconstruction and Development), *Transition Report*, October 1994, London: EBRD.

EBRD (European Bank of Reconstruction and Development), *Transition Report*, October 1997, London: EBRD.

ECE (1993), *Economic Survey of Europe in 1992–93*, UN Economic Commission for Europe, New York: UN.

Eckstein, Harry (1988), 'A culturalist theory of political change' in *American Political Science Review*, **82** (3), pp. 789–804.

Eckstein, Harry (1998), 'Unfinished business. Reflections on the Scope of Comparative Politics', in *Comparative Political Studies*, **31** (4), pp. 505–535.

Eeg, Hans van and Harry Garretsen (1994), 'The Theoretical Foundation of the Reforms in Eastern Europe: Big-Bang versus Gradualism and the Limitations of Neo-Classical Theory', in *Economic Systems*, **18** (1), pp. 1–13.

Eggleston, Roland (1997), 'Belarus: OSCE Report on Movement towards a Totalitarian State', in rferl.org/nca/features/1997/06/F.RU.970604110320. html, RFE/RL.

Ernst & Young, (1995), 'Survey of Business Locations in Europe', *Financial Times*, 24 October.

Evans, Geoffrey and Stephen Whitefield (1995), 'The politics and Economics of Democratic Commitment: Support for Democracy in Transition Societies', in *British Journal of Political Science*, **25**.

Evans, Peter (1992), 'The State as Problem and Solution: Predation, Embedded Autonomy, and Structural Change', pp. 138–181 in Stephan Haggard and Robert R. Kaufman (eds.), *The Politics of Economic Adjustment. International Constraints, Distributive Conflicts, and the State*. Princeton, NJ: Princeton University Press.

Evans, Peter (1995), *Embedded Autonomy, State and Industrial Transformation*, Princeton, NJ: Princeton University Press.

Evans, Peter (1996), 'Government Action, Social Capital and Development: Reviewing the Evidence on Synergy, in *World Development* **24** (6), pp. 1119–1132.

Evans, Peter B. and James E. Rauch (1995), 'Bureaucratic Structures and Economic Performance in Less Developed Countries', in *Working Paper Series*, IRIS, Center for Institutional Reform and the Informal Sector, University of Maryland at College Park.

Fareed, Zakaria (1997), 'The Rise of Illiberal Democracy', in *Foreign Affairs*, **76** (6).

Feinstein, Charles et al. (1991), 'Historical Precedents for Economic Change in Central Europe and the USSR', *Oxford Analytica*.

Fish, Steven M. (1998a), 'The Determinants of Economic Reforms in the Post-communist World', in *East European Politics and Society*, **12** (1).

Fish, Steven M. (1998b), 'Mongolia: Democracy Without Prerequisites', *Journal of Democracy*, **9** (3), pp. 127–141.

Fox, Jonathan (1994), 'The Difficult Transition from Clientism to Citizenship', in *World Politics*, **46** (January).

Frederich, Carl J. (1954) 'The Unique Character of Totalitarian Society', in Frederich (ed.), *Totalitarianism*, Boston, MA: Harvard University Press.

Freedom House (1999), '*Freedom in the world rankings*', "www.freedom-house.org"

Freitag-Wirminghaus, Rainer (1998a), 'Turkmenistan's Place in Central Asia and the World', in T. Atabaki and J. O'Kane (eds.) *Post-Soviet Central Asia*, Leiden: The International Institute for Asian Studies.

Freitag-Wirminghaus, Rainer (1998b), 'Turkmenistan's Place in Cental Asia and the World', in T. Atabaki and J. O'Kane (eds.), *Post-Soviet Central Asia*, London: Tauris Academic Studies.

Frenkel, Roberto and Guillermo O'Donnell (1979), 'The "Stabilization Programs" of the International Monetary Fund and their Intenal Impact', pp. 171–203 in Richard R. Fagen (ed.), *Capitalism and the State in U.S.– Latin American Relations*, Stanford, CA: Stanford University Press.

Frentzel-Zagorska, Janina and Kryssztof Zagorski (1993), 'Polish Public Opinion on Privatization and State Interventionism', in *Europe–Asia Studies* **45** (4), pp. 705–728.

Friederich, Carl, J. Zbigniew and K. Brzezinski (1956), *Totalitarian Dictatorship and Autocracy*, Cambridge, MA: Cambridge University Press.

Frye, Timothy (1997), 'A Politics of Institutional Choice. Post Communist Presidencies', in *Comparative Political Studies*, **30** (5), pp. 523–552.

Galton, F. (1889), 'Comment on E.B. Taylor: On a method of investigating the development of institutions', in *Journal of the Anthropological Institute of Great Britain and Ireland*, pp. 245–275.

Geddes, Barbara (1994), *Politician's Dilemma*, Berkeley, CA: University of California Press.

Geddes, Barbara (1995), 'A Comparative Perspective on the Leninist Legacy in Eastern Europe', in *Comparative Political Studies* **28** (2), pp. 239–274.

Gerner, Kristian, Stefan Hedlund and Niclas Sundström (1995), *Hjärnridån*, Stockholm: Fischer & Co.

Gerschenkron, A. (1962), *Economic Backwardness in Historical Perspective*, New York: Praeger.

Gibson, John and Anna Cielcecka (1995), 'Economic Influences on the Political Support for Market Reform in Post-communist Transitions: Some Evidence from the 1993 Polish Parliamentary Elections', in *Europe–Asia Studies*, **47** (5).

Ginsburg, Tom (1997), 'Mongolia in 1996: Fighting Fire and Ice', *Asian Survey*, **37** (1), p. 60.

Giovanni, Andrea Cornea, Richard Jolly and Francis Stewart (1987), *Adjustment with a Human Face*, vol. I, Oxford: Clarendon Press.

Gowan, Peter (1995), 'Neo-liberal theory and practice for Eastern Europe', in *New Left Review*, **213**.

Greskovits, Béla (1998), *The Political Economy of Protest and Patience. East European and Latin American Transformations Compared*, Budapest: CEU Press.

Griffith, Keith (ed.) (1995), *Poverty and the Transition to a Market Economy in Mongolia*, Chippenham: St. Martin's Press.

Grosfeld, Irena (1995), 'Triggering Evolution: The Case for a Breakthrough in Privatization', pp. 211–228, in Kazimiecz Z. Poznanski (ed.), *The Evolutionary Transition to Capitalism*, Boulder, CO: Westview Press.

Grossman, Gregory (1950), *Soviet Statistics of Physical Output of Industrial Commodities. Their Compilation and Quality*. Princeton, NJ: Princeton University Press.

Gunter, R., P.N. Diamandiuros and H.-J. Puhl (eds.) (1995), *The Politics of Democratic Consolidation: Southern Europe in a Comparative Perspective,* Baltimore, MD: Johns Hopkins University Press.

Hadenius, Axel (1992), *Democracy and Development*, Cambridge: Cambridge University Press.

Haggard, Stephan (1990), *Pathways from the Periphery. The Politics of Growth in the Newly Industrializing Countries*, Ithaca, NY and London: Cornell University Press.

Haggard, Stephan and Robert R. Kaufman (1992), 'The Political Economy of Inflation and Stabilization in Middle-Income Countries', pp. 270–315 in S. Haggard and R. Kaufman (eds.), *The Politics of Economic Adjustment, International Constraints, Distributive Conflicts, and the State*, Princeton, NJ: Princeton University Press.

Haggard, Stephan and Robert R. Kaufman (1994), 'The Challenges of Consolidation', in *Journal of Democracy*, **5** (4).

Haggard, Stephan, J.D. Lafay and C. Morrison (1995), *The Political Feasibility of Adjustment in Developing Countries*, Paris: OECD.

Haggard, Stephan and Steven B. Webb (eds.) (1994), *Voting for reform*, Oxford: The World Bank and Oxford University Press.

Hall, Peter (ed.) (1989), *The Political Power of Economic Ideas*, Princeton, NJ: Princeton University Press.

Hall, Peter A. & Rosemary C.R. Taylor (1996), 'Political Science and the Three New Institutionalisms', in *Political Studies*, **44**.

Hall, Robert E. and Charles I. Jones (1996), 'The Productivity of Nations', in *Working Paper Series*, Cambridge, MA: National Bureau of Economic Research, Inc.

Hansen, John and Piritta Sorsa (1994), 'Estonia: A Shining Star from the Baltics', pp. 115–132 in Constantine Michalopoulos and David G. Tarr (eds.), *Trade in the New Independent States, Studies of Economies in Transformation*, **13**, The World Bank/UNDP.

Hansson, Ardo (1994), 'The Political Economy of Macroeconomic and Foreign Trade Policy in Estonia', pp. 133–140 in Constantine Michalopoulos and David G. Tarr (eds.), *Trade in the New Independent States, Studies of Economies in Transition*, **13**, The World Bank/UNDP.

Hausner, Jerry, Bob Jessop and Klaus Nielsen (1995), *Strategic Choice and Path-Dependency in Post-Socialism: Institutional Dynamics in the Transformation Process*, Aldershot: Edward Elgar.

Hayek, F.A. (1945), 'The Use of Knowledge in Society', in *American Economic Review*, **35**.

Hayek, F.A. (1994), *Hayek on Hayek*, London: Routledge.

Hays, William L. (1974), *Statistics for the Social Sciences*, 2nd ed., London: Holt, Rinehart & Winston.

Hellman, Joel (1996), 'Constitutions and Economic Reforms in Post-Communist Transition', *East European Constitutional Review*, **5** (1).

Hellman, Joel S. (1998), 'The Winners Take All. Post-communist Transitions', in *World Politics*, **50**.

Herz, John (ed.) (1982), *From Dictatorship to Democracy. Coping with the Legacies of Authoritarianism and Totalitarianism*, Westport, CT: Greenwood Press.

Hesse, Joachim Jens (1993), 'From Transformation to Modernization: Administrative Change in Central and Eastern Europe', pp. 219–257 in Joachim Jens Hesse (ed.), *Administrative Transformation in Central and Eastern Europe*, Oxford: Blackwell.

Hettne, Björn (1994), 'The Political Economy of Post-Communist Development', *The European Journal of Development Research*, **6** (1), pp. 39–60.

Higley, John, Judith Kullberg and Jan Pakulski (1996), 'The Persistence of Postcommunist Elites', in *Journal of Democracy*, **7** (2).

Hirschman, Albert (1981), *Essays in Trespassing. Economics to Politics and Beyond*, Cambridge: Cambridge University Press.

Holzmann, R., J. Gacs and G. Winkler (1995), *Output Decline in Eastern Europe*, Dordrecht: Kluwer Academic Press.

Hough, Jerry (1997), *The Soviet Union and Social Science Theory*, Cambridge MA: Cambridge University Press.

Huang, Yashing (1994) 'Information, Bureaucracy, and Economic Reforms in China and the Soviet Union', *World Politics*, **47** (1), pp. 102–133.

Huntington, Samuel P. (1965), 'Political Development and Political Decay', in *World Politics*, **17** (2), pp. 387–430.

Huntington, Samuel P. (1968), *Political Order in Changing Societies*, New Haven, CT: Westview Press.

Huskey, Eugene (1997), 'Kyrgistan: The Fate of Political Liberalisation', in K. Dawisha and B. Parrot (eds), *Conflict, Cleavage, and the Change in Central Asia and the Caucasus*, Cambridge: Cambridge University Press.

Hutton, Will (1995), *The State We're In*, London: Jonathan Cape.

Hyman, Anthony (1994), *Political Change in Post-Soviet Central Asia*, London: The Royal Institute of International Affairs.

IMF Staff Country Report (1997) no. 97/92, 'Mongolia, Recent Economic Developments', Washington DC: International Monetary Fund.

IMF Staff Country Report (1999) no. 99/4 'Mongolia, Selected Issues', Washington, DC: International Monetary Fund.

IMF Staff Country Reports 95/195, 'Latvia – Recent Economic Developments', Washington, DC: International Monetary Fund.

Inglehart, Ronald (1996), *Culture Shifts in Advanced Industrial Society*, Princeton, NJ: Princeton University Press.

Jensen, Donald N. (1998), How Russia is Ruled. Radio Free Europe/Radio Liberty, www.rferl.org.nca/special/ruwhorules/index.html.

Jerschina, Jan and Jaroslaw Górniak (1997), 'Leftism, Achievement Orientation, and Basic Dimensions of the Source – Economic and Political Attitudes in Baltic Countries Versus other Central and East European Countries', in Hood, Kilis and Vahlne (eds.), *The Baltic post-socialist Enterprises and the Development of Organizational Capabilities*, London: Macmillan.

JICA (1997), Country Study for Japan's Official Development Assistance to Mongolia, Tokyo: Japan International Cooperation Agency, Tokyo.

Johannsen, Lars (1999), *The Constitution and Democracy (in postcommunist countries)*, Unpublished Manuscript, Aarhus: Department of Political Science, University of Aarhus.

Johnson, Julit (1994), 'Should Russia Adopt the Chinese Model of Economic Reform?', *Communist and Post-Communist Studies*, **27** (1), pp. 59–75.

Johnson, Simon and Marzena Kowalska (1994), 'Poland: The Political Economy of Shock Therapy', in S. Haggard, and S.B. Webb (eds.), *Voting for Reform*, Oxford: Oxford University Press.

Jones, Charles I. (1998), *Introduction to Economic Growth*, London: W.W. Norton & Co.

Kahler, Miles (1990), 'Orthodoxy and its Alternatives: Explaining Approaches to Stabilization and Adjustment', pp. 33–61 in J.M. Nelson (ed.), *Economic Crises and Policy Choice. The Politics of Adjustment in the Third World*, Princeton, NJ: Princeton University Press.

Karatnycky, Adrian et al. (eds.) (1997), *Nations in Transit 1997*, Freedom House Organization.

Karl, Terry Lynn and Philippe C. Schmitter (1991), 'Modes of Transition in Latin America, Southern and Eastern Europe', in *International Social Science Journal*, **128**, pp. 269–284.

Karpunin, V. (1994), 'Problemy privatizatcii v razvivajushchichsja stranach', *Mirovaja ekonomika i mezhdunarodnye otnoshenija*, **8–9**, pp. 120–125.

Katz, Stanley S. (1991), 'East Europe should learn from Asia', in *Financial Times*, **24** (4).

Keynes, J.N. (1890), *The Scope and Method of Political Economy*, London: Macmillan.

Khrystanovskaya, Olga (1994), 'Transformacii staryj nomenklatura v novyi elit', in *Izvestija*, 18 May, Moscow.

Kikic, Laza (1996), 'Assessing and Measuring Progress in the Transition', *Economies in Transition. Eastern Europe and the Former Soviet Union. Regional Overview*, 2nd Quarter, p. 5, The Economist Intelligence Unit.

Kim, Jae-On and Charles W. Mueller (1983), *Factor Analysis. Statistical Methods and Practical Issues*, Sage University Paper: Quantitative Applications in the Social Sciences, London: Sage University Press.

Kim Jae-On and Charles W. Mueller (1984), *Introduction to Factor Analysis. What it is and how to do it*, Sage University Paper: Quantitative Applications in the Social Sciences, London: Sage University Press.

Knack, S. and P. Keefer (1995), 'Institutions and Economic Performance: Cross-country Tests using Alternative Institutional Measures', in *Economics and Politics*, **7** (3).

Knight, James (1992), *Institutions and Social Conflict*, Cambridge: Cambridge University Press.

König, K. (1992), 'The Transformation of a "Real-Socialist" Administrative System into a Conventional Western European System', *International Review of Administrative Sciences*, **58** (7).

Kornai, Janos (1992), *The Socialist System. The Political Economy of Communism*, Oxford: Clarendon Press.

Korsun, Georges and Peter Murrell (1995), 'Politics and Economics of Mongolia's Privatization program', *Asian Survey*, **35** (5).

Kuhn, Thomas S. (1973), *Videnskabens resolutioner*, Copenhagen: Forlaget Fremad.

Kuz'min, S. (1998), 'Al'ternativnye strategii social'no-ekonomicheskogo razvitija', in *Ekonomist*, **8**.

Kuznets, S. (1970), *Economic Growth and Structure*, New Haven, CT: Yale University Press.

Lainela, Seija and Pekka Sutela (1997), 'Introducing New Currencies in the Baltic Countries', pp. 66–95 in T. Haavisto (ed.), *The Transition to a Market Economy: Transformation and Reform in the Baltic States*, Cheltenham: Edward Elgar.

Lal, Deepak (1976), 'Distribution and Development', *World Development*, **4** (9), pp. 725–738.

Lal, Deepak and H. Myint (1996), *The Political Economy of Poverty, Equity and Growth: A Comparative Study*, Oxford: Clarendon Press.

Le Figaro, quoted in Radio Free Europe (rferl.org/nca/features/1996/07/F.RU. 96071164653838/html.

Leidy, Michael and Ali Ibrahim (1996), 'Recent Trade Policies and an Approach to Further Reform in the Baltics, Russia and other Countries of the FSU', *IMF Working Paper 96/71*, Washington, DC: International Monetary Fund.

Lepekhin, Vladimir (1995), 'Interest Groups in Present Day Russia and Their Role in the Political Process', pp. 59–76 in Klaus Segbergs and Stephan de Spiegeleire (eds.), *Post-Soviet Puzzles*, **II**, Baden-Baden: Nomos Verlagsgesellschaft.

Lewis, W.A. (1955), *The Theory of Economic Growth*, London: Allan and Unwin.

Lijphardt, Arend (1971), 'Comparative Politics and Comparative Method', *American Political Science Review*, **1971**, pp. 682–693.

Lijphardt, Arend (1975), 'The Comparable-Cases Strategy in Comparative Research', *Comparative Political Studies*, **1975**, pp. 158–72.

Lijphart, Arend (1992) (ed.), *Parliamentary versus Presidential Government*, London: Oxford University Press.

Lijphart, Arend (1999), *Patterns of Democracy*, New Haven, CT: Yale University Press.

Lijphardt, Arend and Carlos H. Waisman (1996), 'Institutional Design and Democratization', pp. 1–12 in Arend Lijphardt and Carlos H. Waisman (eds.), *Institutional Design in New Democracies. Eastern Europe and Latin America*, Boulder, CO: Westview Press.

Lijphart, Arend and Carlos H. Waisman (1996), 'The Design of Markets and Democracies: Generalizing across Regions', in Lijphart and Waisman (eds.) *Institutional Design in New Democracies*, Boulder, CO: Westview Press.

Lindblom, Charles E. (1991), *Democracy and Market Systems*, Oslo: Norwegian University Press.

Lindpere, Hanno (1994), 'The Political Economy of Economic Reforms: The Case of Estonia', pp. 134–149 in Jan Åke Dellenbrant and Ole Nørgaard (eds.), *The Politics of Transition in the Baltic States*, Umeå: Umeå University, Department of Political Science, Research Report **2**.

Lipset, Seymor Martin (1959), 'Some Social Requisites of Democracy: Economic Development and Political Legitimacy', *American Political Science Review*, **53**.

Lipton, David & Jeffrey Sachs (1990), 'Creating a Market Economy in Eastern Europe: The Case of Poland', in *Brooking Papers on Economic Activity*, **1**, pp. 75–138.

MacPherson, C.B. (1979), *Democratic Theory. Essays in Retrieval*, Oxford: Clarendon Press.

Mair, Peter (1998), 'Comparative Politics: An overview', pp. 309–335 in Robert E. Goodin and Hans-Dieter Klingermann (eds.), *A new Handbook of Political Science*, Oxford: Oxford University Press.

Makarenko, V.P. (1999), 'Pravitel'stvo i bjurokratija', in *Sociologicheskie Issledovanie*, **1999** (1).

Maravall, José Maria (1994), 'The Myth of the Authoritarian Advantage', *Journal of Democracy*, **5** (4), pp. 17–31.

Marer, Paul and Andres Koves (eds.) (1992), *Foreign Economic Liberalization*, Boulder, CO: Westview Press.

Marples, David (1996), *Belarus. From Soviet Rule to Nuclear Catastrophe*, London: Macmillan.

Mau, Vladimir (1996), *The Political History of Economic Reforms in Russia, 1985–1994*, Centre for Research into Communist Economies.

Mauro, Paolo (1995), 'Corruption and Growth', in *The Quarterly Journal of Economics*, **110**, pp. 681–712.

McFaul, Michael (1994), 'State Power, Institutional Change, and the Politics of Privatization in Russia', *World Politics*, **20**, pp. 210–243.

McGregor, James (1994), 'The Presidency in East Central Europe', in *RFE/RL Research Report*, **3** (2), pp. 23–31.

McKinnon, Ronald I. (1991), *The Order of Economic Liberalization, Financial Control in the Transition to a Market Economy*, Baltimore, MD: The Johns Hopkins University Press.

Micklewright, see Atkinson and Micklewright (1992).

Mihalisko, Katleen J. (1997), 'Belarus: Retreat to Authoritarianism', in K. Dawisha and B. Parrott (eds.), *Democratic Changes and Authoritarian Reactions in Russia, Ukraine, Belarus and Moldova*, Cambridge: Cambridge University Press.

Mikhalev, V. (1994), 'Regulirovanie zarabotnoj platy: opyt tret'ego mira dlja reform v Rossii', *Mirovaja ekonomika i mezhdunarodnye otnoshenija*, nos. **8–9**, pp. 125–130.

Milanovic, Branko (1995), 'Poverty, Inequality, and Social Policy in Transition Economies', in *Policy Research Working Paper 1530*, Washington, DC: The World Bank.

Milanovic, Branko (1998a), 'Income, Inequality and Poverty during the Transition from Planned to Market Economy', World Bank, Regional and Sectoral Studies, Washington, DC: The World Bank.

Milanovic, Branko (1998b), 'Explaining the Increase in Inequality during the Transition', in *Policy Research Working Paper 1995*, Washington, DC: The World Bank.

Millar, James R. (1995), 'Rethinking Soviet Economic Studies', pp. 225–246 in Daniel Orlovsky (ed.), *Beyond Soviet Studies*, Baltimore, MD: The Johns Hopkins University Press.

Moreno, Ramon and Bharat Trehan (1997), *Location and the Growth of Nations*, paper, San Francisco: The Federal Reserve Bank of San Francisco.

Murrell, Peter (1992a), 'Evolutionary and Radical Approaches to Economic Reform', *Economics of Planning*, **25**, pp. 79–95.

Murrell, Peter (1992b), 'Conservative Political Philosophy and the Strategy of Economic Transition', *East European Politics and Societies*, **6** (1), pp. 3–16.

Mytol, Alexander J. (1997), Institutional Legacies and Reform Trajectories, in www.freedomhouse.org.

Nagle, John D. and Alison Mahr (1999), *Democracy and Democratization*, London: Sage Publications.

Naughton, Barry (1995), 'China's Economic Success: Effective Reform Policies or Unique Conditions?', pp. 135–156 in Kazimierz Z. Poznanski (ed.), *The Evolutionary Transition to Capitalism*, Boulder, CO: Westview Press.

Naughton, Barry and John McMillan (1993), 'How to Reform a Planned Economy: Lessons from China', *Oxford Review of Economic Policy*, **8** (1), pp. 130–143.

Nee, Victor and Lian Peng (1994), 'Sleeping with the Enemy: A Dynamic Model of Declining Political Commitment in State Socialism', *Theory and Society*, **23** (April), pp. 152–179.

Nee, Victor and David Stark (1989), *Remaking the Economic Institutions of Socialism*, Stanford, CA: Stanford University Press.

Nelson, Joan M. (1989), *Fragile Coalitions: The Politics of Economic Adjustment*, New Brunswick: Oxford University Press.

Nelson, Joan M. (1990a) (ed.), *Economic Crises and Policy Choice*, Princeton, NJ: Princeton University Press.

Nelson, Joan M. (1990b), 'Introduction: The Politics of Economic Adjustment in Developing Nations', pp. 1–32 in Joan M. Nelson (ed.), *Economic Crises and Policy Choice. The Politics of Adjustment in the Third World*, Princeton, NJ: Princeton University Press.

Nelson, Joan M. (1992), *Economic Crises and Policy Choice*, Princeton, NJ: Princeton University Press.

Nelson, Joan M. (1993), 'The Politics of Economic Transition. Is Third World Experience Relevant in Eastern Europe?', *World Politics*, **45**, pp. 433–463.

Nelson, Joan M. (1994a), *A Precarious Balance. An Overview of Democracy and Economic Reform in Eastern Europe and Latin America*, International Center for Economic Growth and Overseas Development Council, San Francisco.

Nelson, Joan M. (1994b), 'Linkages between Politics and Economics', *Journal of Democracy*, **5** (4), pp. 49–62.

Nelson, Richard R. and Sidney G. Winter (1982), *An Evolutionary Theory of Economic Change*, Cambridge, MA: The Belknap Press of Harvard University Press.

Nielsen, Klaus (1992), *Pluralism, Corporatism and the Negotiated Economy – Perspectives for Post-Communism*, paper for the conference 'Transforming Post-Socialist Societies: Theoretical Perspectives and Future Prospects for Economic and Political Change in Europe'.

Nielsen, Klaus, Bob Jessop and Jazy Hausner (1995), 'Institutional Change in Post-Socialism', pp. 3–44 in J. Hausner et al. (eds.), *Strategic Choice and Path-Dependency in Post-Socialism: Institutional Dynamics in the Transformation Process*, Aldershot: Edward Elgar.

Nikitchenko, A.I. (1999), 'Transnacionalizatcija demokratija (II) 'Tret'ja volna demokratizatsii v svete teorij mirovoj ekonomiki)', in *Polis* **1999** (2).

Nissen, S. (1998), 'Comparative politics. The Case of Case Studies: On the Methodological Discussion in Comparative Political Science', in *Quality & Quantity*, **32** (4), pp. 399–418.

Nohlen, Dieter and Mario Fernández (eds.) (1991), *Presidencialismo versus parlamentarismo*, Caracas: Editorial Nueva Sociedad.

Nørgaard, Ole (1979), *Politisk deltagelse i Sovjetunionen*, Aarhus: Selskabet for Østeuropastudier.

Nørgaard, Ole (1985), *Politik og reformer i Sovjetunionen*, Esbjerg: Sydjysk Universitetsforlag.

Nørgaard, Ole (1988), 'Perestrojka and the Social Sciences in the Soviet Union: Does the Gorbachev Reforms Imply a New Role for the Social Scientists?', *Nordic Journal of Soviet and East European Studies*, **5** (2), pp. 139–155.

Nørgaard, Ole (1992), 'The Political Economy of Transition in Post-Socialist Systems: The Case of the Baltic States', *Scandinavian Political Studies*, **15** (1), pp. 41–60.

Nørgaard, Ole (1995), *The Baltic States after Independence*, Aldershot: Edward Elgar.

Nørgaard, Ole, Per Carlsen and Nikolaj Petersen (1995), 'Danish Ostpolitik 1967–1993: Breakdown of Stability – Unknown Challenges', pp. 133–162 in Carsten Due-Nielsen and Nikolaj Petersen (eds.), *Adaptation and Activism. The Foreign Policy of Denmark, 1967–1993*, Copenhagen: Dansk Udenrigspolitisk Institut, DJØF Publishing.

Nørgaard, Ole and Lars Johannsen (1999), *The Baltic States after Independence*, Aldershot: Edward Elgar.

North, Douglass C. (1990), *Institutions, Institutional Change and Economic Performance*, Cambridge: Cambridge University Press.

North, Douglass C. (1997), *The Contribution of the New Institutional Economics to Understanding of the Transition Problem*, UNU/WIDER 1997 Annual Lecture.

O'Donnell, Guillermo (1996), 'Delegative Democracy', in L. Diamond and M.F. Platner (eds.), *The Global Resurgence of Democracy*, Baltimore, MD: The Johns Hopkins University Press.

O'Neil, Helen (1994), 'Development Studies in Europe in 1993: Plus ca Change?', *The European Journal of Development Research*, **6** (1), pp. 18–38.

Ochs, Michael (1997), 'Turkmenistan: The Quest for Stability and Control', in K. Dawisha and B. Parrott (eds.), *Conflict, Cleavage, and Change in Central Asia and the Caucasus*, Cambridge: Cambridge University Press.

Olson, Mancur (1965), *The Logic of Collective Action*, Cambridge MA: Harvard University Press.

Olson, Mancur (1982), *The Rise and Decline of Nations*, New Haven, CT: Yale University Press.

Olson, Mancur (1987), 'Economic Nationalism and Economic Progress', *World Economy*, **10**, pp. 241–264.

Olson, Mancur (1990a) 'The Logic of Collective Action in Soviet-type Societies', in *Journal of Soviet Nationalities*, **1** (2).

Olson, Mancur (1990b), 'The Logic of Collective Action in Soviet-type Societies', in *Journal of Soviet Nationalities*, **1** (2), pp. 8–33.

Olson, Mancur (1996), 'Big Bills Left on the Sidewalk: Why Some Nations Are Rich and Others Poor', *Journal of Economic Perspectives*, **10** (2), pp. 3-24.

Onikienko, A. (1994), 'Ispol'sovanie vneshnego faktora: opyt K-itaja', *Mirovaja ekonomika i mezhdunarodnye otnoshenija*, **8–9**, pp. 130–134.

Orenstein, Mitchell (1998), 'Lawlessness from Above and Below: Economic Radicalism and Political Institutions', in *SAIS Review*, **18** (1), pp. 35–50.

Pacek, Alexander C. (1994), 'Macroeconomic Conditions and Electoral Politics in East Central Europe', in *American Journal of Political Science*, **38** (3).

Pachomov, Ju. (1998), 'Ukraina i Rossija na volnach globalizatsii. Ekonomicheskij aspekt', in *Polis*, **1998** (3), pp. 115–123.

Partnoy, Frank (1998), *F.I.A.S.C.O. Blood in the Water on Wall Street*, London: Profile Books.

Pedersen, Karin Hilmer (1998), *Rusland mod årtusindskiftet. Feudalstat, retsstat, velfærdsstat, eller....?*, Copenhagen: Jurist- og Økonomforbundets Forlag.

Pedersen, Ove K. (1992), *Evolution of Interest Representation and the Development of the Labour Market in Post-Socialist Countries*, paper for the conference 'Transforming Post-Socialist Societies: Theoretical Perspectives and Future Prospects for Economic and Political Change in Europe'.

Pei, Minxin (1996), 'Microfoundations of State-socialism and Patterns of Economic Transformation', in *Communist and Post-communist Studies*, **29** (2), pp. 121–145.

Pereira, Luiz Carlos Bresser, José Maria Maravall, and Adam Przeworski (1993), *Economic Reforms in New Democracies*, Cambridge: Cambridge University Press.

Persson, Torsten and Guido Tabellini (1994), 'Is Inequality Harmful for Growth', in *The Economic Review*, **84** (3).

Peters, B. Guy (1993), *The Politics of Taxation: A Comparative Perspective*, Oxford: Blackwell.

Peters, B. Guy (1998), *Comparative Politics. Theory and Methods*, New York: New York University Press.

Peters, B. Guy (1999), *Institutional Theory in Political Science. The 'New Institutionalism'*, London: Pinter.

Petersen, Mogens M. (1977), 'Om den rette brug af historiske materialer i statskundskaben: Nogle didaktiske overvejelser', pp. 235–272 in *Festskrift til Erik Rasmussen*, Aarhus: Politica.

Pinder, J. (1994), *Prospective Europeans, New Members for the European Union*, J. Redmond (ed.), New York, NY: Harvester/Wheatsheaf.

Pockney, B.P. (1991), *Soviet Statistics since 1950*, Aldershot: Dartmouth.

Poole, Theresa (1998), 'Mongolia Reels from Shock Therapy', *Independent* August 3, p. 12, London.

Popov, Vladimir (1997), 'The investment decline in transition economies: Policy versus non-policy factors', in *Research in Progress*, UNU/WIDER, Helsinki.

Popov, Vladimir (1998), 'Will Russia Achieve Fast Economic Growth?', in *Communist Economics and Economic Transformation*, **10** (4), pp. 421–449.

Popova, Marina (1996), 'Income Inequality and Poverty of Economies in Transition, in *Luxemburg Income Studies*, Luxemburg: Working Paper No. 144, Centre d'Etudes des Populations de Pouvreté et det Politiques Socio-Economiques.

Poznanski, Kazimierz Z. (1995), 'Institutional Perspectives on Post-communist Recession in Eastern Europe', pp. 3–30 in Kazimierz Z. Poznanski (ed.), *The Evolutionary Transition to Capitalism*, Boulder, CO: Westview Press.

Przeworski, Adam (1987), 'Methods of Cross-National Research, 1970–83: An overview', pp. 31–49 in M. Dierkes, H.N. Weiler and A. Berthoin Antal (eds.), *Comparative Policy Research,* Aldershot: Gower.

Przeworski, Adam (1991), *Democracy and the Market*, Cambridge: Cambridge University Press.

Przeworski, A. and H. Teune (1970), *The Logic of Comparative Social Inquiery*, New York: Wiley-Interscience.

Przeworski, Adam and Fernando Limongo (1993), 'Political Regimes and Economic Growth', *Journal of Economic Perspectives*, **7** (3), pp. 51–69.

Public Administration and Development (1993), 'Reforming Public Sector Management in Centrally Planned and Transitional Economies', special issue of *Public Administration and Development*, **13** (4).

Putnam, Robert D. (1993), *Making Democracy Work*, Princeton, NJ: Princeton University Press.

Ragin, Charles C. (1987), *The Comparative Method*, Berkeley, CA: University of California Press.

Rasch, Bjørn-Erik (1996), 'Presidentstyrets utfordringer. Demokraisk institusjonsformning i Latin-Amerika og Chile', in *Norsk Statsvitenskapelig Tidsskrift*, **3** (4).

Reich, R. (1990), *The Power of Public Ideas*, Cambridge, MA: Cambridge University Press.

Reinecke, Gerhard (1995), 'Politische Entwicklung im nachsowjetischen Mittelasien: Demokratisierung in Kirgistan', in *Berichte des Bundesinstitut für ostwissenschaftliche und internationale Studien*, Bundesinstitut für ostwissenschaftliche und internationale Studien, Köln.

Reisinger, W., A. Miller, W. Hesli and H. Mahler (1994), 'Political Values in Russia, Ukraine and Lithuania: Sources and Implications for Democracy', in *British Journal of Political Science* **24** (2), pp. 183–223.

Remmer, Karen L. (1993), 'The Political Economy of Elections in Latin America', in *American Political Science Review*, **87** (2), pp. 393–407.

Rhodes, Martin and Bastian van Apeldorn (1997), Capitalism versus Capitalism in Western Europe, in *Developments in West European Politics*, London: Macmillan.

Rodrik, Dani (1996), 'Understanding Economic Policy Reform', in *Journal of Economic Literature*, (**34**).

Roland, Gérard (1997), 'Political Transition and the Transition Experience', pp. 169–187 in Salvatore Zeccini (ed.), *Lessons of Economic Transition*, London: Kluwer Academic Publishers.

Rose, Richard (1995a), 'Economic Conditions of Nationalities in the Baltics', in *Post Soviet Geography*, **36** (8).

Rose, Richard (1995b), 'Micro-economic Conditions of Baltic Nationalities', *Studies in Public Policy 254*, Glasgow: University of Strathclyde.

Rose, Richard (1997), 'Micro-economic Differences Between or Within Nationalities', pp. 109–128 in Neil Hood, Robert Kilis and Jan-Erik Vahlne (eds.), *The Baltic Post-Socialist Enterprises and the Development of Organizational Capabilities*, London: Macmillan Press.

Rose, Richard and A. McAllister (1996), 'Is Money the Measure of Welfare in Russia?', in *Review of Income and Wealth*, **42** (1), pp. 75–90.

Rose, Richard, Neil Monroe and Tom Mackie (1998), 'Election in Central and Eastern Europe since 1990', *Studies in Public Policies*, **300**, Center for the Study of Public Policy.

Rose, Richard and Doh Chull Chin (1998), *Democratization Backwards: The Problems of Third World Democracies*. Unpublished paper.

Rossabi, Morris (1997), 'Mongolia in the 1990s: from Commissars to Capitalists?'

Roth, P.A. (1987), *Meaning and Method in the Social Sciences*, Ithaca, NY: Cornell University Press.

Ruggie, John G. (1982), 'International Regimes, Transactions, and Change: Embedded Liberalism in the Postwar Economic Order', in *International Organisation*, **36** (spring).

Rummel, R.J. (1972), *The Dimensions of Nations*, London: Sage Publications.

Rummel, R.J. (1979), *National Attributes and Behavior*, London: Sage Publications.

Rummel, R.J. (1995), 'Democracy, Power, Genocide and Mass Murder', *Journal of Conflict Resolution*, **39**, pp. 3–26.

Saavalainen, Tapio (1995), *Stabilization in the Baltic States: A Comparative Analysis*, IMF Working Paper, Washington, D.C.: IMF.

Sachs, Jeffrey D. (1996a), 'The Transition at Mid Decade', in *AEA Papers and Proceedings*, **86** (2).

Sachs, Jeffrey D. (1996b), *Reforms in Eastern Europe and the Former Soviet Union in Light of the East Asian Experiences*, Working Paper 5404. Cambridge, MA: National Bureau of Economic Research, IUC.

Sachs, Jeffrey D. and Andrew M. Warner (1996), *Achieving Rapid Growth in the Transition Economies of Central Europe*, Development Discussion paper no. 544, Cambridge, MA: Harvard Institute for International Development.

Sachs, Jeffrey and Wing Thye Woo (1994), 'Structural Factors in the Economic Reforms of China, Eastern Europe and the Former Soviet Union', *Economic Policy*, **18** (April), pp. 102-145.

Sanford, Georg (1999), *Poland – the Conquest of History*, Amsterdam: Harwood Academic Publishers.

Sartori, Giovani (1991), 'Comparing and Miscomparing', in *Journal of Theoretical Politics*, **3** (4), pp. 243–257.

Saxonberg, Steven (1998), *The Fall. A Comparative Study of the End of Communism in Czecho-slovakia, East Germany and Poland*, Reading, MA: Gordon & Breach (forthcoming).

Schleifer, Andrei and Robert W. Vishny (1998), *The Grabbing Hand. Government Pathologies and their Cures*, Cambridge, MA: Harvard University Press.

Schmitt, Jason (1997), 'Winding road. Democratization in Kyrgyzstan', in *Harvard International Review*, **19** (3).

Schmitter, Philippe C., with Terry Linn Karl (1994), 'The Conceptual Travels of Transitologists and Consolodologists: How far to the East should they Attempt to go?', *Slavic Review*, **53** (1), pp. 173–185.

Schroeder, Gertrude (1979), 'The Soviet Economy on a Treadmill of Reforms', *The Soviet Economy in a Time of Change*, Washington, DC: Joint Economic Committee, U.S. Congress.

Schroeder, Gertrude (1997), 'The Economic Transformation Process in the Post-Soviet States', pp. 243–276 in K. Dawisha (ed.), *The International Dimension of Post-Communist Transitions in Russia and the New States of Eurasia*, Aremonk, NY: M.E. Sharpe.

Schumpeter, Joseph A. (1994), *Capitalism, Socialism and Democracy*. London: Routledge.

Scully, Gerald W. (1992), *Constitutional Environments and Economic Growth*, Princeton, NJ: Princeton University Press.

Senik-Legoyne, C. and G. Hughes (1992), 'Industrial Profitability and Trade among the Former Soviet Republics', *Economic Policy*, **15** (October), pp. 353–386.

Shin, Don Chull (1994), 'On the Third Wave of Democratization', in *World Politics*, **47** (October), pp. 135–170.

Shistikto (1995), 'Neoklassicheskaja ekonomicheskaja teorija: Kriticheskij analiz predposylok', in *Mirovaja ekonomika i mezhidukasodnye otnoshenija*, **10**, pp. 18–31.

Sikkink, Kathryn (1991), *Ideas and Institutions. Developmentalism in Brazil and Argentina*, Ithaca, NY: Cornell University Press.

Skilling, Gordon S. and F. Griffiths (1971), *Interest Groups in Soviet Politics*, Princeton, NJ: Princeton University Press.

Skocpol, Theda and Margaret Somers (1980), 'The Use of Comparative History in Macrosocial Inquiry', *Comparative Studies in Society and History*, **22** (2), pp. 174–197.

Smol'kov, V.G. (1999), 'Bjurokratizm', in *Sociologicheskie issledovanii*, Rossijskaja Akademja Nauk, **1999** (1).

Solnik, Steven L. (1996), 'The Breakdown of Hierarchies in the Soviet Union and China. A Neo-Institutional Perspective', *World Politics* **24** pp. 209–238.

Sørensen, Curt (1997), 'Social Classes and Democracy – Different Trajectories', in L.B. Sørensen and L.B. Eliason (eds.), *Forward to the Past*, Aarhus: Aarhus University Press.

Sørensen, Georg (1991), *Democracy, Dictatorship and Development: Economic Development in Selected Regimes of the Third World*, London: Macmillan.

Sørensen, Georg (1993), *Democracy and Democratization*, Boulder, CO: Westview Press.

Sørensen, Lene Bøgh (1995), *Political Development and Regime Transformations. The Hungarian case*, Aarhus: University of Aarhus, Department of Political Science, Ph.D. dissertation.

Sorsa, Piritta (1994a), 'Latvia: Trade Issues in Transition', pp. 141–156 in Constantine Michalopoulos and David G. Tarr (eds.), *Trade in the New Independent States, Studies of Economies in Transformation* **13**, The World Bank/UNDP.

Sorsa, Piritta (1994b), 'Lithuania: Trade Issues in Transition', pp. 157–70 in Constantine Michalopoulos and David G. Tarr (eds), *Trade in the New Independent States, Studies of Economies in Transformation*, **13**, The World Bank/UNDP.

Spiegeleire, Stephan De (1995), 'Levels and Units of Analyses in Post-Soviet Studies', in K. Segbers and S. De Spiegeleire (eds.) *Post-Soviet Puzzles. Mapping the Political Economy of the Former Soviet Union*, Baden-Baden: Nomos Verlagsgesellschaft.

Stalling, Barbara (1992), 'International Influence on Economic Policy: Debt, Stabilization and Structural Reforms', pp. 41–88 in S. Haggard and R. Kaufman (eds.), *The Politics of Economic Adjustment*, Princeton, NJ: Princeton University Press.

Staniszkis, Jadwiga (1994), 'Dillemata der Demokratie in Osteuropa', in R. Deppe et al. (eds.), *Demokratischer Umbruch in Osteuropa*, Frankfurt A.M.: Suhrkamp.

Stark, David (1992), 'Path Dependence and Privatization Strategies in East Central Europe', *East European Politics and Societies*, **6** (1), pp. 17–54.

Stark, David and Victor Nee (1989), 'Toward an Institutional Analysis of State Socialism', in V. Nee and D. Stark (eds.), *Remaking the Economic Institutions of Socialism*, Stanford, CA: Stanford University Press.

Steen, Anton (1996), 'Elites, Democracy and Policy Development in Post Communist States', *Research Report 02/96*, Oslo: Oslo University, Department of Political Science.

Steinmo, S., K. Thelen and F. Longstreth (1992), *Structuring Politics: Historical Institutionalism in Comparative Analyses*, Cambridge: Cambridge University Press.

Stephan, Alfred and Cindy Skach (1993), 'Constitutional Frameworks and Democratic Consolidation', in *World Politics*, **46** (1).

Stern, Nicholas (1997), 'Transition in Eastern Europe and the Former Soviet Union: Some Strategic Lessons from the Experience of 25 Countries over Six Years', in S. Zeccini (ed.), *Lessons of Economic Transtion*, London: Kluwer Academic Publishers.

Stiglitz, Joseph E. (1998), 'More instruments and broader goals: Moving towards the post-Washington Consensus', *Wider Annual Lectures 2*, www.wider.unu.edu/ stiglitx.htm.

Stol, Kruglyj (1994), 'Ekonomicheskie reformy v razvivajushchich stran', *Mirovaja ekonomika i mezhdunarodnye otnoshenija*, **8–9**, pp. 12–14.

Stoner-Weiss, Kathrine (1997), *Local Heroes. The political economy of Russian Regional Governance*, Princeton, NJ: Princeton University Press.

Sundakov, Alexander (1994), *Measuring the Progress of Economic Reform in the Countries of the Former Soviet Union*, IMF paper on Policy Analyses and Assessments, Washington, DC: IMF.

Surdej, Alexander (1992), *Distributional Coalitions and Economic Reforms*, paper for the conference 'Transforming Post-Socialist Societies: Theoretical Perspectives and Future Prospects for Economic and Political Change in Europe'.

Surdej, Alexander (1993), 'Distributional Coalitions and Economic Reforms', in *Post-Soviet Affairs*, **10** (1).

Szule, Adam (1996), 'Economic Transition and Poverty: The Case of the Vysehrad Countries', Luxemburg: Working Paper No. 138, Centre *d'Etudes* des Populations de Pouvreté et de Politiques Socio-Economiques.

Taagepera, Rein and Matthew Soberg Shugart (1989), *Seats & Votes: The Effects and Determinants of Electoral Systems*, New Haven, CT: Yale University Press.

Taylor, Lance (1983), *Structures and Macroeconomics*, New York: Basic Books.

Taylor, Lance (1987), *Varieties of Stabilization Experience: Toward Sensible Macroeconomics in the Third World*, Unpublished Manuscript, Massachusetts Institute of Technology.

Thomsen, Søren Risbjerg (1997), *Om anvendelse af signifikanstest i ikkestikprøve sistuationer*, Unpublished paper. Aarhus: University of Aarhus, Department of Political Science.

Tilly, Charles (1984), *Big Structures, Large Processes, Huge Comparisons*, New York: Russell Sage Foundation.

Toye, John (1990), 'In Search of a Manual for Technopols', pp. 35–43 in John Williamson (ed.), *The Political Economy of Policy Reform*, Washington DC: Institute for International Economics.

Tranøy, Bent Sofus (1993), 'Komparativ metode – mellem ideografiske og nomotetiske idealer', *Sociologi i dag*, **4**, pp. 17–40.

Treisman, Daniel S. (1998), 'Fighting Inflation in a Transitional Regime. Russia's Anomalous Stabilization', in *World Politics*, **50**.

UNDP (1997), *Human Development Report 1997*, Oxford: Oxford University Press.

UNDP (1997), *Human Development Report, Mongolia 1997*, Ulaanbaator, Mongolia: UNDP.

UNDP (1999), *Human Development Report 1999*, http://www.undp.org/hdro/report.html.

UNICEF International Child Development Centre (1997), *Children at Risk in Central and Eastern Europe: Perils and Promises*. Florence: UNICEF International Child Development Centre.

UNICEF (1993), The United Nations Children's Fund, *Public Policy and Social Conditions: Central and Eastern Europe in Transition*, Regional Monitoring Report, no. 1, November 1993, Florence, Italy: UNICEF International Child Development Centre.

UNICEF (1994), *Crisis in Mortality, Health and Nutrition. Central and Eastern Europe in Transition. Public Policy and Social Conditions*, Regional Monitoring Report, no. 2, August 1994, Florence: UNICEF International Child Development Centre.

United Nations (1991), *Economic Bulletin for Europe*, **43**.

Vecernik, Jiri (1995), 'Incomes in East Central Europe: Distribution, Patterns and Perceptions', *Working Paper no. 129*, Luxemburg Income Study, Centre d'Etudes de Populations.

Walton, John and David Seddon (1994), *Free Markets & Food Riots*, Oxford: Blackwell.

Waterbury, John (1992), 'The Heart of the Matter? Public Enterprise and the Adjustment Process', pp. 182–220 in Stephan Haggard and Robert R. Kaufman (eds.), *The Politics of Economic Adjustment. International Constraints, Distributive Conflicts, and the State*, Princeton, NJ: Princeton University Press.

Weaver, R. Kent and Bert A. Rockman (1993), 'Assessing the effects of institutions', in *Do Institutions Matter?*, R.K. Weaver and B.A. Rockman (eds.), Washington, DC: The Brookings Institution.

Weber, Max (1992), *Economy and Society*, ed. by Guenther Roth and Claus Wittick, New York: Bedminster Press.

Weingast, Barry R. (1995), 'The Economic Role of Political Institutions: Market-preserving Federalism and Economic Development', in *The Journal of Law, Economics & Organization*, **11** (1).

Wellhofer, E. Spencer (1989), 'The Comparative Method and the Study of Development, Differences and Social Change', *Comparative Political Studies*, pp. 315–342.

Wesolowsky, W. (1995), 'The Nature of Social Ties and the Future of Postcommunist Society: Poland after Solidarity', in John A. Hall (ed.), *Civil society. Theory, History, Comparison*, Cambridge: Cambridge University Press.

Weydenthal, Jan de (1996), 'Dealing with Belarus' Lukashenko', Radio Free Europe (rferl.org/nca/features/1996/07/F.RU.96071164653838/html).

Whitely, Paul (1998), 'Economic Growth and Social Capital', in *ECPR News*, **9** (3).

Wiatr, Jerzy (1994), 'From Communist Party to Socialist Democracy of the Polish Republic', in Kay Larsen (ed.), *How Parties Work*, Westport, CT: Praeger.

Wiesenthal, Helmut (1996), 'Organised Interests in Contemporary East Central Europe: Theoretical Perspectives and Tentative Hypotheses', in A. Agh and G. Ilonski (eds.), *Parliaments and Organised Interests in Central Europe: The Second Steps*, Budapest: Hungarian Centre for Democracy Studies.

Williamson, John (1990), 'What Washington Means by Policy Reform', pp. 7–38 in *Latin American Adjustment: How Much Has Happened?*, Washington, DC: Institute for International Economics.

Williamson, John (1993), 'In Search for a Manual for Technopols', pp. 9–48 in John Williamson (ed.), *The Political Economy of Policy Reform*, Washington, DC: Institute for International Economics.

Williamson, John (1994) (ed.), *The Political Economy of Policy Reform*, Washington, DC: Institute for International Economics.

Williamson, John and Stephan Haggard (1994), 'The Political Conditions for Economic Reform', in John Williamson (ed.), *The Political Economy of Policy Reform*, Washington, DC: Institute for International Economics.

Winiecki, Jan (1990), *Resistance to Change in the Soviet Economic System. A Property Rights Approach*, New York: Routledge.

Wolfensohn, James D. (1996), 'The other Crises', Address to the Board of Governors, The World Bank Group, Washington, DC, October 6.

Woo, Wing Thye (1994), 'The art of reforming centrally planned economies: Comparing China, Poland and Russia', in *Journal of Comparative Economics*, **18**, pp. 276–78.

World Bank (1996), *From Plan to Market, World Development Report 1996*, Oxford: Oxford University Press.

World Bank (1997), *The State in a Developing World, World Development Report 1997*, Oxford: Oxford University Press.

World Value Studies (1996), http://www.za.unikoeln.de/research/en/ eurolabor/el_other. htm#Values.

Zaprudnik, Jan and Michael Urban (1997), 'Belarus: from statehood to empire?', in I. Bremmer and R. Taras (eds.), *New states – new politics*, Cambridge: Cambridge University Press.

Zubek, Voytek (1997), 'The end of liberalism', in *Communist and Post-Communist Studies*, **30** (2).

Index